# THE
# TRAGIC SENSE OF LIFE

## IN MEN AND IN PEOPLES

BY

## MIGUEL DE UNAMUNO

TRANSLATED BY

### J. E. CRAWFORD FLITCH
M.A. (Cantab.)

WITH AN INTRODUCTORY ESSAY BY

### SALVADOR DE MADARIAGA

MACMILLAN AND CO., LIMITED
ST. MARTIN'S STREET, LONDON
1921

# CONTENTS

# V

## THE RATIONALIST DISSOLUTION

# VI

## IN THE DEPTHS OF THE ABYSS

# VII

## LOVE, SUFFERING, PITY, AND PERSONALITY

# VIII

## FROM GOD TO GOD

# IX

## FAITH, HOPE, AND CHARITY

# INTRODUCTORY ESSAY

## DON MIGUEL DE UNAMUNO

I SAT, several years ago, at the Welsh National Eisteddfod, under the vast tent in which the Bard of Wales was being crowned. After the small golden crown had been placed in unsteady equilibrium on the head of a clever-looking pressman, several Welsh bards came on the platform and recited little epigrams. A Welsh bard is, if young, a pressman, and if of maturer years, a divine. In this case, as England was at war, they were all of the maturer kind, and, while I listened to the music of their ditties—the sense thereof being, alas! beyond my reach —I was struck by the fact that all of them, though different, closely resembled Don Miguel de Unamuno. It is not my purpose to enter into the wasp-nest of racial disquisitions. If there is a race in the world over which more sense and more nonsense can be freely said for lack of definite information than the Welsh, it is surely this ancient Basque people, whose greatest contemporary figure is perhaps Don Miguel de Unamuno. I am merely setting down that intuitional fact for what it may be worth, though I do not hide my opinion that such promptings of the inner, untutored man are worth more than cavefuls of bones and tombfuls of undecipherable papers.

This reminiscence, moreover, which springs up into the light of my memory every time I think of Don Miguel de Unamuno, has to my mind a further value in that in it the image of Don Miguel does not appear as evoked by one man, but by many, though many of one species, many who in depth are but one man, one type, the Welsh divine. Now, this unity underlying a multiplicity, these many faces, moods, and movements, traceable to one only type, I find deeply connected in my mind with Unamuno's person and with what he signifies in Spanish life and letters. And when I further delve into my impression, I first realize an undoubtedly physical relation between the many-one Welsh divines and the many-one Unamuno. A tall, broad-shouldered, bony man, with high cheeks, a beak-like nose, pointed grey beard, and a complexion the colour of the red hematites on which Bilbao, his native town, is built, and which Bilbao ruthlessly plucks from its very body to exchange for gold in the markets of England—and in the deep sockets under the high aggressive forehead prolonged by short iron-grey hair, two eyes like gimlets eagerly watching the world through spectacles which seem to be purposely pointed at the object like microscopes; a fighting expression, but of noble fighting, above the prizes of the passing world, the contempt for which is shown in a peculiar attire whose blackness invades even that little triangle of white which worldly men leave on their breast for the necktie of frivolity and the decorations of vanity, and, blinding it, leaves but the thinnest rim of white collar to emphasize, rather than relieve, the priestly effect of the whole. Such is Don Miguel de Unamuno.

Such is, rather, his photograph. For Unamuno himself is ever changing. A talker, as all good Spaniards are nowadays, but a talker in earnest and with his heart in it, he is varied, like the subjects of his conversation, and, still more, like the passions which they awake in him. And here I find an unsought reason in intellectual support of that intuitional observation which I noted down in starting—that Unamuno resembles the Welsh in that he is not ashamed of showing his passions—a thing which he has often to do, for he is very much alive and feels therefore plenty of them. But a word of caution may here be necessary, since that term, "passion," having been diminished—that is, made meaner— by the world, an erroneous impression might be conveyed by what precedes, of the life and ways of Unamuno. So that it may not be superfluous to say that Don Miguel de Unamuno is a Professor of Greek in the University of Salamanca, an ex-Rector of it who left behind the reputation of being a strong ruler; a father of a numerous family, and a man who has sung the quiet and deep joys of married life with a restraint, a vigour, and a nobility which it would be difficult to match in any literature. *Yet* a passionate man—or, as he would perhaps prefer to say, *therefore* a passionate man. But in a major, not in a minor key; of strong, not of weak passions.

The difference between the two lies perhaps in that the man with strong passions lives them, while the man with weak passions is lived by them, so that while weak passions paralyze the will, strong passions urge man to action. It is such an urge towards life, such a vitality ever awake, which inspires Unamuno's multifarious activities in the realm of the mind. The duties of his chair of Greek are the first claim upon his time. But then, his reading is prodigious, as any reader of this book will realize for himself. Not only is he familiar with the stock-in-trade of every intellectual worker—the Biblical, Greek, Roman, and Italian cultures—but there is hardly anything worth reading in Europe and America which he has not read, and, but for the Slav languages, in the original. Though never out of Spain, and seldom out of Salamanca, he has succeeded in establishing direct connections with most of the intellectual leaders of the world, and in gathering an astonishingly accurate knowledge of the spirit and literature of foreign peoples.   It was in his library at Salamanca that he once explained to an Englishman the meaning of a particular Scotticism in Robert Burns; and it was there that he congratulated another Englishman on his having read *Rural Rides,* "the hall-mark," he said, "of the man of letters who is no mere man of letters, but also a man." From that corner of Castile, he has poured out his spirit in essays, poetry, criticism, novels, philosophy, lectures, and public meetings, and that daily toil of press article writing which is the duty rather than the privilege of most present-day writers in Spain.   Such are the many faces, moods, and movements in which Unamuno appears before Spain and the world.   And yet, despite this multiplicity and this dispersion, the dominant impression which his personality leaves behind is that of a vigorous unity, an unswerving concentration both of mind and purpose.   Bagaria, the national caricaturist, a genius of rhythm and character which the war revealed, but who was too good not to be overshadowed by the facile art of Raemaekers (imagine Goya overshadowed by Reynolds!), once represented Unamuno as an owl. A marvellous thrust at the heart of Unamuno's character.   For all this vitality and ever-moving activity of mind is shot through by the absolute immobility of two owlish eyes piercing the darkness of spiritual night. And this intense gaze into the mystery is the steel axis round which his spirit revolves and revolves in desperation; the unity under his multiplicity; the one fire under his passions and the inspiration of his whole work and life.

*        *        *        *        *

It was Unamuno himself who once said that the Basque is the alkaloid of the Spaniard.   The saying is true, so far as it goes.   But it would be more accurate to say "one of the two alkaloids."   It is probable that if the Spanish character were analyzed—always provided that the Mediterranean aspect of it be left aside as a thing apart—two main principles would be recognized in it—*i.e.*, the Basque, richer in concentration, substance, strength; and the Andalusian, more given to observation, grace, form. The two types are to this day socially opposed. The Andalusian is a people which has lived down many civilizations, and in which even illiterate peasants possess a kind of innate education. The Basques are a primitive people of mountaineers and fishermen, in which even scholars have a peasant-like roughness not unlike the roughness of Scotch tweeds—or character. It is the even balancing of these two elements—the force of the Northerner with the grace of the Southerner—which gives the Castilian his admirable poise and explains the graceful virility of men such as Fray Luis de León and the feminine strength of women such as Queen Isabel and Santa Teresa. We are therefore led to expect in so forcible a representative of the Basque race as Unamuno the more substantial and earnest features of the Spanish spirit.

Our expectation is not disappointed. And to begin with it appears in that very concentration of his mind and soul on the mystery of man's destiny on earth. Unamuno is in earnest, in dead earnest, as to this matter. This earnestness is a distinct Spanish, nay, Basque feature in him. There is something of the stern attitude of Loyola about his "tragic sense of life," and on this subject—under one form or another, his only subject—he admits no joke, no flippancy, no subterfuge. A true heir of those great Spanish saints and mystics whose lifework was devoted to the exploration of the kingdoms of faith, he is more human than they in that he has lost hold of the firm ground where they had stuck their anchor. Yet, though loose in the modern world, he refuses to be drawn away from the main business of the Christian, the saving of his soul, which, in his interpretation, means the conquest of his immortality, his own immortality.

An individualist. Certainly. And he proudly claims the title. Nothing more refreshing in these days of hoggish communistic cant than this great voice asserting the divine, the eternal rights of the individual. But it is not with political rights that he is concerned. Political individualism, when not a mere blind for the unlimited freedom of civil privateering, is but the outcome of that abstract idea of man which he so energetically condemns as pedantic—that is, inhuman. His opposition of the individual to society is not that of a puerile anarchist to a no less puerile socialist. There is nothing childish about Unamuno. His assertion that society is for the individual, not the individual for society, is made on a transcendental plane. It is not the argument of liberty against authority—which can be easily answered on the rationalistic plane by showing that authority is in its turn the liberty of the social or collective being, a higher, more complex, and longer-living " individual " than the individual pure and simple. It is rather the unanswerable argument of eternity against duration. Now that argument must rest on a religious basis. And it is on a religious basis that Unamuno founds his individualism. Hence the true Spanish flavour of his social theory, which will not allow itself to be set down and analyzed into principles of ethics and politics, with their inevitable tendency to degenerate into mere economics, but remains free and fluid and absolute, like the spirit.

Such an individualism has therefore none of the features of that childish half-thinking which inspires most anarchists. It is, on the contrary, based on high thinking, the highest of all, that which refuses to dwell on anything less than man's origin and destination. We are here confronted with that humanistic tendency of the Spanish mind which can be observed as the dominant feature of her arts and literature. All races are of course predominantly concerned with man. But they all manifest their concern with a difference. Man is in Spain a concrete being, the man of flesh and bones, and the whole man. He is neither subtilized into an idea by pure thinking nor civilized into a gentleman by social laws and prejudices. Spanish art and letters deal with concrete, tangible persons. Now, there is no more concrete, no more tangible person for every one of us than ourself. Unamuno is therefore right in the line of Spanish tradition in dealing predominantly—one might almost say always—with his own person. The feeling of the awareness of one's own personality has seldom been more forcibly expressed than by Unamuno. This is primarily due to the fact that he is himself obsessed by it. But in his expression of it Unamuno derives also some strength from his own sense of matter and the material—again a typically Spanish element of his character. Thus his human beings are as much body as soul, or rather body and soul all in one, a union which he admirably renders by bold mixtures of physical and spiritual metaphors, as in *gozarse uno la carne del alma* (to enjoy the flesh of one's own soul).

In fact, Unamuno, as a true Spaniard which he is, refuses to surrender life to ideas, and that is why he runs shy of abstractions, in which he sees but shrouds wherewith we cover dead thoughts. He is solely concerned with his own life, nothing but his life, and the whole of his life. An egotistical position? Perhaps. Unamuno, however, can and does answer the charge. We can only know and feel humanity in the one human being which we have at hand. It is by penetrating deep into ourselves that we find our brothers in us—branches of the same trunk which can only touch each other by seeking their common origin. This searching within, Unamuno has undertaken with a sincerity, a fearlessness which cannot be excelled. Nowhere will the reader find the inner contradictions of a modern human being, who is at the same time healthy and capable of thought, set down with a greater respect for truth. Here the uncom-

promising tendency of the Spanish race, whose eyes
never turn away from nature, however unwelcome the
sight, is strengthened by that passion for life which
burns in Unamuno. The suppression of the slightest
thought or feeling for the sake of intellectual order would
appear to him as a despicable worldly trick. Thus it is
precisely because he does sincerely feel a passionate love
of his own life that he thinks out with such scrupulous
accuracy every argument which he finds in his mind—
his own mind, a part of his life—against the possibility
of life after death; but it is also because he feels that,
despite such conclusive arguments, his will to live perseveres, that he refuses to his intellect the power to kill
his faith. A knight-errant of the spirit, as he himself
calls the Spanish mystics, he starts for his adventures
after having, like Hernán Cortés, burnt his ships.
But, is it necessary to enhance his figure by literary
comparison? He is what he wants to be, a man—in
the striking expression which he chose as a title for one
of his short stories, *nothing less than a whole man*. Not
a mere thinking machine, set to prove a theory, nor an
actor on the world stage, singing a well-built poem, well
built at the price of many a compromise; but a whole
man, with all his affirmations and all his negations, all
the pitiless thoughts of a penetrating mind that denies,
and all the desperate self-assertions of a soul that yearns
for eternal life.

This strife between enemy truths, the truth thought
and the truth felt, or, as he himself puts it, between
veracity and sincerity, is Unamuno's *raison d'être*. And
it is because the "*Tragic Sense of Life*" is the most
direct expression of it that this book is his masterpiece.
The conflict is here seen as reflected in the person of the
author. The book opens by a definition of the Spanish
man, the "man of flesh and bones," illustrated by the
consideration of the real living men who stood behind
the bookish figures of great philosophers and consciously

or unconsciously shaped and misshaped their doctrines in order to satisfy their own vital yearnings. This is followed by the statement of the will to live or hunger for immortality, in the course of which the usual subterfuges with which this all-important issue is evaded in philosophy, theology, or mystic literature, are exposed and the real, concrete, " flesh and bones " character of the immortality which men desire is reaffirmed. The Catholic position is then explained as the *vital* attitude in the matter, summed up in Tertullian's *Credo quia absurdum,* and this is opposed to the critical attitude which denies the possibility of individual survival in the sense previously defined. Thus Unamuno leads us to his inner deadlock : his reason can rise no higher than scepticism, and, unable to become vital, dies sterile; his faith, exacting anti-rational affirmations and unable therefore to be apprehended by the logical mind, remains incommunicable. From the bottom of this abyss Unamuno builds up his theory of life. But is it a theory? Unamuno does not claim for it such an intellectual dignity. He knows too well that in the constructive part of his book his vital self takes the leading part and repeatedly warns his reader of the fact, lest critical objections might be raised against this or that assumption or self-contradiction. It is on the survival of his will to live, after all the onslaughts of his critical intellect, that he finds the basis for his belief—or rather for his effort to believe. Self-compassion leads to self-love, and this self-love, founded as it is on a universal conflict, widens into love of all that lives and therefore wants to survive. So, by an act of love, springing from our own hunger for immortality, we are led to give a conscience to the Universe—that is, to create God.

Such is the process by which Unamuno, from the transcendental pessimism of his inner contradiction, extracts an everyday optimism founded on love. His symbol of this attitude is the figure of Don Quixote, of whom he truly says that his creed " can hardly be called idealism, since he did not fight for ideas : it was spiritualism, for he fought for the spirit." Thus he opposes a synthetical to an analytical attitude; a religious to an ethico-scientific ideal; Spain, his Spain— *i.e.*, the spiritual manifestation of the Spanish race—to Europe, his Europe—*i.e.*, the intellectual manifestation of the white race, which he sees in Franco-Germany; and heroic love, even when comically unpractical, to culture, which, in this book, written in 1912, is already prophetically spelt Kultura.

This courageous work is written in a style which is the man—for Buffon's saying, seldom true, applies here to the letter. It is written as Carlyle wrote, not merely with the brain, but with the whole soul and the whole body of the man, and in such a vivid manner that one can without much effort imagine the eager gesticulation which now and then underlines, interprets, despises, argues, denies, and above all asserts. In his absolute subservience to the matter in hand this manner of writing has its great precedent in Santa Teresa. The differences, and they are considerable, are not of art, absent in either case, but of nature. They are such deep and obvious differences as obtain between the devout, ignorant, graceful nun of sixteenth-century Avila and the free-thinking, learned, wilful professor of twentieth-century Salamanca. In the one case, as in the other, the language is the most direct and simple required. It is also the least literary and the most popular. Unamuno, who lives in close touch with the people, has enriched the Spanish literary language by returning to it many a popular term. His vocabulary abounds in racy words of the soil, and his writings gain from them an almost peasant-like pith and directness which suits his own Basque primitive nature. His expression occurs simultaneously with the thoughts and feelings to be expressed, the flow of which, but loosely controlled by the

critical mind, often breaks through the meshes of established diction and gives birth to new forms created under
the pressure of the moment.   This feature Unamuno has
also in common with Santa Teresa, but what in the Saint
was a self-ignorant charm becomes in Unamuno a
deliberate manner inspired, partly by an acute sense of
the symbolical and psychological value of word-connec-
tions, partly by that genuine need for expansion of the
language which all true original thinkers or " feelers "
must experience, but partly also by an acquired habit of
juggling with words which is but natural in a philologist
endowed with a vigorous imagination.   Unamuno revels
in words.   He positively enjoys stretching them beyond
their usual meaning, twisting them, composing, opposing, and transposing them in all sorts of possible ways.
This game—not wholly unrewarded now and then by
striking intellectual finds—seems to be the only relaxa-
tion which he allows his usually austere mind.   It
certainly is the only light feature of a style the merit of
which lies in its being the close-fitting expression of a
great mind earnestly concentrated on a great idea.

       \*       \*       \*       \*       \*

The earnestness, the intensity, and the oneness of his
predominant passion are the main cause of the strength
of Unamuno's philosophic work.   They remain his
main asset, yet become also the principal cause of his
weakness, as a creative artist.   Great art can only
flourish in the temperate zone of the passions, on the
return journey from the torrid.   Unamuno, as a creator,
has none of the failings of those artists who have never
felt deeply.   But he does show the limitations of those
artists who cannot cool down.   And the most striking
of them is that at bottom he is seldom able to put himself
in a purely esthetical mood.   In this, as in many other
features, Unamuno curiously resembles Wordsworth—
whom, by the way, he is one of the few Spaniards to

read and appreciate.[1]  Like him, Unamuno is an essentially purposeful and utilitarian mind.  Of the two qualities which the work of art requires for its inception —earnestness and detachment—both Unamuno and Wordsworth possess the first; both are deficient in the second.  Their interest in their respective leading thought—survival in the first, virtue in the second—is too direct, too pressing, to allow them the "distance" necessary for artistic work.  Both are urged to work by a lofty utilitarianism—the search for God through the individual soul in Unamuno, the search for God through the social soul in Wordsworth—so that their thoughts and sensations are polarized and their spirit loses that impartial transparence for nature's lights without which no great art is possible.  Once suggested, this parallel is too rich in sidelights to be lightly dropped.  This single-mindedness which distinguishes them explains that both should have consciously or unconsciously chosen a life of semi-seclusion, for Unamuno lives in Salamanca very much as Wordsworth lived in the Lake District—

> in a still retreat
> Sheltered, but not to social duties lost,

hence in both a certain proclivity towards ploughing a solitary furrow and becoming self-centred.  There are no doubt important differences.  The Englishman's sense of nature is both keener and more concrete; while the Spaniard's knowledge of human nature is not barred by the subtle inhibitions and innate limitations which tend to blind its more unpleasant aspects to the eye of the Englishman.  There is more courage and passion in the Spaniard; more harmony and goodwill in the Englishman; the one is more like fire, the other like

---

[1] In what follows, I confess to refer not so much to the generally admitted opinion on Wordsworth as to my own views on him and his poetry, which I tried to explain in my essay: "The Case of Wordsworth" (*Shelley and Calderón, and other Essays*, Constable and Co., 1920).

light. For Wordsworth, a poem is above all an essay, a means for conveying a lesson in forcible and easily remembered terms to those who are in need of improvement. For Unamuno, a poem or a novel (and he holds that a novel is but a poem) is the outpouring of a man's passion, the overflow of the heart which cannot help itself and lets go. And it may be that the essential difference between the two is to be found in this difference between their respective purposes: Unamuno's purpose is more intimately personal and individual; Wordsworth's is more social and objective. Thus both miss the temperate zone, where emotion takes shape into the moulds of art; but while Wordsworth is driven by his ideal of social service this side of it, into the cold light of both moral and intellectual self-control, Unamuno remains beyond, where the molten metal is too near the fire of passion, and cannot cool down into shape.

Unamuno is therefore not unlike Wordsworth in the insufficiency of his sense of form. We have just seen the essential cause of this insufficiency to lie in the non-esthetical attitude of his mind, and we have tried to show one of the roots of such an attitude in the very loftiness and earnestness of his purpose. Yet, there are others, for living nature is many-rooted as it is many-branched. It cannot be doubted that a certain refractoriness to form is a typical feature of the Basque character. The sense of form is closely in sympathy with the feminine element in human nature, and the Basque race is strongly masculine. The predominance of the masculine element—strength without grace—is as typical of Unamuno as it is of Wordsworth. The literary gifts which might for the sake of synthesis be symbolized in a smile are absent in both. There is as little humour in the one as in the other. Humour, however, sometimes occurs in Unamuno, but only in his ill-humoured moments, and then with a curious bite of its own which adds an un-

conscious element to its comic effect. Grace only visits
them in moments of inspiration, and then it is of a noble
character, enhanced as it is by the ever-present gift of
strength. And as for the sense for rhythm and music,
both Unamuno and Wordsworth seem to be limited to
the most vigorous and masculine gaits. This feature
is particularly pronounced in Unamuno, for while
Wordsworth is painstaking, all-observant, and too good
a " teacher " to underestimate the importance of pleasure
in man's progress, Unamuno knows no compromise.
His aim is not to please but to strike, and he deliberately
seeks the naked, the forceful, even the brutal word for
truth. There is in him, however, a cause of formless-
ness from which Wordsworth is free—namely, an eagerness for sincerity and veracity which brushes aside all
preparation, ordering or planning of ideas as suspect of
"dishing up," intellectual trickery, and juggling with
spontaneous truths.

*    *    *    *    *

Such qualities—both the positive and the negative—
are apparent in his poetry. In it, the appeal of force
and sincerity is usually stronger than that of art. This
is particularly the case in his first volume (*Poesías*, 1907),
in which a lofty inspiration, a noble attitude of mind,
a rich and racy vocabulary, a keen insight into the spirit
of places, and above all the overflowing vitality of a
strong man in the force of ripeness, contend against the
still awkward gait of the Basque and a certain rebellious-
ness of rhyme. The dough of the poetic language is
here seen heavily pounded by a powerful hand, bent on
reducing its angularities and on improving its plasticity.
Nor do we need to wait for further works in order to
enjoy the reward of such efforts, for it is attained in this
very volume more than once, as for instance in *Muere
en el mar el ave que voló del nido*, a beautiful poem in
which emotion and thought are happily blended into
exquisite form.

In his last poem, *El Cristo de Velázquez* (1920),
Unamuno undertakes the task of giving a poetical
rendering of his tragic sense of life, in the form of a
meditation on the Christ of Velázquez, the beautiful and
pathetic picture in the Prado. Why Velázquez's and
not Christ himself? The fact is that, though in his
references to actual forms, Unamuno closely follows
Velázquez's picture, the spiritual interpretation of it
which he develops as the poem unfolds itself is wholly
personal. It would be difficult to find two great
Spaniards wider apart than Unamuno and Velázquez,
for if Unamuno is the very incarnation of the masculine
spirit of the North—all strength and substance—Velázquez is the image of the feminine spirit of the South—
all grace and form. Velázquez is a limpid mirror, with
a human depth, yet a mirror. That Unamuno has departed from the image of Christ which the great Sevillian
reflected on his immortal canvas was therefore to be
expected. But then Unamuno has, while speaking of
Don Quixote, whom he has also freely and personally
interpreted,[1] taken great care to point out that a work of
art is, for each of us, all that we see in it. And, moreover,
Unamuno has not so much departed from Velázquez's
image of Christ as delved into its depths, expanded,
enlarged it, or, if you prefer, seen in its limpid surface
the immense figure of his own inner Christ. However
free and unorthodox in its wide scope of images and
ideas, the poem is in its form a regular meditation in the
manner approved by the Catholic Church, and it is
therefore meet that it should rise from a concrete, tangible
object as it is recommended to the faithful. To this
concrete character of its origin, the poem owes much of
its suggestiveness, as witness the following passage
quoted here, with a translation sadly unworthy of the
original, as being the clearest link between the poetical

---

[1] *Vida de Don Quijote y Sancho, explicada y comentada*, por M de
Unamuno Madrid, Fernando Fé, 1905

meditation and the main thought that underlies all the
work and the life of Unamuno.

### NUBE NEGRA

O es que una nube negra de los cielos
ese negror le dió a tu cabellera
de nazareno, cual de mustio sauce
de una noche sin luna sobre el río?
¿ Es la sombra del ala sin perfiles
del ángel de la nada negadora,
de Luzbel, que en su caída inacabable
— fondo no puede dar—su eterna cuita
clava en tu frente, en tu razón?  ¿ Se vela
el claro Verbo en Ti con esa nube,
negra cual de Luzbel las negras alas,
mientras brilla el Amor, todo desnudo,
con tu desnudo pecho por cendal ?

### BLACK CLOUD

Or was it then that a black cloud from heaven
Such blackness gave to your Nazarene's hair,
As of a languid willow o'er the river
Brooding in moonless night?   Is it the shadow
Of the profileless wing of Luzbel, the Angel
Of denying nothingness, endlessly falling—
Bottom he ne'er can touch—whose grief eternal
He nails on to Thy forehead, to Thy reason ?
Is the clear Word in Thee with that cloud veiled
—A cloud as black as the black wings of Luzbel—
While Love shines naked within Thy naked breast?

The poem, despite its length, easily maintains this
lofty level throughout, and if he had written nothing
else Unamuno would still remain as having given to
Spanish letters the noblest and most sustained lyrical
flight in the language.  It abounds in passages of ample
beauty and often strikes a note of primitive strength in
the true Old Testament style.  It is most distinctively a
poem in a major key, in a group with *Paradise Lost*
and *The Excursion*, but in a tone halfway between the
two; and, as coming from the most Northern-minded
and substantial poet that Spain ever had, wholly free

from that tendency towards grandiloquence and Ciceronian drapery which blighted previous similar efforts
in Spain. Its weakness lies in a certain monotony due to
the interplay of Unamuno's two main limitations as an
artist : the absolute surrender to one dominant thought
and a certain deficiency of form bordering here on contempt. The plan is but a loose sequence of meditations
on successive aspects of Christ as suggested by images
or advocations of His divine person, or even of parts of
His human body : Lion, Bull, Lily, Sword, Crown,
Head, Knees. Each meditation is treated in a period
of blank verse, usually of a beautiful texture, the splen-
dour of which is due less to actual images than to the
inner vigour of ideas and the eagerness with which even
the simplest facts are interpreted into significant symbols.
Yet, sometimes, this blank verse becomes hard and
stony under the stubborn hammering of a too insistent
mind, and the device of ending each meditation with a
line accented on its last syllable tends but to increase the
monotony of the whole.

Blank verse is never the best medium for poets of a
strong masculine inspiration, for it does not sufficiently
correct their usual deficiency in form. Such poets are
usually at their best when they bind themselves to the
discipline of existing forms and particularly when they
limit the movements of their muse to the "sonnet's
scanty plot of ground." Unamuno's best poetry, as
Wordsworth's, is in his sonnets. His *Rosario de
Sonetos Líricos,* published in 1911, contains some of the
finest sonnets in the Spanish language. There is variety
in this volume—more at least than is usual in Unamuno :
from comments on events of local politics (sonnet lii.)
which savour of the more prosaic side of Wordsworth, to meditations on space and time such as that
sonnet xxxvii., so reminiscent of Shelley's *Ozymandias
of Egypt;* from a suggestive homily to a " Don Juan of
Ideas " whose thirst for knowledge is " not love of truth,

but intellectual lust," and whose " thought is therefore
sterile " (sonnet cvii.), to an exquisitely rendered moonlight love scene (sonnet civ.).   The author's main theme
itself, which of course occupies a prominent part in the
series, appears treated under many different lights and
in genuinely poetical moods which truly do justice to
the inherent wealth of poetical inspiration which it contains.   Many a sonnet might be quoted here, and in
particular that sombre and fateful poem *Nihil Novum
sub Sole* (cxxiii.), which defeats its own theme by the
striking originality of its inspiration.

So active, so positive is the inspiration of this poetry
that the question of outside influences does not even arise.
Unamuno is probably the Spanish contemporary poet
whose manner owes least, if anything at all, to modern
developments of poetry such as those which take their
source in Baudelaire and Verlaine.   These over-sensitive
and over-refined artists have no doubt enriched the
sensuous, the formal, the sentimental, even the intellectual aspects of verse with an admirable variety of
exquisite shades, lacking which most poetry seems old-
fashioned to the fastidious palate of modern men.
Unamuno is too genuine a representative of the spiritual
and masculine variety of Spanish genius, ever impervious
to French, and generally, to intellectual, influences, to
be affected by the esthetic excellence of this art.   Yet,
for all his disregard of the modern resources which it
adds to the poetic craft, Unamuno loses none of his
modernity.   He is indeed more than modern.   When,
as he often does, he strikes the true poetic note, he is
outside time.   His appeal is not in complexity but in
strength.   He is not refined : he is final.

      *       *       *       *       *

In the Preface to his *Tres Novelas Ejemplares y un
Prólogo* (1921) Unamuno says : " . . . novelist—that is,
poet . . . a novel—that is, a poem."   Thus, with characteristic decision, he sides with the lyrical conception

of the novel. There is of course an infinite variety of types of novels. But they can probably all be reduced to two classes—*i.e.*, the dramatic or objective, and the lyrical or subjective, according to the mood or inspiration which predominates in them. The present trend of the world points towards the dramatic or objective type. This type is more in tune with the detached and scientific character of the age. The novel is often nowadays considered as a document, a " slice of life," a piece of information, a literary photograph representing places and people which purse or time prevents us from seeing with our own eyes. It is obvious, given what we now know of him, that such a view of the novel cannot appeal to Unamuno. He is a utilitarian, but not of worldly utilities. His utilitarianism transcends our daily wants and seeks to provide for our eternal ones. He is, moreover, a mind whose workings turn in spiral form towards a central idea and therefore feels an instinctive antagonism to the dispersive habits of thought and sensation which such detailed observation of life usually entails. For at bottom the opposition between the lyrical and the dramatic novel may be reduced to that between the poet and the dramatist. Both the dramatist and the poet create in order to link up their soul and the world in one complete circle of experience, but this circle is travelled in opposite directions. The poet goes inwards first, then out to nature full of his inner experience, and back home. The dramatist goes outwards first, then comes back to himself, his harvest of wisdom gathered in reality. It is the recognition of his own lyrical inward-looking nature which makes Unamuno pronounce the identity of the novel and the poem.

Whatever we may think of it as a general theory, there is little doubt that this opinion is in the main sound in so far as it refers to Unamuno's own work. His novels are created within. They are—and their author is the first to declare it so—novels which happen in the king-

dom of the spirit. Outward points of reference in time
and space are sparingly given—in fact, reduced to a bare
minimum. In some of them, as for instance *Niebla*
(1914), the name of the town in which the action takes
place is not given, and such scanty references to the
topography and general features as are supplied would
equally apply to any other provincial town of Spain.
Action, in the current sense of the word, is correspond-
ingly simplified, since the material and local elements on
which it usually exerts itself are schematized, and in their
turn made, as it were, spiritual. Thus a street, a river
of colour for some, for others a series of accurately
described shops and dwellings, becomes in Unamuno
(see *Niebla*) a loom where the passions and desires of
men and women cross and recross each other and weave
the cloth of daily life. Even the physical description of
characters is reduced to a standard of utmost simplicity.
So that, in fine, Unamuno's novels, by eliminating all
other material, appear, if the boldness of the metaphor
be permitted, as the spiritual skeletons of novels, con-
flicts between souls.

Nor is this the last stage in his deepening and narrow-
ing of the creative furrow. For these souls are in their
turn concentrated so that the whole of their vitality burns
into one passion. If a somewhat fanciful comparison
from another art may throw any light on this feature of
his work we might say that his characters are to those of
Galdós, for instance, as counterpoint music to the complex modern symphony. Joaquín Monegro, the true
hero of his *Abel Sánchez* (1917), is the personification of
hatred. Raquel in *Dos Madres*[1] and Catalina in *El
Marqués de Lumbría*[1] are two widely different but
vigorous, almost barbarous, " maternities." Alejandro,
the hero of his powerful *Nada Menos que Todo un
Hombre*,[1] is masculine will, pure and unconquerable,

[1] These three novels appeared together as *Tres Novelas y un Prólogo*
Calpe, Madrid, 1921.

save by death.  Further still, in most if not all of his main characters, we can trace the dominant passion which is their whole being to a mere variety of the one and only passion which obsesses Unamuno himself, the hunger for life, a full life, here and after.  Here is, for instance, *Abel Sánchez,* a sombre study of hatred, a modern paraphrase of the story of Cain.  Joaquín Monegro, the Cain of the novel, has been reading Byron's poem, and writes in his diary : " It was when I read how Lucifer declared to Cain that he, Cain, was immortal, that I began in terror to wonder whether I also was immortal and whether in me would be also immortal my hatred.  'Have I a soul?' I said to myself then.  'Is this my hatred soul?' And I came to think that it could not be otherwise, that such a hatred cannot be the function of a body. . . . A corruptible organism could not hate as I hated."

Thus Joaquín Monegro, like every other main character in his work, appears preoccupied by the same central pieoccupation of Unamuno.  In one word, all Unamuno's characters are but incarnations of himself. But that is what we expected to find in a lyrical novelist.

There are critics who conclude from this observation that these characters do not exist, that they are mere arguments on legs, personified ideas.  Here and there, in Unamuno's novels, there are passages which lend some colour of plausibility to this view.  Yet, it is in my opinion mistaken.  Unamuno's characters may be schematized, stripped of their complexities, reduced to the mainspring of their nature; they may, moreover, reveal mainsprings made of the same steel.  But that they are alive no one could deny who has a sense for life.  The very restraint in the use of physical details which Unamuno has made a feature of his creative work may have led his critics to forget the intensity of those— admirably chosen—which are given.  It is significant that the eyes play an important part in his description of characters and in his narrative too.  His sense of the interpenetration of body and soul is so deep that he does not for one moment let us forget how bodily his " souls " are, and how pregnant with spiritual significance is every one of their words and gestures. No. These characters are not arguments on legs. They truly are men and women of " flesh and bones," human, terribly human.

In thus emphasizing a particular feature in their nature, Unamuno imparts to his creations a certain deformity which savours of romantic days. Yet Unamuno is not a romanticist, mainly because Romanticism was an esthetic attitude, and his attitude is seldom purely esthetic. For all their show of passion, true Romanticists seldom gave their real selves to their art. They created a stage double of their own selves for public exhibitions. They sought the picturesque. Their form was lyrical, but their substance was dramatic. Unamuno, on the contrary, even though he often seeks expression in dramatic form, is essentially lyrical. And if he is always intense, he never is exuberant. He follows the Spanish tradition for restraint—for there is one, along its opposite tradition for grandiloquence—and, true to the spirit of it, he seeks the maximum of effect through the minimum of means. Then, he never shouts. Here is an example of his quiet method, the rhythmical beauty of which is unfortunately almost untranslatable :

" Y así pasaron días de llanto y de negrura hasta que las lágrimas fueron yéndose hacia adentro y la casa fué derritiendo los negrores " (*Niebla*) (And thus, days of weeping and mourning went by, till the tears began to flow inward and the blackness to melt in the home).

\* \* \* \* \*

Miguel de Unamuno is to-day the greatest literary figure of Spain. Baroja may surpass him in variety of external experience, Azorín in delicate art, Ortega y Gasset in philosophical subtlety, Ayala in intellectual elegance, Valle Inclán in rhythmical grace. Even in

vitality he may have to yield the first place to that over-
whelming athlete of literature, Blasco Ibáñez. But
Unamuno is head and shoulders above them all in the
highness of his purpose and in the earnestness and
loyalty with which, Quixote-like, he has served all
through his life his unattainable Dulcinea. Then there
is another and most important reason which explains
his position as first, *princeps*, of Spanish letters, and it
is that Unamuno, by the cross which he has chosen to
bear, incarnates the spirit of modern Spain. His eternal
conflict between faith and reason, between life and
thought, between spirit and intellect, between heaven
and civilization, is the conflict of Spain herself. A
border country, like Russia, in which East and West
mix their spiritual waters, Spain wavers between two
life-philosophies and cannot rest. In Russia, this conflict emerges in literature during the nineteenth century,
when Dostoievsky and Tolstoy stand for the East while
Turgeniev becomes the West's advocate. In Spain, a
country less articulate, and, moreover, a country in which
the blending of East and West is more intimate, for both
found a common solvent in centuries of Latin civilization, the conflict is less clear, less on the surface. To-
day Ortega y Gasset is our Turgeniev—not without
mixture. Unamuno is our Dostoievsky, but painfully
aware of the strength of the other side within him, and
full of misgivings. Nor is it sure that when we speak of
East in this connection we really mean East. There is
a third country in Europe in which the " Eastern " view
is as forcibly put and as deeply understood as the
" Western," a third border country—England. England, particularly in those of her racial elements conven-
tionally named Celtic, is closely in sympathy with the
" East." Ireland is almost purely " Eastern " in this
respect. That is perhaps why Unamuno feels so strong
an attraction for the English language and its literature,
and why, even to this day, he follows so closely the

movements of English thought.[1]  For his own nature,
of a human being astride two enemy ideals, draws him
instinctively towards minds equally placed in opposition,
yet a co-operating opposition, to progress.  Thus
Unamuno, whose literary qualities and defects make him
a genuine representative of the more masculine variety
of the Spanish genius, becomes in his spiritual life the
true living symbol of his country and his time.  And
that he is great enough to bear this incarnation is a sufficient measure of his greatness.

S. DE MADARIAGA.

[1] " Me va interesando ese Dean Inge," he wrote to me last year.

# AUTHOR'S PREFACE

I INTENDED at first to write a short Prologue to this English translation of my *Del Sentimiento Trágico de la Vida,* which has been undertaken by my friend Mr. J. E. Crawford Flitch. But upon further consideration I have abandoned the idea, for I reflected that after all I wrote this book not for Spaniards only, but for all civilized and Christian men—Christian in particular, whether consciously so or not—of whatever country they may be.

Furthermore, if I were to set about writing an Introduction in the light of all that we see and feel now, after the Great War, and, still more, of what we foresee and forefeel, I should be led into writing yet another book. And that is a thing to be done with deliberation and only after having better digested this terrible peace, which is nothing else but the war's painful convalescence.

As for many years my spirit has been nourished upon the very core of English literature—evidence of which the reader may discover in the following pages—the translator, in putting my *Sentimiento Trágico* into English, has merely converted not a few of the thoughts and feelings therein expressed back into their original form of expression. Or retranslated them, perhaps. Whereby they emerge other than they originally were, for an idea does not pass from one language to another without change.

The fact that this English translation has been carefully revised here, in my house in this ancient city of Salamanca, by the translator and myself, implies not merely some guarantee of exactitude, but also something more—namely, a correction, in certain respects, of the original.

The truth is that, being an incorrigible Spaniard, I am naturally given to a kind of extemporization and to neglectfulness of a filed niceness in my works. For this reason my original work—and likewise the Italian and French translations of it—issued from the press with a certain number of errors, obscurities, and faulty references. The labour which my friend Mr. J. E. Crawford Flitch fortunately imposed upon me in making me revise his translation obliged me to correct these errors, to clarify some obscurities, and to give greater exactitude to certain quotations from foreign writers. Hence this English translation of my *Sentimiento Trágico* presents in some ways a more purged and correct text than that of the original Spanish. This perhaps compensates for what it may lose in the spontaneity of my Spanish thought, which at times, I believe, is scarcely translatable.

It would advantage me greatly if this translation, in opening up to me a public of English-speaking readers, should some day lead to my writing something addressed to and concerned with this public. For just as a new friend enriches our spirit, not so much by what he gives us of himself, as by what he causes us to discover in our own selves, something which, if we had never known him, would have lain in us undeveloped, so it is with a new public. Perhaps there may be regions in my own Spanish spirit—my Basque spirit, and therefore doubly Spanish—unexplored by myself, some corner hitherto uncultivated, which I should have to cultivate in order to offer the flowers and fruits of it to the peoples of English speech.

And now, no more.

God give my English readers that inextinguishable thirst for truth which I desire for myself.

MIGUEL DE UNAMUNO.

SALAMANCA,
   *April*, 1921.

------

## TRANSLATOR'S NOTE

FOOTNOTES added by the Translator, other than those which merely supplement references to writers or their works mentioned in the text, are distinguished by his initials

# I

## THE MAN OF FLESH AND BONE

*Homo sum; nihil humani a me alienum puto,* said the
Latin playwright. And I would rather say, *Nullum
hominem a me alienum puto:* I am a man; no other
man do I deem a stranger. For to me the adjective
*humanus* is no less suspect than its abstract substantive
*humanitas,* humanity. Neither "the human" nor
"humanity," neither the simple adjective nor the
substantivized adjective, but the concrete substantive—
man. The man of flesh and bone; the man who is born,
suffers, and dies—above all, who dies; the man who eats
and drinks and plays and sleeps and thinks and wills;
the man who is seen and heard; the brother, the real
brother.

For there is another thing which is also called man,
and he is the subject of not a few lucubrations, more or
less scientific. He is the legendary featherless biped,
the ζῷον πολιτικόν of Aristotle, the social contractor of
Rousseau, the *homo economicus* of the Manchester
school, the *homo sapiens* of Linnæus, or, if you like,
the vertical mammal. A man neither of here nor there,
neither of this age nor of another, who has neither sex
nor country, who is, in brief, merely an idea. That is
to say, a no-man.

The man we have to do with is the man of flesh and
bone—I, you, reader of mine, the other man yonder, all
of us who walk solidly on the earth.

And this concrete man, this man of flesh and bone,
is at once the subject and the supreme object of all

1

philosophy, whether certain self-styled philosophers like
it or not.

In most of the histories of philosophy that I know,
philosophic systems are presented to us as if growing
out of one another spontaneously, and their authors,
the philosophers, appear only as mere pretexts. The
inner biography of the philosophers, of the men who
philosophized, occupies a secondary place. And yet it
is precisely this inner biography that explains for us
most things.

It behoves us to say, before all, that philosophy lies
closer to poetry than to science. All philosophic systems
which have been constructed as a supreme concord of
the final results of the individual sciences have in every
age possessed much less consistency and life than those
which expressed the integral spiritual yearning of their
authors.

And, though they concern us so greatly, and are,
indeed, indispensable for our life and thought, the
sciences are in a certain sense more foreign to us than
philosophy. They fulfil a more objective end—that is
to say, an end more external to ourselves. They are
fundamentally a matter of economics. A new scientific
discovery, of the kind called theoretical, is, like a
mechanical discovery—that of the steam-engine, the
telephone, the phonograph, or the aeroplane—a thing
which is useful for something else. Thus the telephone
may be useful to us in enabling us to communicate at a
distance with the woman we love. But she, wherefore is
she useful to us? A man takes an electric tram to go to
hear an opera, and asks himself, Which, in this case, is
the more useful, the tram or the opera?

Philosophy answers to our need of forming a complete
and unitary conception of the world and of life, and as a
result of this conception, a feeling which gives birth to
an inward attitude and even to outward action. But the
fact is that this feeling, instead of being a consequence

of this conception, is the cause of it. Our philosophy—
that is, our mode of understanding or not understanding
the world and life—springs from our feeling towards life
itself. And life, like everything affective, has roots in
subconsciousness, perhaps in unconsciousness.

It is not usually our ideas that make us optimists or
pessimists, but it is our optimism or our pessimism, of
physiological or perhaps pathological origin, as much
the one as the other, that makes our ideas.

Man is said to be a reasoning animal. I do not know
why he has not been defined as an affective or feeling
animal. Perhaps that which differentiates him from
other animals is feeling rather than reason. More often
I have seen a cat reason than laugh or weep. Perhaps
it weeps or laughs inwardly—but then perhaps, also
inwardly, the crab resolves equations of the second
degree.

And thus, in a philosopher, what must needs most
concern us is the man.

Take Kant, the man Immanuel Kant, who was born
and lived at Königsberg, in the latter part of the eighteenth century and the beginning of the nineteenth. In
the philosophy of this man Kant, a man of heart and head
—that is to say, a man—there is a significant somersault,
as Kierkegaard, another man—and what a man !—would
have said, the somersault from the *Critique of Pure Reason*
to the *Critique of Practical Reason*. He reconstructs in
the latter what he destroyed in the former, in spite of what
those may say who do not see the man himself. After
having examined and pulverized with his analysis the
traditional proofs of the existence of God, of the Aristotelian God, who is the God corresponding to the
ζῷον πολιτικόν, the abstract God, the unmoved prime
Mover, he reconstructs God anew; but the God of the
conscience, the Author of the moral order—the Lutheran
God, in short. This transition of Kant exists already in
embryo in the Lutheran notion of faith.

The first God, the rational God, is the projection to the outward infinite of man as he is by definition—that is to say, of the abstract man, of the man no-man ; the other God, the God of feeling and volition, is the projection to the inward infinite of man as he is by life, of the concrete man, the man of flesh and bone.

Kant reconstructed with the heart that which with the head he had overthrown. And we know, from the testimony of those who knew him and from his testimony in his letters and private declarations, that the man Kant, the more or less selfish old bachelor who professed philosophy at Königsberg at the end of the century of the Encyclopedia and the goddess of Reason, was a man much preoccupied with the problem—I mean with the only real vital problem, the problem that strikes at the very root of our being, the problem of our individual and personal destiny, of the immortality of the soul. The man Kant was not resigned to die utterly. And because he was not resigned to die utterly he made that leap, that immortal somersault,[1] from the one Critique to the other.

Whosoever reads the *Critique of Practical Reason* carefully and without blinkers will see that, in strict fact, the existence of God is therein deduced from the immortality of the soul, and not the immortality of the soul from the existence of God. The categorical imperative leads us to a moral postulate which necessitates in its turn, in the teleological or rather eschatological order, the immortality of the soul, and in order to sustain this immortality God is introduced. All the rest is the jugglery of the professional of philosophy.

The man Kant felt that morality was the basis of eschatology, but the professor of philosophy inverted the terms.

[1] " *Salto inmortal.*"    There is a play here upon the term *salto mortal*, used to denote the dangerous aerial somersault of the acrobat, which cannot be rendered in English —J E C F.

Another professor, the professor and man William James, has somewhere said that for the generality of men God is the provider of immortality. Yes, for the generality of men, including the man Kant, the man James, and the man who writes these lines which you, reader, are reading.

Talking to a peasant one day, I proposed to him the hypothesis that there might indeed be a God who governs heaven and earth, a Consciousness[1] of the Universe, but that for all that the soul of every man may not be immortal in the traditional and concrete sense. He replied : "Then wherefore God?" So answered, in the secret tribunal of their consciousness, the man Kant and the man James. Only in their capacity as professors they were compelled to justify rationally an attitude in itself so little rational. Which does not mean, of course, that the attitude is absurd.

Hegel made famous his aphorism that all the rational is real and all the real rational; but there are many of us who, unconvinced by Hegel, continue to believe that the real, the really real, is irrational, that reason builds upon irrationalities. Hegel, a great framer of definitions, attempted with definitions to reconstruct the universe, like that artillery sergeant who said that cannon were made by taking a hole and enclosing it with steel.

Another man, the man Joseph Butler, the Anglican bishop who lived at the beginning of the eighteenth century and whom Cardinal Newman declared to be the greatest man in the Anglican Church, wrote, at the conclusion of the first chapter of his great work, *The Analogy of Religion,* the chapter which treats of a future life, these pregnant words : "This credibility of a future life, which has been here insisted upon, how little soever it may satisfy our curiosity, seems to answer all the pur-

---

[1] "*Conciencia.*" The same word is used in Spanish to denote both consciousness and conscience. If the latter is specifically intended, the qualifying adjective "*moral*" or "*religiosa*" is commonly added.—J. E. C. F

poses of religion, in like manner as a demonstrative proof would. Indeed a proof, even a demonstrative one, of a future life, would not be a proof of religion. For, that we are to live hereafter, is just as reconcilable with the scheme of atheism, and as well to be accounted for by it, as that we are now alive is : and therefore nothing can be more absurd than to argue from that scheme that there can be no future state."

The man Butler, whose works were perhaps known to the man Kant, wished to save the belief in the immortality of the soul, and with this object he made it independent of belief in God. The first chapter of his *Analogy* treats, as I have said, of the future life, and the second of the government of God by rewards and punishments. And the fact is that, fundamentally, the good Anglican bishop deduces the existence of God from the immortality of the soul. And as this deduction was the good Anglican bishop's starting-point, he had not to make that somersault which at the close of the same century the good Lutheran philosopher had to make. Butler, the bishop, was one man and Kant, the professor, another man.

To be a man is to be something concrete, unitary, and substantive ; it is to be a thing—*res*. Now we know what another man, the man Benedict Spinoza, that Portuguese Jew who was born and lived in Holland in the middle of the seventeenth century, wrote about the nature of things. The sixth proposition of Part III. of his *Ethic* states : *unaquæque res, qualenus in se est, in suo esse perseverare conatur*—that is, Everything, in so far as it is in itself, endeavours to persist in its own being. Everything in so far as it is in itself—that is to say, in so far as it is substance, for according to him substance is *id quod in se est et per se concipitur*—that which is in itself and is conceived by itself. And in the following proposition, the seventh, of the same part, he adds : *conatus, quo unaquæque res in suo esse perseverare*

*conatur, nihil est præter ipsius rei actualem essentiam*—
that is, the endeavour wherewith everything endeavours .
to persist in its own being is nothing but the actual
essence of the thing itself.   This means that your essence,
reader, mine, that of the man Spinoza, that of the man
Butler, of the man Kant, and of every man who is a man,
is nothing but the endeavour, the effort, which he makes
to continue to be a man, not to die.   And the other
proposition which follows these two, the eighth, says :
*conatus, quo unaquæque res in suo esse perseverare*
*conatur, nullum tempus finitum, sed indefinitum in-*
*volvit*—that is, The endeavour whereby each individual
thing endeavours to persist involves no finite time but
indefinite time.   That is to say that you, I, and Spinoza
wish never to die and that this longing of ours never to
die is our actual essence.   Nevertheless, this poor Portuguese Jew, exiled in the mists of Holland, could never
attain to believing in his own personal immortality, and
all his philosophy was but a consolation which he con-
trived for his lack of faith.   Just as other men have a
pain in hand or foot, heart-ache or head-ache, so he had
God-ache.   Unhappy man !   And unhappy fellow-men !

And man, this thing, is he a thing ?   How absurd
soever the question may appear, there are some who have
propounded it.   Not long ago there went abroad a certain
doctrine called Positivism, which did much good and
much ill.   And among other ills that it wrought was the
introduction of a method of analysis whereby facts were
pulverized, reduced to a dust of facts.   Most of the facts
labelled as such by Positivism were really only fragments
of facts.   In psychology its action was harmful.   There
were even scholastics meddling in literature—I will not
say philosophers meddling in poetry, because poet and
philosopher are twin brothers, if not even one and the
same—who carried this Positivist psychological analysis
into the novel and the drama, where the main business is
to give act and motion to concrete men, men of flesh and

bone, and by dint of studying states of consciousness, consciousness itself disappeared. The same thing happened to them which is said often to happen in the examination and testing of certain complicated, organic, living chemical compounds, when the reagents destroy the very body which it was proposed to examine and all that is obtained is the products of its decomposition.

Taking as their starting-point the evident fact that contradictory states pass through our consciousness, they did not succeed in envisaging consciousness itself, the " I." To ask a man about his " I " is like asking him about his body. And note that in speaking of the " I," I speak of the concrete and personal " I," not of the " I " of Fichte, but of Fichte himself, the man Fichte.

That which determines a man, that which makes him one man, one and not another, the man he is and not the man he is not, is a principle of unity and a principle of continuity. A principle of unity firstly in space, thanks to the body, and next in action and intention. When we walk, one foot does not go forward and the other backward, nor, when we look, if we are normal, does one eye look towards the north and the other towards the south. In each moment of our life we entertain some purpose, and to this purpose the synergy of our actions is directed. Notwithstanding the next moment we may change our purpose. And in a certain sense a man is so much the more a man the more unitary his action. Some there are who throughout their whole life follow but one single purpose, be it what it may.

Also a principle of continuity in time. Without entering upon a discussion—an unprofitable discussion— as to whether I am or am not he who I was twenty years ago, it appears to me to be indisputable that he who I am to-day derives, by a continuous series of states of consciousness, from him who was in my body twenty years ago. Memory is the basis of individual personality, just as tradition is the basis of the collective personality of a people. We live in memory and by memory, and our spiritual life is at bottom simply the effort of our memory to persist, to transform itself into hope, the effort of our past to transform itself into our future.

All this, I know well, is sheer platitude; but in going about in the world one meets men who seem to have no feeling of their own personality. One of my best friends with whom I have walked and talked every day for many years, whenever I spoke to him of this sense of one's own personality, used to say: "But I have no sense of myself; I don't know what that is."

On a certain occasion this friend remarked to me: "I should like to be So-and-so" (naming someone), and I said: "That is what I shall never be able to understand—that one should want to be someone else. To want to be someone else is to want to cease to be he who one is. I understand that one should wish to have what someone else has, his wealth or his knowledge; but to be someone else, that is a thing I cannot comprehend." It has often been said that every man who has suffered misfortunes prefers to be himself, even with his misfortunes, rather than to be someone else without them. For unfortunate men, when they preserve their normality in their misfortune—that is to say, when they endeavour to persist in their own being—prefer misfortune to non-existence. For myself I can say that as a youth, and even as a child, I remained unmoved when shown the most moving pictures of hell, for even then nothing appeared to me quite so horrible as nothingness itself. It was a furious hunger of being that possessed me, an appetite for divinity, as one of our ascetics has put it.[1]

To propose to a man that he should be someone else, that he should become someone else, is to propose to him that he should cease to be himself. Everyone defends his own personality, and only consents to a change in his mode of thinking or of feeling in so far as this change is

[1] San Juan de los Angeles.

able to enter into the unity of his spirit and become
involved in its continuity; in so far as this change can
harmonize and integrate itself with all the rest of his
mode of being, thinking and feeling, and can at the
same time knit itself with his memories.  Neither of a
man nor of a people—which is, in a certain sense, also a
man—can a change be demanded which breaks the unity
and continuity of the person.  A man can change greatly,
almost completely even, but the change must take place
within his continuity.

It is true that in certain individuals there occur what
are called changes of personality; but these are pathological cases, and as such are studied by alienists.  In
these changes of personality, memory, the basis of consciousness, is completely destroyed, and all that is left
to the sufferer as the substratum of his individual continuity, which has now ceased to be personal, is the
physical organism.  For the subject who suffers it, such
an infirmity is equivalent to death—it is not equivalent
to death only for those who expect to inherit his fortune,
if he possesses one!  And this infirmity is nothing less
than a revolution, a veritable revolution.

A disease is, in a certain sense, an organic dissocia-
tion; it is a rebellion of some element or organ of the
living body which breaks the vital synergy and seeks an
end distinct from that which the other elements co-
ordinated with it seek.  Its end, considered in itself—
that is to say, in the abstract—may be more elevated,
more noble, more anything you like; but it is different.
To fly and breathe in the air may be better than to swim
and breathe in the water; but if the fins of a fish aimed
at converting themselves into wings, the fish, as a fish,
would perish.  And it is useless to say that it would end
by becoming a bird, if in this becoming there was not a
process of continuity.  I do not precisely know, but
perhaps it may be possible for a fish to engender a bird,
or another fish more akin to a bird than itself; but a fish,

this fish, cannot itself and during its own lifetime become a bird.

Everything in me that conspires to break the unity and continuity of my life conspires to destroy me and consequently to destroy itself. Every individual in a people who conspires to break the spiritual unity and continuity of that people tends to destroy it and to destroy himself as a part of that people. What if some other people is better than our own ?  Very possibly, although perhaps we do not clearly understand what is meant by better or worse.  Richer ?  Granted.  More cultured ?  Granted likewise.  Happier ?  Well, happiness . . . but still, let it pass !  A conquering people (or what is called conquering) while we are conquered ?  Well and good.  All this is good—but it is something different.  And that is enough.  Because for me the becoming other than I am, the breaking of the unity and continuity of my life, is to cease to be he who I am—that is to say, it is simply to cease to be.  And that—no !  Anything rather than that !

Another, you say, might play the part that I play as well or better ?  Another might fulfil my function in society ?  Yes, but it would not be I.

" I, I, I, always I !" some reader will exclaim; " and who are you ?"  I might reply in the words of Obermann, that tremendous man Obermann : " For the universe, nothing—for myself, everything "; but no, I would rather remind him of a doctrine of the man Kant—to wit, that we ought to think of our fellow-men not as means but as ends.  For the question does not touch me alone, it touches you also, grumbling reader, it touches each and all.  Singular judgments have the value of universal judgments, the logicians say.  The singular is not particular, it is universal.

Man is an end, not a means.  All civilization addresses itself to man, to each man, to each I.  What is that idol, call it Humanity or call it what you like, to which all men and each individual man must be sacrificed ?  For

I sacrifice myself for my neighbours, for my fellow-countrymen, for my children, and these sacrifice themselves in their turn for theirs, and theirs again for those that come after them, and so on in a never-ending series of generations. And who receives the fruit of this sacrifice?

Those who talk to us about this fantastic sacrifice, this dedication without an object, are wont to talk to us also about the right to live. What is this right to live? They tell me I am here to realize I know not what social end; but I feel that I, like each one of my fellows, am here to realize myself, to live.

Yes, yes, I see it all!—an enormous social activity, a mighty civilization, a profuseness of science, of art, of industry, of morality, and afterwards, when we have filled the world with industrial marvels, with great factories, with roads, museums, and libraries, we shall fall exhausted at the foot of it all, and it will subsist—for whom? Was man made for science or was science made for man?

"Why!" the reader will exclaim again, "we are coming back to what the Catechism says: ' *Q*. For whom did God create the world? *A*. For man.'" Well, why not?—so ought the man who is a man to reply. The ant, if it took account of these matters and were a person, would reply "For the ant," and it would reply rightly. The world is made for consciousness, for each consciousness.

A human soul is worth all the universe, someone—I know not whom—has said and said magnificently. A human soul, mind you! Not a human life. Not this life. And it happens that the less a man believes in the soul—that is to say in his conscious immortality, personal and concrete—the more he will exaggerate the worth of this poor transitory life. This is the source from which springs all that effeminate, sentimental ebullition against war. True, a man ought not to wish to die, but the death to be renounced is the death of the soul. "Whosoever will save his life shall lose it," says the Gospel; but it does not say "whosoever will save his soul," the immortal soul—or, at any rate, which we believe and wish to be immortal.

And what all the objectivists do not see, or rather do not wish to see, is that when a man affirms his " I," his personal consciousness, he affirms man, man concrete and real, affirms the true humanism—the humanism of man, not of the things of man—and in affirming man he affirms consciousness. For the only consciousness of which we have consciousness is that of man.

The world is for consciousness. Or rather this *for*, this notion of finality, and feeling rather than notion, this teleological feeling, is born only where there is consciousness. Consciousness and finality are fundamentally the same thing.

If the sun possessed consciousness it would think, no doubt, that it lived in order to give light to the worlds; but it would also and above all think that the worlds existed in order that it might give them light and enjoy itself in giving them light and so live. And it would think well.

And all this tragic fight of man to save himself, this immortal craving for immortality which caused the man Kant to make that immortal leap of which I have spoken, all this is simply a fight for consciousness. If consciousness is, as some inhuman thinker has said, nothing more than a flash of light between two eternities of darkness, then there is nothing more execrable than existence.

Some may espy a fundamental contradiction in everything that I am saying, now expressing a longing for unending life, now affirming that this earthly life does not possess the value that is given to it. Contradiction? To be sure! The contradiction of my heart that says Yes and of my head that says No! Of course there is contradiction. Who does not recollect those words of the Gospel, "Lord, I believe, help thou my unbelief"? Contradiction! Of course! Since we only live in and by contradictions, since life is tragedy and the tragedy is perpetual struggle, without victory or the hope of victory, life is contradiction.

The values we are discussing are, as you see, values of the heart, and against values of the heart reasons do not avail. For reasons are only reasons—that is to say, they are not even truths. There is a class of pedantic labelmongers, pedants by nature and by grace, who remind me of that man who, purposing to console a father whose son has suddenly died in the flower of his years, says to him, "Patience, my friend, we all must die!" Would you think it strange if this father were offended at such an impertinence? For it is an impertinence. There are times when even an axiom can become an impertinence. How many times may it not be said—

*Para pensar cual tú, sólo es preciso*
*no tener nada mas que inteligencia.*[1]

There are, in fact, people who appear to think only with the brain, or with whatever may be the specific thinking organ; while others think with all the body and all the soul, with the blood, with the marrow of the bones, with the heart, with the lungs, with the belly, with the life. And the people who think only with the brain develop into definition-mongers; they become the professionals of thought. And you know what a professional is? You know what a product of the differentiation of labour is?

Take a professional boxer. He has learnt to hit with such economy of effort that, while concentrating all his strength in the blow, he only brings into play just those muscles that are required for the immediate and definite

[1] To be lacking in everything but intelligence is the necessary qualification for thinking like you

object of his action—to knock out his opponent. A blow given by a non-professional will not have so much immediate, objective efficiency; but it will more greatly vitalize the striker, causing him to bring into play almost the whole of his body. The one is the blow of a boxer, the other that of a man. And it is notorious that the Hercules of the circus, the athletes of the ring, are not, as a rule, healthy. They knock out their opponents, they lift enormous weights, but they die of phthisis or dyspepsia.

If a philosopher is not a man, he is anything but a philosopher; he is above all a pedant, and a pedant is a caricature of a man. The cultivation of any branch of science—of chemistry, of physics, of geometry, of philology—may be a work of differentiated specialization, and even so only within very narrow limits and restrictions; but philosophy, like poetry, is a work of integration and synthesis, or else it is merely pseudo-philosophical erudition.

All knowledge has an ultimate object. Knowledge for the sake of knowledge is, say what you will, nothing but a dismal begging of the question. We learn something either for an immediate practical end, or in order to complete the rest of our knowledge. Even the knowledge that appears to us to be most theoretical—that is to say, of least immediate application to the non-intellectual necessities of life—answers to a necessity which is no less real because it is intellectual, to a reason of economy in thinking, to a principle of unity and continuity of consciousness. But just as a scientific fact has its finality in the rest of knowledge, so the philosophy that we would make our own has also its extrinsic object—it refers to our whole destiny, to our attitude in face of life and the universe. And the most tragic problem of philosophy is to reconcile intellectual necessities with the necessities of the heart and the will. For it is on this rock that every philosophy that pretends to resolve the eternal and tragic contradiction, the basis of our existence, breaks to pieces.    But do all men face this contradiction squarely?

Little can be hoped from a ruler, for example, who has not at some time or other been preoccupied, even if only confusedly, with the first beginning and the ultimate end of all things, and above all of man, with the "why" of his origin and the "wherefore" of his destiny.

And this supreme preoccupation cannot be purely rational, it must involve the heart.    It is not enough to think about our destiny : it must be felt.    And the would-be leader of men who affirms and proclaims that he pays no heed to the things of the spirit, is not worthy to lead them.    By which I do not mean, of course, that any ready-made solution is to be required of him. Solution ?    Is there indeed any ?

So far as I am concerned, I will never willingly yield myself, nor entrust my confidence, to any popular leader who is not penetrated with the feeling that he who orders a people orders men, men of flesh and bone, men who are born, suffer, and, although they do not wish to die, die ; men who are ends in themselves, not merely means ; men who must be themselves and not others ; men, in fine, who seek that which we call happiness. It is inhuman, for example, to sacrifice one generation of men to the generation which follows, without having any feeling for the destiny of those who are sacrificed, without having any regard, not for their memory, not for their names, but for them themselves.

All this talk of a man surviving in his children, or in his works, or in the universal consciousness, is but vague verbiage which satisfies only those who suffer from affective stupidity, and who, for the rest, may be persons of a certain cerebral distinction.    For it is possible to possess great talent, or what we call great talent, and yet to be stupid as regards the feelings and even morally imbecile.    There have been instances.

These clever-witted, affectively stupid persons are wont

to say that it is useless to seek to delve in the unknowable or to kick against the pricks. It is as if one should say to a man whose leg has had to be amputated that it does not help him at all to think about it. And we all lack something; only some of us feel the lack and others do not. Or they pretend not to feel the lack, and then they are hypocrites.

A pedant who beheld Solon weeping for the death of a son said to him, "Why do you weep thus, if weeping avails nothing?" And the sage answered him, "Precisely for that reason—because it does not avail." It is manifest that weeping avails something, even if only the alleviation of distress; but the deep sense of Solon's reply to the impertinent questioner is plainly seen. And I am convinced that we should solve many things if we all went out into the streets and uncovered our griefs, which perhaps would prove to be but one sole common grief, and joined together in beweeping them and crying aloud to the heavens and calling upon God. And this, even though God should hear us not; but He would hear us. The chiefest sanctity of a temple is that it is a place to which men go to weep in common. A *miserere* sung in common by a multitude tormented by destiny has as much value as a philosophy. It is not enough to cure the plague: we must learn to weep for it. Yes, we must learn to weep! Perhaps that is the supreme wisdom. Why? Ask Solon.

There is something which, for lack of a better name, we will call the tragic sense of life, which carries with it a whole conception of life itself and of the universe, a whole philosophy more or less formulated, more or less conscious. And this sense may be possessed, and is possessed, not only by individual men but by whole peoples. And this sense does not so much flow from ideas as determine them, even though afterwards, as is manifest, these ideas react upon it and confirm it. Sometimes it may originate in a chance illness—

2

dyspepsia, for example; but at other times it is constitutional. And it is useless to speak, as we shall see, of men who are healthy and men who are not healthy. Apart from the fact there is no normal standard of health, nobody has proved that man is necessarily cheerful by nature. And further, man, by the very fact of being man, of possessing consciousness, is, in comparison with the ass or the crab, a diseased animal. Consciousness is a disease.

Among men of flesh and bone there have been typical examples of those who possess this tragic sense of life. I recall now Marcus Aurelius, St. Augustine, Pascal, Rousseau, *René*, *Obermann*, Thomson,[1] Leopardi, Vigny, Lenau, Kleist, Amiel, Quental, Kierkegaard—men burdened with wisdom rather than with knowledge.

And there are, I believe, peoples who possess this tragic sense of life also.

It is to this that we must now turn our attention, beginning with this matter of health and disease.

[1] James Thomson, author of *The City of Dreadful Night*.

# II.

## THE STARTING-POINT

To some, perhaps, the foregoing reflections may seem to possess a certain morbid character. Morbid? But what is disease precisely? And what is health?

May not disease itself possibly be the essential condition of that which we call progress and progress itself a disease?

Who does not know the mythical tragedy of Paradise? Therein dwelt our first parents in a state of perfect health and perfect innocence, and Jahwé gave them to eat of the tree of life and created all things for them; but he commanded them not to taste of the fruit of the tree of the knowledge of good and evil. But they, tempted by the serpent—Christ's type of prudence—tasted of the fruit of the tree of the knowledge of good and evil, and became subject to all diseases, and to death, which is their crown and consummation, and to labour and to progress. For progress, according to this legend, springs from original sin. And thus it was the curiosity of Eve, of woman, of her who is most thrall to the organic necessities of life and of the conservation of life, that occasioned the Fall and with the Fall the Redemption, and it was the Redemption that set our feet on the way to God and made it possible for us to attain to Him and to be in Him.

Do you want another version of our origin? Very well then. According to this account, man is, strictly speaking, merely a species of gorilla, orang-outang, chimpanzee, or the like, more or less hydrocephalous. Once on a time an anthropoid monkey had a diseased offspring—diseased from the strictly animal or zoological

point of view, really diseased; and this disease, although
a source of weakness, resulted in a positive gain in the
struggle for survival. The only vertical mammal at last
succeeded in standing erect—man. The upright position freed him from the necessity of using his hands as
means of support in walking; he was able, therefore, to
oppose the thumb to the other four fingers, to seize hold
of objects and to fashion tools; and it is well known that
the hands are great promoters of the intelligence. This
same position gave to the lungs, trachea, larynx, and
mouth an aptness for the production of articulate speech,
and speech is intelligence. Moreover, this position,
causing the head to weigh vertically upon the trunk,
facilitated its development and increase of weight, and
the head is the seat of the mind. But as this necessitated
greater strength and resistance in the bones of the pelvis
than in those of species whose head and trunk rest upon
all four extremities, the burden fell upon woman, the
author of the Fall according to Genesis, of bringing forth
larger-headed offspring through a harder framework of
bone. And Jahwé condemned her, for having sinned,
to bring forth her children in sorrow.

The gorilla, the chimpanzee, the orang-outang, and
their kind, must look upon man as a feeble and infirm
animal, whose strange custom it is to store up his dead.
Wherefore?

And this primary disease and all subsequent diseases
—are they not perhaps the capital element of progress?
Arthritis, for example, infects the blood and introduces
into it scoriæ, a kind of refuse, of an imperfect organic
combustion; but may not this very impurity happen to
make the blood more stimulative? May not this impure
blood promote a more active cerebration precisely because
it is impure? Water that is chemically pure is un-
drinkable. And may not also blood that is physiolo-
gically pure be unfit for the brain of the vertical mammal
that has to live by thought?

The history of medicine, moreover, teaches us that progress consists not so much in expelling the germs of disease, or rather diseases themselves, as in accommodating them to our organism and so perhaps enriching it, in dissolving them in our blood. What but this is the meaning of vaccination and all the serums, and immunity from infection through lapse of time?

If this notion of absolute health were not an abstract category, something which does not strictly exist, we might say that a perfectly healthy man would be no longer a man, but an irrational animal. Irrational, because of the lack of some disease to set a spark to his reason. And this disease which gives us the appetite of knowing for the sole pleasure of knowing, for the delight of tasting of the fruit of the tree of the knowledge of good and evil, is a real disease and a tragic one.

Πάντες ἄνθρωποι τὸν εἰδέναι ὀρέγονται φύσει, "all men naturally desire to know." Thus Aristotle begins his Metaphysic, and it has been repeated a thousand times since then that curiosity or the desire to know, which according to Genesis led our first mother to sin, is the origin of knowledge.

But it is necessary to distinguish here between the desire or appetite for knowing, apparently and at first sight for the love of knowledge itself, between the eagerness to taste of the fruit of the tree of knowledge, and the necessity of knowing for the sake of living. The latter, which gives us direct and immediate knowledge, and which in a certain sense might be called, if it does not seem too paradoxical, unconscious knowledge, is common both to men and animals, while that which distinguishes us from them is reflective knowledge, the knowing that we know.

Man has debated at length and will continue to debate at length—the world having been assigned as a theatre for his debates—concerning the origin of knowledge; but, apart from the question as to what the real truth

about this origin may be, which we will leave until later,
it is a certainly ascertained fact that in the apparential
order of things, in the life of beings who are endowed
with a certain more or less cloudy faculty of knowing
and perceiving, or who at any rate appear to act as if
they were so endowed, knowledge is exhibited to us as
bound up with the necessity of living and of procuring
the wherewithal to maintain life.  It is a consequence of
that very essence of being, which according to Spinoza
consists in the effort to persist indefinitely in its own
being.  Speaking in terms in which concreteness verges
upon grossness, it may be said that the brain, in so far as
its function is concerned, depends upon the stomach.
In beings which rank in the lowest scale of life, those
actions which present the characteristics of will, those
which appear to be connected with a more or less clear
consciousness, are actions designed to procure nourish-
ment for the being performing them.

Such then is what we may call the historical origin of
knowledge, whatever may be its origin from another
point of view.  Beings which appear to be endowed with
perception, perceive in order to be able to live, and only
perceive in so far as they require to do so in order to live.
But perhaps this stored-up knowledge, the utility in
which it had its origin being exhausted, has come to
constitute a fund of knowledge far exceeding that required for the bare necessities of living.

Thus we have, first, the necessity of knowing in order
to live, and next, arising out of this, that other knowledge which we might call superfluous knowledge or
knowledge *de luxe*, which may in its turn come to constitute a new necessity.  Curiosity, the so-called innate
desire of knowing, only awakes and becomes operative
after the necessity of knowing for the sake of living is
satisfied; and although sometimes in the conditions
under which the human race is actually living it may not
so befall, but curiosity may prevail over necessity and

knowledge over hunger, nevertheless the primordial fact is that curiosity sprang from the necessity of knowing in order to live, and this is the dead weight and gross matter carried in the matrix of science. Aspiring to be knowledge for the sake of knowledge, to know the truth for the sake of the truth itself, science is forced by the necessities of life to turn aside and put it itself at their service. While men believe themselves to be seeking truth for its own sake, they are in fact seeking life in truth. The variations of science depend upon the variations of human needs, and men of science are wont to work, willingly or unwillingly, wittingly or unwittingly, in the service of the powerful or in that of a people that demands from them the confirmation of its own desires.

But is this really a dead weight that impedes the progress of science, or is it not rather its innermost redeeming essence? It is in fact the latter, and it is a gross stupidity to presume to rebel against the very condition of life.          .

Knowledge is employed in the service of the necessity of life and primarily in the service of the instinct of personal preservation. This necessity and this instinct have created in man the organs of knowledge and given them such capacity as they possess. Man sees, hears, touches, tastes, and smells that which it is necessary for him to see, hear, touch, taste, and smell in order to preserve his life. The decay or the loss of any of these senses increases the risks with which his life is environed, and if it increases them less in the state of society in which we are actually living, the reason is that some see, hear, touch, and smell for others. A blind man, by himself and without a guide, could not live long. Society is an additional sense; it is the true common sense.

Man, then, in his quality of an isolated individual, only sees, hears, touches, tastes, and smells in so far as is necessary for living and self-preservation. If he does not perceive colours below red or above violet, the reason perhaps is that the colours which he does perceive suffice for the purposes of self-preservation. And the senses themselves are simplifying apparati which eliminate from objective reality everything that it is not necessary to know in order to utilize objects for the purpose of preserving life. In complete darkness an animal, if it does not perish, ends by becoming blind. Parasites which live in the intestines of other animals upon the nutritive juices which they find ready prepared for them by these animals, as they do not need either to see or hear, do in fact neither see nor hear; they simply adhere, a kind of receptive bag, to the being upon whom they live. For these parasites the visible and audible world does not exist. It is enough for them that the animals, in whose intestines they live, see and hear.

Knowledge, then, is primarily at the service of the instinct of self-preservation, which is indeed, as we have said with Spinoza, its very essence. And thus it may be said that it is the instinct of self-preservation that makes perceptible for us the reality and truth of the world; for it is this instinct that cuts out and separates that which exists for us from the unfathomable and illimitable region of the possible. In effect, that which has existence for us is precisely that which, in one way or another, we need to know in order to exist ourselves; objective existence, as we know it, is a dependence of our own personal existence. And nobody can deny that there may not exist, and perhaps do exist, aspects of reality unknown to us, to-day at any rate, and perhaps unknowable, because they are in no way necessary to us for the preservation of our own actual existence.

But man does not live alone; he is not an isolated individual, but a member of society. There is not a little truth in the saying that the individual, like the atom, is an abstraction. Yes, the atom apart from the universe is as much an abstraction as the universe apart from the atom. And if the individual maintains his existence by the instinct of self-preservation, society owes its being and maintenance to the individual's instinct of perpetuation. And from this instinct, or rather from society, springs reason.

Reason, that which we call reason, reflex and reflective knowledge, the distinguishing mark of man, is a social product.

It owes its origin, perhaps, to language. We think articulately—i.e., reflectively—thanks to articulate language, and this language arose out of the need of communicating our thought to our neighbours. To think is to talk with oneself, and each one of us talks with himself, thanks to our having had to talk with one another. In everyday life it frequently happens that we hit upon an idea that we were seeking and succeed in giving it form—that is to say, we obtain the idea, drawing it forth from the mist of dim perceptions which it represents, thanks to the efforts which we make to present it to others. Thought is inward language, and the inward language originates in the outward. Hence it results that reason is social and common. A fact pregnant with consequences, as we shall have occasion to see.

Now if there is a reality which, in so far as we have knowledge of it, is the creation of the instinct of personal preservation and of the senses at the service of this instinct, must there not be another reality, not less real than the former, the creation, in so far as we have knowledge of it, of the instinct of perpetuation, the instinct of the species, and of the senses at the service of this instinct? The instinct of preservation, hunger, is the foundation of the human individual; the instinct of perpetuation, love, in its most rudimentary and physiological form, is the foundation of human society. And just as man knows that which he needs to know in order that he may preserve his existence, so society, or man in so far as he is a social being, knows that which he needs to know in order that he may perpetuate himself in society.

There is a world, the sensible world, that is the child of hunger, and there is another world, the ideal world, that is the child of love. And just as there are senses employed in the service of the knowledge of the sensible world, so there are also senses, at present for the most part dormant, for social consciousness has scarcely awakened, employed in the service of the knowledge of the ideal world. And why must we deny objective reality to the creations of love, of the instinct of perpetuation, since we allow it to the creations of hunger or the instinct of preservation? For if it be said that the former creations are only the creations of our imagination, without objective value, may it not equally be said of the latter that they are only the creations of our senses? Who can assert that there is not an invisible and intangible world, perceived by the inward sense that lives in the service of the instinct of perpetuation?

Human society, as a society, possesses senses which the individual, but for his existence in society, would lack, just as the individual, man, who is in his turn a kind of society, possesses senses lacking in the cells of which he is composed. The blind cells of hearing, in their dim consciousness, must of necessity be unaware of the existence of the visible world, and if they should hear it spoken of they would perhaps deem it to be the arbitrary creation of the deaf cells of sight, while the latter in their turn would consider as illusion the audible world which the hearing cells create.

We have remarked before that the parasites which live in the intestines of higher animals, feeding upon the nutritive juices which these animals supply, do not need either to see or hear, and therefore for them the visible and audible world does not exist. And if they possessed a certain degree of consciousness and took account of the fact that the animal at whose expense they live

believed in a world of sight and hearing, they would
perhaps deem such belief to be due merely to the
extravagance of its imagination.  And similarly there
are social parasites, as Mr. A. J. Balfour admirably
observes,[1] who, receiving from the society in which they
live the motives of their moral conduct, deny that belief
in God and the other life is a necessary foundation for
good conduct and for a tolerable life, society having
prepared for them the spiritual nutriment by which they
live.  An isolated individual can endure life and live it
well and even heroically without in any sort believing
either in the immortality of the soul or in God, but he
lives the life of a spiritual parasite.  What we call the
sense of honour is, even in non-Christians, a Christian
product.  And I will say further, that if there exists in
a man faith in God joined to a life of purity and moral
elevation, it is not so much the believing in God that
makes him good, as the being good, thanks to God,
that makes him believe in Him.  Goodness is the best
source of spiritual clear-sightedness.

I am well aware that it may be objected that all this
talk of man creating the sensible world and love the ideal
world, of the blind cells of hearing and the deaf cells of
sight, of spiritual parasites, etc., is merely metaphor.
So it is, and I do not claim to discuss otherwise than by
metaphor.  And it is true that this social sense, the
creature of love, the creator of language, of reason, and
of the ideal world that springs from it, is at bottom
nothing other than what we call fancy or imagination.

[1] *The Foundations of Belief, being Notes Introductory to the Study of
Theology,* by the Right Hon. Arthur James Balfour    London, 1895
"So it is with those persons who claim to show by their example that
naturalism is practically consistent with the maintenance of ethical ideals with
which naturalism has no natural affinity  Their spiritual life is parasitic , it is
sheltered by convictions which belong, not to them, but to the society of
which they form a part ; it is nourished by processes in which they take no
share.  And when those convictions decay, and those processes come to an
end, the alien life which they have maintained can scarce be expected to
outlast them" (Chap. iv.)

Out of fancy springs reason. And if by imagination is understood a faculty which fashions images capriciously, I will ask : What is caprice ? And in any case the senses and reason are also fallible.

We shall have to enquire what is this inner social faculty, the imagination which personalizes everything, and which, employed in the service of the instinct of perpetuation, reveals to us God and the immortality of the soul—God being thus a social product.

But this we will reserve till later.

And now, why does man philosophize?—that is to say, why does he investigate the first causes and ultimate ends of things? Why does he seek the disinterested truth ? For to say that all men have a natural tendency to know is true; but wherefore?

Philosophers seek a theoretic or ideal starting-point for their human work, the work of philosophizing; but they are not usually concerned to seek the practical and real starting-point, the purpose. What is the object in making philosophy, in thinking it and then expounding it to one's fellows ? What does the philosopher seek in it and with it? The truth for the truth's own sake ? The truth, in order that we may subject our conduct to it and determine our spiritual attitude towards life and the universe comformably with it?

Philosophy is a product of the humanity of each philosopher, and each philosopher is a man of flesh and bone who addresses himself to other men of flesh and bone like himself. And, let him do what he will, he philosophizes not with the reason only, but with the will, with the feelings, with the flesh and with the bones, with the whole soul and the whole body. It is the man that philosophizes.

I do not wish here to use the word " I " in connection with philosophizing, lest the impersonal " I " should be understood in place of the man that philosophizes, for this concrete, circumscribed " I," this " I " of flesh and bone, that suffers from tooth-ache and finds life insupportable if death is the annihilation of the personal consciousness, must not be confounded with that other counterfeit " I," the theoretical " I " which Fichte smuggled into philosophy, nor yet with the Unique, also theoretical, of Max Stirner. It is better to say " we," understanding, however, the " we " who are circumscribed in space.

Knowledge for the sake of knowledge! Truth for truth's sake! This is inhuman. And if we say that theoretical philosophy addresses itself to practical philosophy, truth to goodness, science to ethics, I will ask : And to what end is goodness? Is it, perhaps, an end in itself? Good is simply that which contributes to the preservation, perpetuation, and enrichment of consciousness. Goodness addresses itself to man, to the maintenance and perfection of human society which is composed of men. And to what end is this? " So act that your action may be a pattern to all men," Kant tells us. That is well, but wherefore? We must needs seek for a wherefore.

In the starting-point of all philosophy, in the real starting-point, the practical not the theoretical, there is a wherefore. The philosopher philosophizes for something more than for the sake of philosophizing. *Primum vivere, deinde philosophari*, says the old Latin adage ; and as the philosopher is a man before he is a philosopher, he must needs live before he can philosophize, and, in fact, he philosophizes in order to live. And usually he philosophizes either in order to resign himself to life, or to seek some finality in it, or to distract himself and forget his griefs, or for pastime and amusement. A good illustration of this last case is to be found in that terrible Athenian ironist, Socrates, of whom Xenophon relates in his *Memorabilia* that he discovered to Theodata, the courtesan, the wiles that she ought to make use of in order to lure lovers to her

house so aptly, that she begged him to act as her companion in the chase, συνθηρατής, her pimp, in a word.
And philosophy is wont, in fact, not infrequently to
convert itself into a kind of art of spiritual pimping.
And sometimes into an opiate for lulling sorrows to
sleep.

I take at random a book of metaphysics, the first that
comes to my hand, *Time and Space, a Metaphysical
Essay,* by Shadworth H. Hodgson. I open it, and in
the fifth paragraph of the first chapter of the first part
I read :

"Metaphysics is, properly speaking, not a science
but a philosophy—that is, it is a science whose end is in
itself, in the gratification and education of the minds
which carry it on, not in external purpose, such as the
founding of any art conducive to the welfare of life."
Let us examine this. We see that metaphysics is not,
properly speaking, a science—that is, it is a science
whose end is in itself. And this science, which, properly
speaking, is not a science, has its end in itself, in the
gratification and education of the minds that cultivate
it. But what are we to understand? Is its end in itself
or is it to gratify and educate the minds that cultivate it?
Either the one or the other ! Hodgson afterwards adds
that the end of metaphysics is not any external purpose,
such as that of founding an art conducive to the welfare
of life. But is not the gratification of the mind of him
who cultivates philosophy part of the well-being of his
life? Let the reader consider this passage of the
English metaphysician and tell me if it is not a tissue
of contradictions.

Such a contradiction is inevitable when an attempt is
made to define humanly this theory of science, of knowledge, whose end is in itself, of knowing for the sake
of knowing, of attaining truth for the sake of truth.
Science exists only in personal consciousness and thanks
to it; astronomy, mathematics, have no other reality

than that which they possess as knowledge in the minds of those who study and cultivate them. And if some day all personal consciousness must come to an end on the earth; if some day the human spirit must return to the nothingness—that is to say, to the absolute unconsciousness—from whence it sprang; and if there shall no more be any spirit that can avail itself of all our accumulated knowledge—then to what end is this knowledge? For we must not lose sight of the fact that the problem of the personal immortality of the soul involves the future of the whole human species.

This series of contradictions into which the Englishman falls in his desire to explain the theory of a science whose end is in itself, is easily understood when it is remembered that it is an Englishman who speaks, and that the Englishman is before everything else a man. Perhaps a German specialist, a philosopher who had made philosophy his speciality, who had first murdered his humanity and then buried it in his philosophy, would be better able to explain this theory of a science whose end is in itself and of knowledge for the sake of knowledge.

Take the man Spinoza, that Portuguese Jew exiled in Holland; read his *Ethic* as a despairing elegiac poem, which in fact it is, and tell me if you do not hear, beneath the disemburdened and seemingly serene propositions *more geometrico*, the lugubrious echo of the prophetic psalms. It is not the philosophy of resignation but of despair. And when he wrote that the free man thinks of nothing less than of death, and that his wisdom consists in meditating not on death but on life— *homo liber de nulla re minus quam de morte cogitat et eius sapientia non mortis, sed vitæ meditatio est (Ethic,* Part IV., Prop. LXVII.)—when he wrote that, he felt, as we all feel, that we are slaves, and he did in fact think about death, and he wrote it in a vain endeavour to free himself from this thought. Nor in writing Proposition

XLII. of Part V., that "happiness is not the reward of
virtue but virtue itself," did he feel, one may be sure,
what he wrote.   For this is usually the reason why men
philosophize—in order to convince themselves, even
though they fail in the attempt.   And this desire of
convincing oneself—that is to say, this desire of doing
violence to one's own human nature—is the real starting-
point of not a few philosophies.

Whence do I come and whence comes the world in
which and by which I live?   Whither do I go and
whither goes everything that environs me?   What does
it all mean?   Such are the questions that man asks as
soon as he frees himself from the brutalizing necessity
of labouring for his material sustenance.   And if we
look closely, we shall see that beneath these questions
lies the wish to know not so much the "why" as the
"wherefore," not the cause but the end.   Cicero's
definition of philosophy is well known—" the knowledge
of things divine and human and of the causes in which
these things are contained," *rerum divinarum et
humanarum, causarumque quibus hæ res continentur;*
but in reality these causes are, for us, ends.   And what
is the Supreme Cause, God, but the Supreme End?
The "why" interests us only in view of the "wherefore."   We wish to know whence we came only in order
the better to be able to ascertain whither we are going.

This Ciceronian definition, which is the Stoic definition, is also found in that formidable intellectualist,
Clement of Alexandria, who was canonized by the
Catholic Church, and he expounds it in the fifth chapter
of the first of his *Stromata.*   But this same Christian
philosopher—Christian?—in the twenty-second chapter
of his fourth *Stroma* tells us that for the gnostic—that is
to say, the intellectual—knowledge, *gnosis*, ought to
suffice, and he adds: "I will dare aver that it is not
because he wishes to be saved that he, who devotes himself to knowledge for the sake of the divine science itself,

chooses knowledge. For the exertion of the intellect by exercise is prolonged to a perpetual exertion. And the perpetual exertion of the intellect is the essence of an intelligent being, which results from an uninterrupted process of admixture, and remains eternal contemplation, a living substance. Could we, then, suppose anyone proposing to the gnostic whether he would choose the knowledge of God or everlasting salvation, and if these, which are entirely identical, were separable, he would without the least hesitation choose the knowledge of God?" May He, may God Himself, whom we long to enjoy and possess eternally, deliver us from this Clementine gnosticism or intellectualism!

Why do I wish to know whence I come and whither I go, whence comes and whither goes everything that environs me, and what is the meaning of it all? For I do not wish to die utterly, and I wish to know whether I am to die or not definitely. If I do not die, what is my destiny? and if I die, then nothing has any meaning for me. And there are three solutions : (a) I know that I shall die utterly, and then irremediable despair, or (b) I know that I shall not die utterly, and then resignation, or (c) I cannot know either one or the other, and then resignation in despair or despair in resignation, a desperate resignation or a resigned despair, and hence conflict.

" It is best," some reader will say, " not to concern yourself with what cannot be known." But is it possible? In his very beautiful poem, *The Ancient Sage,* Tennyson said :

> Thou canst not prove the Nameless, O my son,
> Nor canst thou prove the world thou movest in,
> Thou canst not prove that thou art body alone,
> Thou canst not prove that thou art spirit alone,
> Nor canst thou prove that thou art both in one .
> Nor canst thou prove thou art immortal, no,
> Nor yet that thou art mortal—nay, my son,
> Thou canst not prove that I, who speak with thee,

3

Am not thyself in converse with thyself,
For nothing worthy proving can be proven,
Nor yet disproven · wherefore thou be wise,
Cleave ever to the sunnier side of doubt,
Cling to Faith beyond the forms of Faith !

Yes, perhaps, as the Sage says, "nothing worthy
proving can be proven, nor yet disproven"; but can
we restrain that instinct which urges man to wish to
know, and above all to wish to know the things which
may conduce to life, to eternal life? Eternal life, not
eternal knowledge, as the Alexandrian gnostic said.
For living is one thing and knowing is another; and,
as we shall see, perhaps there is such an opposition
between the two that we may say that everything vital
is anti-rational, not merely irrational, and that everything rational is anti-vital. And this is the basis of the
tragic sense of life.

The defect of Descartes' *Discourse of Method* lies not
in the antecedent methodical doubt; not in his beginning
by resolving to doubt everything, a merely intellectual
device; but in his resolution to begin by emptying himself of himself, of Descartes, of the real man, the man of
flesh and bone, the man who does not want to die, in
order that he might be a mere thinker—that is, an
abstraction. But the real man returned and thrust
himself into the philosophy.

"*Le bon sens est la chose du monde la mieux
partagée.*" Thus begins the *Discourse of Method,* and
this good sense saved him. He continues talking about
himself, about the man Descartes, telling us among
other things that he greatly esteemed eloquence and
loved poetry; that he delighted above all in mathematics
because of the evidence and certainty of its reasons, and
that he revered our theology and claimed as much as any
to attain to heaven—*et prétendais autant qu'aucun autre
à gagner le ciel.* And this pretension—a very laudable
one, I think, and above all very natural—was what

prevented him from deducing all the consequences of his methodical doubt. The man Descartes claimed, as much as any other, to attain to heaven, "but having learned as a thing very sure that the way to it is not less open to the most ignorant than to the most learned, and that the revealed truths which lead thither are beyond our intelligence, I did not dare submit them to my feeble reasonings, and I thought that to undertake to examine them and to succeed therein, I should want some extraordinary help from heaven and need to be more than man." And here we have the man. Here we have the man who "did not feel obliged, thank God, to make a profession (*métier*) of science in order to increase his means, and who did not pretend to play the cynic and despise glory." And afterwards he tells us how he was compelled to make a sojourn in Germany, and there, shut up in a stove (*poêle*) he began to philosophize his method. But in Germany, shut up in a stove! And such his discourse is, a stove-discourse, and the stove a German one, although the philosopher shut up in it was a Frenchman who proposed to himself to attain to heaven.

And he arrives at the *cogito ergo sum,* which St. Augustine had already anticipated; but the *ego* implicit in this enthymeme, *ego cogito, ergo ego sum,* is an unreal —that is, an ideal—*ego* or I, and its *sum,* its existence, something unreal also. " I think, therefore I am," can only mean " I think, therefore I am a thinker "; this being of the " I am," which is deduced from " I think," is merely a knowing; this being is knowledge, but not life. And the primary reality is not that I think, but that I live, for those also live who do not think. Although this living may not be a real living. God! what contradictions when we seek to join in wedlock life and reason !

The truth is *sum, ergo cogito*—I am, therefore I think, although not everything that is thinks. Is not consciousness of thinking above all consciousness of being? Is pure thought possible, without consciousness of self, without personality? Can there exist pure knowledge without feeling, without that species of materiality which feeling lends to it? Do we not perhaps feel thought, and do we not feel ourselves in the act of knowing and willing? Could not the man in the stove have said: "I feel, therefore I am"? or "I will, therefore I am"? And to feel oneself, is it not perhaps to feel oneself imperishable? To will oneself, is it not to wish oneself eternal—that is to say, not to wish to die? What the sorrowful Jew of Amsterdam called the essence of the thing, the effort that it makes to persist indefinitely in its own being, self-love, the longing for immortality, is it not perhaps the primal and fundamental condition of all reflective or human knowledge? And is it not therefore the true base, the real starting-point, of all philosophy, although the philosophers, perverted by intellectualism, may not recognize it?

And, moreover, it was the *cogito* that introduced a distinction which, although fruitful of truths, has been fruitful also of confusions, and this distinction is that between object, *cogito*, and subject, *sum*. There is scarcely any distinction that does not also lead to confusion. But we will return to this later.

For the present let us remain keenly suspecting that the longing not to die, the hunger for personal immortality, the effort whereby we tend to persist indefinitely in our own being, which is, according to the tragic Jew, our very essence, that this is the affective basis of all knowledge and the personal inward starting-point of all human philosophy, wrought by a man and for men. And we shall see how the solution of this inward affective problem, a solution which may be but the despairing renunciation of the attempt at a solution, is that which colours all the rest of philosophy. Underlying even the so-called problem of knowledge there is simply this human feeling, just as underlying the enquiry into the "why," the cause, there is simply the search for the "wherefore," the end. All the rest is either to deceive oneself or to wish to deceive others; and to wish to deceive others in order to deceive oneself.

And this personal and affective starting-point of all philosophy and all religion is the tragic sense of life. Let us now proceed to consider this.

# III

## THE HUNGER OF IMMORTALITY

LET us pause to consider this immortal yearning for immortality—even though the gnostics or intellectuals may be able to say that what follows is not philosophy but rhetoric. Moreover, the divine Plato, when he discussed the immortality of the soul in his *Phædo*, said that it was proper to clothe it in legend, μυθολογεῖν.

First of all let us recall once again—and it will not be for the last time—that saying of Spinoza that every being endeavours to persist in itself, and that this endeavour is its actual essence, and implies indefinite time, and that the soul, in fine, sometimes with a clear and distinct idea, sometimes confusedly, tends to persist in its being with indefinite duration, and is aware of its persistency (*Ethic*, Part III., Props. VI.-X.).

It is impossible for us, in effect, to conceive of ourselves as not existing, and no effort is capable of enabling consciousness to realize absolute unconsciousness, its own annihilation. Try, reader, to imagine to yourself, when you are wide awake, the condition of your soul when you are in a deep sleep; try to fill your consciousness with the representation of no-consciousness, and you will see the impossibility of it. The effort to comprehend it causes the most tormenting dizziness. We cannot conceive ourselves as not existing.

The visible universe, the universe that is created by the instinct of self-preservation, becomes all too narrow for me. It is like a cramped cell, against the bars of which my soul beats its wings in vain. Its lack of air stifles me. More, more, and always more ! I want to be myself, and yet without ceasing to be myself to be others as well, to merge myself into the totality of things visible and invisible, to extend myself into the illimitable of space and to prolong myself into the infinite of time. Not to be all and for ever is as if not to be—at least, let me be my whole self, and be so for ever and ever. And to be the whole of myself is to be everybody else. Either all or nothing!

All or nothing! And what other meaning can the Shakespearean "To be or not to be" have, or that passage in *Coriolanus* where it is said of Marcius "He wants nothing of a god but eternity"? Eternity, eternity!—that is the supreme desire! The thirst of eternity is what is called love among men, and whosoever loves another wishes to eternalize himself in him. Nothing is real that is not eternal.

From the poets of all ages and from the depths of their souls this tremendous vision of the flowing away of life like water has wrung bitter cries—from Pindar's "dream of a shadow," σκιᾶς ὄναρ, to Calderón's "life is a dream" and Shakespeare's "we are such stuff as dreams are made on," this last a yet more tragic sentence than Calderón's, for whereas the Castilian only declares that our life is a dream, but not that we ourselves are the dreamers of it, the Englishman makes us ourselves a dream, a dream that dreams.

The vanity of the passing world and love are the two fundamental and heart-penetrating notes of true poetry. And they are two notes of which neither can be sounded without causing the other to vibrate. The feeling of the vanity of the passing world kindles love in us, the only thing that triumphs over the vain and transitory, the only thing that fills life again and eternalizes it. In appearance at any rate, for in reality . . . And love, above all when it struggles against destiny, overwhelms us with the feeling of the vanity of this world of appearances and gives us a glimpse of another world, in which destiny is overcome and liberty is law.

Everything passes ! Such is the refrain of those who have drunk, lips to the spring, of the fountain of life, of those who have tasted of the fruit of the tree of the knowledge of good and evil.

To be, to be for ever, to be without ending ! thirst of being, thirst of being more ! hunger of God ! thirst of love eternalizing and eternal ! to be for ever ! to be God !

" Ye shall be as gods !" we are told in Genesis that the serpent said to the first pair of lovers (Gen. iii. 5). " If in this life only we have hope in Christ, we are of all men most miserable," wrote the Apostle (1 Cor. xv. 19); and all religion has sprung historically from the cult of the dead—that is to say, from the cult of immortality.

The tragic Portuguese Jew of Amsterdam wrote that the free man thinks of nothing less than of death ; but this free man is a dead man, free from the impulse of life, for want of love, the slave of his liberty. This thought that I must die and the enigma of what will come after death is the very palpitation of my consciousness. When I contemplate the green serenity of the fields or look into the depths of clear eyes through which shines a fellow-soul, my consciousness dilates, I feel the diastole of the soul and am bathed in the flood of the life that flows about me, and I believe in my future; but instantly the voice of mystery whispers to me, " Thou shalt cease to be !" the angel of Death touches me with his wing, and the systole of the soul floods the depths of my spirit with the blood of divinity.

Like Pascal, I do not understand those who assert that they care not a farthing for these things, and this indifference " in a matter that touches themselves, their eternity, their all, exasperates me rather than moves me to compassion, astonishes and shocks me," and he who feels thus " is for me," as for Pascal, whose are the words just quoted, " a monster."

It has been said a thousand times and in a thousand

books that ancestor-worship is for the most part the
source of primitive religions, and it may be strictly said
that what most distinguishes man from the other animals
is that, in one form or another, he guards his dead and
does not give them over to the neglect of teeming mother
earth; he is an animal that guards its dead. And from
what does he thus guard them? From what does he so
futilely protect them? The wretched consciousness
shrinks from its own annihilation, and, just as an
animal spirit, newly severed from the womb of the
world, finds itself confronted with the world and knows
itself distinct from it, so consciousness must needs
desire to possess another life than that of the world itself.
And so the earth would run the risk of becoming a vast
cemetery before the dead themselves should die again.

When mud huts or straw shelters, incapable of resisting the inclemency of the weather, sufficed for the living,
tumuli were raised for the dead, and stone was used for
sepulchres before it was used for houses. It is the
strong-builded houses of the dead that have withstood
the ages, not the houses of the living; not the temporary
lodgings but the permanent habitations.

This cult, not of death but of immortality, originates
and preserves religions. In the midst of the delirium of
destruction, Robespierre induced the Convention to
declare the existence of the Supreme Being and "the
consolatory principle of the immortality of the soul,"
the Incorruptible being dismayed at the idea of having
himself one day to turn to corruption.

A disease? Perhaps; but he who pays no heed to his
disease is heedless of his health, and man is an animal
essentially and substantially diseased. A disease?
Perhaps it may be, like life itself to which it is thrall,
and perhaps the only health possible may be death; but
this disease is the fount of all vigorous health. From
the depth of this anguish, from the abyss of the feeling
of our mortality, we emerge into the light of another

heaven, as from the depth of Hell Dante emerged to behold the stars once again—

*e quindi uscimmo a riveder le stelle.*

Although this meditation upon mortality may soon induce in us a sense of anguish, it fortifies us in the end. Retire, reader, into yourself and imagine a slow dissolution of yourself—the light dimming about you—all things becoming dumb and soundless, enveloping you in silence—the objects that you handle crumbling away between your hands—the ground slipping from under your feet—your very memory vanishing as if in a swoon —everything melting away from you into nothingness and you yourself also melting away—the very consciousness of nothingness, merely as the phantom harbourage of a shadow, not even remaining to you.

I have heard it related of a poor harvester who died in a hospital bed, that when the priest went to anoint his hands with the oil of extreme unction, he refused to open his right hand, which clutched a few dirty coins, not considering that very soon neither his hand nor he himself would be his own any more. And so we close and clench, not our hand, but our heart, seeking to clutch the world in it.

A friend confessed to me that, foreseeing while in the full vigour of physical health the near approach of a violent death, he proposed to concentrate his life and spend the few days which he calculated still remained to him in writing a book. Vanity of vanities!

If at the death of the body which sustains me, and which I call mine to distinguish it from the self that is I, my consciousness returns to the absolute unconsciousness from which it sprang, and if a like fate befalls all my brothers in humanity, then is our toil-worn human race nothing but a fatidical procession of phantoms, going from nothingness to nothingness, and humanitarianism the most inhuman thing known.

And the remedy is not that suggested in the quatrain that runs—

> *Cada vez que considero*
> *que me tengo de morir,*
> *tiendo la capa en el suelo*
> *y no me harto de dormir.*[1]

No! The remedy is to consider our mortal destiny without flinching, to fasten our gaze upon the gaze of the Sphinx, for it is thus that the malevolence of its spell is discharmed.

If we all die utterly, wherefore does everything exist? Wherefore? It is the Wherefore of the Sphinx; it is the Wherefore that corrodes the marrow of the soul; it is the begetter of that anguish which gives us the love of hope.

Among the poetic laments of the unhappy Cowper there are some lines written under the oppression of delirium, in which, believing himself to be the mark of the Divine vengeance, he exclaims—

> Hell might afford my miseries a shelter.

This is the Puritan sentiment, the preoccupation with sin and predestination; but read the much more terrible words of Sénancour, expressive of the Catholic, not the Protestant, despair, when he makes his Obermann say, "L'homme est périssable. Il se peut; mais périssons en résistant, et, si le néant nous est réservé, ne faisons pas que ce soit une justice." And I must confess, painful though the confession be, that in the days of the simple faith of my childhood, descriptions of the tortures of hell, however terrible, never made me tremble, for I always felt that nothingness was much more terrifying. He who suffers lives, and he who lives suffering, even though over the portal of his abode is written "Abandon all hope!" loves and hopes. It is better to live in pain

---

[1] Each time that I consider that it is my lot to die, I spread my cloak upon the ground and am never surfeited with sleeping.

than to cease to be in peace.  The truth is that I could
not believe in this atrocity of Hell, of an eternity of
punishment, nor did I see any more real hell than
nothingness and the prospect of it.  And I continue in
the belief that if we all believed in our salvation from
nothingness we should all be better.

What is this *joie de vivre* that they talk about nowadays?  Our hunger for God, our thirst of immortality,
of survival, will always stifle in us this pitiful enjoyment
of the life that passes and abides not.  It is the frenzied
love of life, the love that would have life to be unending,
that most often urges us to long for death.  "If it is
true that I am to die utterly," we say to ourselves, "then
once I am annihilated the world has ended so far as I
am concerned—it is finished.  Why, then, should it not
end forthwith, so that no new consciousnesses, doomed
to suffer the tormenting illusion of a transient and
apparential existence, may come into being?  If, the
illusion of living being shattered, living for the mere
sake of living or for the sake of others who are likewise
doomed to die, does not satisfy the soul, what is the
good of living?  Our best remedy is death."  And thus
it is that we chant the praises of the never-ending rest
because of our dread of it, and speak of liberating death.

Leopardi, the poet of sorrow, of annihilation, having
lost the ultimate illusion, that of believing in his immortality—

*Peri l'inganno estremo*
*ch'eterno io mi credei,*

spoke to his heart of *l'infinita vanitá del tutto,* and perceived how close is the kinship between love and death,
and how "when love is born deep down in the heart,
simultaneously a languid and weary desire to die is felt
in the breast."  The greater part of those who seek
death at their own hand are moved thereto by love; it
is the supreme longing for life, for more life, the longing

to prolong and perpetuate life, that urges them to death, once they are persuaded of the vanity of this longing.

The problem is tragic and eternal, and the more we seek to escape from it, the more it thrusts itself upon us. Four-and-twenty centuries ago, in his dialogue on the immortality of the soul, the serene Plato—but was he serene?—spoke of the uncertainty of our dream of being immortal and of the *risk* that the dream might be vain, and from his own soul there escaped this profound cry— Glorious is the risk!—καλὸς γὰρ ὁ κίνδυνος, glorious is the risk that we are able to run of our souls never dying—a sentence that was the germ of Pascal's famous argument of the wager.

Faced with this risk, I am presented with arguments designed to eliminate it, arguments demonstrating the absurdity of the belief in the immortality of the soul; but these arguments fail to make any impression upon me, for they are reasons and nothing more than reasons, and it is not with reasons that the heart is appeased. I do not want to die—no; I neither want to die nor do I want to want to die; I want to live for ever and ever and ever. I want this " I " to live—this poor " I " that I am and that I feel myself to be here and now, and therefore the problem of the duration of my soul, of my own soul, tortures me.

I am the centre of my universe, the centre of the universe, and in my supreme anguish I cry with Michelet, "Mon moi, ils m'arrachent mon moi!" What is a man profited if he shall gain the whole world and lose his own soul? (Matt. xvi. 26). Egoism, you say? There is nothing more universal than the individual, for what is the property of each is the property of all. Each man is worth more than the whole of humanity, nor will it do to sacrifice each to all save in so far as all sacrifice themselves to each. That which we call egoism is the principle of psychic gravity, the necessary postulate. "Love thy neighbour as thyself," we are told, the presupposition being that each man loves himself; and it is not said "Love thyself." And, nevertheless, we do not know how to love ourselves.

Put aside the persistence of your own self and ponder what they tell you. Sacrifice yourself to your children! And sacrifice yourself to them because they are yours, part and prolongation of yourself, and they in their turn will sacrifice themselves to their children, and these children to theirs, and so it will go on without end, a sterile sacrifice by which nobody profits. I came into the world to create my self, and what is to become of all our selves? Live for the True, the Good, the Beautiful! We shall see presently the supreme vanity and the supreme insincerity of this hypocritical attitude.

"That art thou!" they tell me with the Upanishads. And I answer: Yes, I am that, if that is I and all is mine, and mine the totality of things. As mine I love the All, and I love my neighbour because he lives in me and is part of my consciousness, because he is like me, because he is mine.

Oh, to prolong this blissful moment, to sleep, to eternalize oneself in it! Here and now, in this discreet and diffused light, in this lake of quietude, the storm of the heart appeased and stilled the echoes of the world! Insatiable desire now sleeps and does not even dream; use and wont, blessed use and wont, are the rule of my eternity; my disillusions have died with my memories, and with my hopes my fears.

And they come seeking to deceive us with a deceit of deceits, telling us that nothing is lost, that everything is transformed, shifts and changes, that not the least particle of matter is annihilated, not the least impulse of energy is lost, and there are some who pretend to console us with this! Futile consolation! It is not my matter or my energy that is the cause of my disquiet, for they are not mine if I myself am not mine—that is, if I am not eternal. No, my longing is not to be submerged in the vast All, in an infinite and eternal Matter or Energy, or in God; not to be possessed by God, but to possess Him, to become myself God, yet without ceasing to be I myself, I who am now speaking to you. Tricks of monism avail us nothing; we crave the substance and not the shadow of immortality.

Materialism, you say? Materialism? Without doubt; but either our spirit is likewise some kind of matter or it is nothing. I dread the idea of having to tear myself away from my flesh; I dread still more the idea of having to tear myself away from everything sensible and material, from all substance. Yes, perhaps this merits the name of materialism; and if I grapple myself to God with all my powers and all my senses, it is that He may carry me in His arms beyond death, looking into these eyes of mine with the light of His heaven when the light of earth is dimming in them for ever. Self-illusion? Talk not to me of illusion—let me live!

They also call this pride—"stinking pride" Leopardi called it—and they ask us who are we, vile earthworms, to pretend to immortality; in virtue of what? wherefore? by what right? "In virtue of what?" you ask; and I reply, In virtue of what do we now live? "Wherefore?"—and wherefore do we now exist? "By what right?"—and by what right are we? To exist is just as gratuitous as to go on existing for ever. Do not let us talk of merit or of right or of the wherefore of our longing, which is an end in itself, or we shall lose our reason in a vortex of absurdities. I do not claim any right or merit; it is only a necessity; I need it in order to live.

And you, who are you? you ask me; and I reply with Obermann, "For the universe, nothing; for myself, everything!" Pride? Is it pride to want to be immortal? Unhappy men that we are! 'Tis a tragic fate, without a doubt, to have to base the affirmation of immortality upon the insecure and slippery foundation of the desire for immortality; but to condemn this

desire on the ground that we believe it to have been
proved to be unattainable, without undertaking the proof,
is merely supine.  I am dreaming . . .?  Let me dream,
if this dream is my life.  Do not awaken me from it.  I
believe in the immortal origin of this yearning for immortality, which is the very substance of my soul.  But
do I really believe in it . . .?  And wherefore do you
want to be immortal? you ask me, wherefore?  Frankly,
I do not understand the question, for it is to ask the
reason of the reason, the end of the end, the principle of
the principle.

But these are things which it is impossible to discuss.

It is related in the book of the Acts of the Apostles
how wherever Paul went the Jews, moved with envy, were
stirred up to persecute him.  They stoned him in
Iconium and Lystra, cities of Lycaonia, in spite of the
wonders that he worked therein ; they scourged him in
Philippi of Macedonia and persecuted his brethren in
Thessalonica and Berea.  He arrived at Athens, however, the noble city of the intellectuals, over which
brooded the sublime spirit of Plato—the Plato of the
gloriousness of the risk of immortality; and there Paul
disputed with Epicureans and Stoics.  And some said of
him, " What doth this babbler (σπερμολόγος) mean?"
and others, " He seemeth to be a setter forth of strange
gods " (Acts xvii. 18), " and they took him and brought
him unto Areopagus, saying, May we know what this
new doctrine, whereof thou speakest, is? for thou
bringest certain strange things to our ears; we would
know, therefore, what these things mean " (verses 19-20).
And then follows that wonderful characterization of those
Athenians of the decadence, those dainty connoisseurs of
the curious, " for all the Athenians and strangers which
were there spent their time in nothing else, but either to
tell or to hear some new thing " (verse 21).  A wonderful
stroke which depicts for us the condition of mind of those
who had learned from the *Odyssey* that the gods plot and

achieve the destruction of mortals in order that their posterity may have something to narrate!

Here Paul stands, then, before the subtle Athenians, before the *græuli,* men of culture and tolerance, who are ready to welcome and examine every doctrine, who neither stone nor scourge nor imprison any man for professing these or those doctrines—here he stands where liberty of conscience is respected and every opinion is given an attentive hearing. And he raises his voice in the midst of the Areopagus and speaks to them as it was fitting to speak to the cultured citizens of Athens, and all listen to him, agog to hear the latest novelty. But when he begins to speak to them of the resurrection of the dead their stock of patience and tolerance comes to an end, and some mock him, and others say: " We will hear thee again of this matter!" intending not to hear him. And a similar thing happened to him at Cæsarea when he came before the Roman prætor Felix, likewise a broadminded and cultured man, who mitigated the hardships of his imprisonment, and wished to hear and did hear him discourse of righteousness and of temperance; but when he spoke of the judgement to come, Felix said, terrified (ἔμφοβος γενόμενος): " Go thy way for this time; when I have a convenient season I will call for thee" (Acts xxiv. 22-25). And in his audience before King Agrippa, when Festus the governor heard him speak of the resurrection of the dead, he exclaimed: " Thou art mad, Paul; much learning hath made thee mad" (Acts xxvi. 24).

Whatever of truth there may have been in Paul's discourse in the Areopagus, and even if there were none, it is certain that this admirable account plainly shows how far Attic tolerance goes and where the patience of the intellectuals ends. They all listen to you, calmly and smilingly, and at times they encourage you, saying: " That's strange!" or, " He has brains!" or "That's suggestive," or " How fine!" or " Pity that a thing so

4

beautiful should not be true!" or "This makes one think!" But as soon as you speak to them of resurrection and life after death, they lose their patience and cut short your remarks and exclaim, "Enough of this! We will talk about this another day!" And it is about this, my poor Athenians, my intolerant intellectuals, it is about this that I am going to talk to you here.

And even if this belief be absurd, why is its exposition less tolerated than that of others much more absurd? Why this manifest hostility to such a belief? Is it fear? Is it, perhaps, spite provoked by inability to share it?

And sensible men, those who do not intend to let themselves be deceived, keep on dinning into our ears the refrain that it is no use giving way to folly and kicking against the pricks, for what cannot be is impossible. The manly attitude, they say, is to resign oneself to fate; since we are not immortal, do not let us want to be so; let us submit ourselves to reason without tormenting ourselves about what is irremediable, and so making life more gloomy and miserable. This obsession, they add, is a disease. Disease, madness, reason . . . the everlasting refrain! Very well then—No! I do not submit to reason, and I rebel against it, and I persist in creating by the energy of faith my immortalizing God, and in forcing by my will the stars out of their courses, for if we had faith as a grain of mustard seed we should say to that mountain, "Remove hence," and it would remove, and nothing would be impossible to us (Matt. xvii. 20).

There you have that "thief of energies," as he[1] so obtusely called Christ who sought to wed nihilism with the struggle for existence, and he talks to you about courage. His heart craved the eternal All while his head convinced him of nothingness, and, desperate and mad to defend himself from himself, he cursed that which he

[1] Nietzsche

most loved. Because he could not be Christ, he blasphemed against Christ. Bursting with his own self, he wished himself unending and dreamed his theory of eternal recurrence, a sorry counterfeit of immortality, and, full of pity for himself, he abominated all pity. And there are some who say that his is the philosophy of strong men ! No, it is not. My health and my strength urge me to perpetuate myself. His is the doctrine of weaklings who aspire to be strong, but not of the strong who are strong. Only the feeble resign themselves to final death and substitute some other desire for the longing for personal immortality. In the strong the zeal for perpetuity overrides the doubt of realizing it, and their superabundance of life overflows upon the other side of death.

Before this terrible mystery of mortality, face to face with the Sphinx, man adopts different attitudes and seeks in various ways to console himself for having been born. And now it occurs to him to take it as a diversion, and he says to himself with Renan that this universe is a spectacle that God presents to Himself, and that it behoves us to carry out the intentions of the great Stage-Manager and contribute to make the spectacle the most brilliant and the most varied that may be. And they have made a religion of art, a cure for the metaphysical evil, and invented the meaningless phrase of art for art's sake.

And it does not suffice them. If the man who tells you that he writes, paints, sculptures, or sings for his own amusement, gives his work to the public, he lies; he lies if he puts his name to his writing, painting, statue, or song. He wishes, at the least, to leave behind a shadow of his spirit, something that may survive him. If the *Imitation of Christ* is anonoymous, it is because its author sought the eternity of the soul and did not trouble himself about that of the name. The man of letters who shall tell you that he despises fame is a lying rascal.

Of Dante, the author of those three-and-thirty vigorous
verses (*Purg.* xi. 85-117) on the vanity of worldly glory,
Boccaccio says that he relished honours and pomps more
perhaps than suited with his conspicuous virtue. The
keenest desire of his condemned souls is that they may be
remembered and talked of here on earth, and this is the
chief solace that lightens the darkness of his Inferno.
And he himself confessed that his aim in expounding the
concept of Monarchy was not merely that he might be of
service to others, but that he might win for his own glory
the palm of so great prize (*De Monarchia*, lib. i., cap. i.).
What more? Even of that holy man, seemingly the
most indifferent to worldly vanity, the Poor Little One
of Assisi, it is related in the *Legenda Trium Sociorum*
that he said : *Adhuc adorabor per totum mundum!*—You
will see how I shall yet be adored by all the world!
(II. *Celano*, i. 1). And even of God Himself the
theologians say that He created the world for the manifestation of His glory.

When doubts invade us and cloud our faith in the
immortality of the soul, a vigorous and painful impulse
is given to the anxiety to perpetuate our name and fame,
to grasp at least a shadow of immortality. And hence
this tremendous struggle to singularize ourselves, to
survive in some way in the memory of others and of
posterity. It is this struggle, a thousand times more
terrible than the struggle for life, that gives its tone,
colour, and character to our society, in which the
medieval faith in the immortal soul is passing away.
Each one seeks to affirm himself, if only in appearance.

Once the needs of hunger are satisfied—and they are
soon satisfied—the vanity, the necessity—for it is a necessity—arises of imposing ourselves upon and surviving
in others. Man habitually sacrifices his life to his purse,
but he sacrifices his purse to his vanity. He boasts even
of his weaknesses and his misfortunes, for want of anything better to boast of, and is like a child who, in order

to attract attention, struts about with a bandaged finger. And vanity, what is it but eagerness for survival?

The vain man is in like case with the avaricious—he takes the means for the end; forgetting the end he pursues the means for its own sake and goes no further. The seeming to be something, conducive to being it, ends by forming our objective. We need that others should believe in our superiority to them in order that we may believe in it ourselves, and upon their belief base our faith in our own persistence, or at least in the persistence of our fame. We are more grateful to him who congratulates us on the skill with which we defend a cause than we are to him who recognizes the truth or the goodness of the cause itself. A rabid mania for originality is rife in the modern intellectual world and characterizes all individual effort. We would rather err with genius than hit the mark with the crowd. Rousseau has said in his *Émile* (book iv.) : "Even though philosophers should be in a position to discover the truth, which of them would take any interest in it? Each one knows well that his system is not better founded than the others, but he supports it because it is his. There is not a single one of them who, if he came to know the true and the false, would not prefer the falsehood that he had found to the truth discovered by another. Where is the philosopher who would not willingly deceive mankind for his own glory? Where is he who in the secret of his heart does not propose to himself any other object than to distinguish himself? Provided that he lifts himself above the vulgar, provided that he outshines the brilliance of his competitors, what does he demand more? The essential thing is to think differently from others. With believers he is an atheist; with atheists he would be a believer." How much substantial truth there is in these gloomy confessions of this man of painful sincerity!

This violent struggle for the perpetuation of our name extends backwards into the past, just as it aspires to conquer the future; we contend with the dead because we, the living, are obscured beneath their shadow. We are jealous of the geniuses of former times, whose names, standing out like the landmarks of history, rescue the ages from oblivion. The heaven of fame is not very large, and the more there are who enter it the less is the share of each. The great names of the past rob us of our place in it; the space which they fill in the popular memory they usurp from us who aspire to occupy it. And so we rise up in revolt against them, and hence the bitterness with which all those who seek after fame in the world of letters judge those who have already attained it and are in enjoyment of it. If additions continue to be made to the wealth of literature, there will come a day of sifting, and each one fears lest he be caught in the meshes of the sieve. In attacking the masters, irreverent youth is only defending itself; the iconoclast or image-breaker is a Stylite who erects himself as an image, an *icon*. "Comparisons are odious," says the familiar adage, and the reason is that we wish to be unique. Do not tell Fernandez that he is one of the most talented Spaniards of the younger generation, for though he will affect to be gratified by the eulogy he is really annoyed by it; if, however, you tell him that he is the most talented man in Spain—well and good! But even that is not sufficient : one of the worldwide reputations would be more to his liking, but he is only fully satisfied with being esteemed the first in all countries and all ages. The more alone, the nearer to that unsubstantial immortality, the immortality of the name, for great names diminish one another.

What is the meaning of that irritation which we feel when we believe that we are robbed of a phrase, or a thought, or an image, which we believed to be our own, when we are plagiarized? Robbed? Can it indeed be ours once we have given it to the public? Only because it is ours we prize it; and we are fonder of the false money

that preserves our impress than of the coin of pure gold
from which our effigy and our legend has been effaced.
It very commonly happens that it is when the name of a
writer is no longer in men's mouths that he most influences his public, his mind being then disseminated
and infused in the minds of those who have read him,
whereas he was quoted chiefly when his thoughts and
sayings, clashing with those generally received, needed
the guarantee of a name.    What was his now belongs to
all, and he lives in all.    But for him the garlands have
faded, and he believes himself to have failed.    He hears
no more either the applause or the silent tremor of the
heart of those who go on reading him.    Ask any sincere
artist which he would prefer, whether that his work
should perish and his memory survive, or that his work
should survive and his memory perish, and you will see
what he will tell you, if he is really sincere.    When a
man does not work merely in order to live and carry on,
he works in order to survive.    To work for the work's
sake is not work but play.    And play?    We will talk
about that later on.

A tremendous passion is this longing that our memory
may be rescued, if it is possible, from the oblivion which
overtakes others.    From it springs envy, the cause,
according to the biblical narrative, of the crime with
which human history opened : the murder of Abel by his
brother Cain.    It was not a struggle for bread—it was a
struggle to survive in God, in the divine memory.    Envy
is a thousand times more terrible than hunger, for it is
spiritual hunger.    If what we call the problem of life,
the problem of bread, were once solved, the earth would
be turned into a hell by the emergence in a more violent
form of the struggle for survival.

For the sake of a name man is ready to sacrifice not
only life but happiness—life as a matter of course.    " Let
me die, but let my fame live !" exclaimed Rodrigo Arias
in *Las Mocedades del Cid* when he fell mortally wounded

by Don Ordóñez de Lara. "Courage, Girolamo, for
you will long be remembered; death is bitter, but fame
eternal!" cried Girolamo Olgiati, the disciple of Cola
Montano and the murderer, together with his fellow-
conspirators Lampugnani and Visconti, of Galeazzo
Sforza, tyrant of Milan. And there are some who covet
even the gallows for the sake of acquiring fame, even
though it be an infamous fame : *avidus malæ famæ*, as
Tacitus says.

And this erostratism, what is it at bottom but the longing for immortality, if not for substantial and concrete
immortality, at any rate for the shadowy immortality of
the name?

And in this there are degrees. If a man despises the
applause of the crowd of to-day, it is because he seeks to
survive in renewed minorities for generations. "Posterity is an accumulation of minorities," said Gounod.
He wishes to prolong himself in time rather than in
space. The crowd soon overthrows its own idols and
the statue lies broken at the foot of the pedestal without
anyone heeding it; but those who win the hearts of the
elect will long be the objects of a fervent worship in
some shrine, small and secluded no doubt, but capable
of preserving them from the flood of oblivion. The
artist sacrifices the extensiveness of his fame to its
duration; he is anxious rather to endure for ever in some
little corner than to occupy a brilliant second place in the
whole universe; he prefers to be an atom, eternal and
conscious of himself, rather than to be for a brief moment
the consciousness of the whole universe; he sacrifices
infinitude to eternity.

And they keep on wearying our ears with this chorus
of Pride! stinking Pride! Pride, to wish to leave an
ineffaceable name? Pride? It is like calling the thirst
for riches a thirst for pleasure. No, it is not so much the
longing for pleasure that drives us poor folk to seek
money as the terror of poverty, just as it was not the

desire for glory but the terror of hell that drove men in the Middle Ages to the cloister with its *acedia*. Neither is this wish to leave a name pride, but terror of extinction. We aim at being all because in that we see the only means of escaping from being nothing. We wish to save our memory—at any rate, our memory. How long will it last? At most as long as the human race lasts. And what if we shall save our memory in God?

Unhappy, I know well, are these confessions; but from the depth of unhappiness springs new life, and only by draining the lees of spiritual sorrow can we at last taste the honey that lies at the bottom of the cup of life. Anguish leads us to consolation.

This thirst for eternal life is appeased by many, especially by the simple, at the fountain of religious faith; but to drink of this is not given to all. The institution whose primordial end is to protect this faith in the personal immortality of the soul is Catholicism; but Catholicism has sought to rationalize this faith by converting religion into theology, by offering a philosophy, and a philosophy of the thirteenth century, as a basis for vital belief. This and its consequences we will now proceed to examine.

# IV

## THE ESSENCE OF CATHOLICISM

LET us now approach the Christian, Catholic, Pauline, or Athanasian solution of our inward vital problem, the hunger of immortality.

Christianity sprang from the confluence of two mighty spiritual streams—the one Judaic, the other Hellenic— each of which had already influenced the other, and Rome finally gave it a practical stamp and social permanence.

It has been asserted, perhaps somewhat precipitately, that primitive Christianity was an-eschatological, that faith in another life after death is not clearly manifested in it, but rather a belief in the proximate end of the world and establishment of the kingdom of God, a belief known as chiliasm. But were they not fundamentally one and the same thing? Faith in the immortality of the soul, the nature of which was not perhaps very precisely defined, may be said to be a kind of tacit understanding or supposition underlying the whole of the Gospel; and it is the mental orientation of many of those who read it to-day, an orientation contrary to that of the Christians from among whom the Gospel sprang, that prevents them from seeing this. Without doubt all that about the second coming of Christ, when he shall come among the clouds, clothed with majesty and great power, to judge the quick and the dead, to open to some the kingdom of heaven and to cast others into Gehenna, where there shall be weeping and gnashing of teeth, may be understood in a chiliastic sense; and it is even said of Christ in the Gospel (Mark ix. 1), that there were with

58

him some who should not taste of death till they had
seen the kingdom of God—that is, that the kingdom
should come during their generation.   And in the same
chapter, verse 10, it is said of Peter and James and John,
who went up with Jesus to the Mount of Transfiguration
and heard him say that he would rise again from the
dead, that "they kept that saying within themselves,
questioning one with another what the rising from the
dead should mean."   And at all events the Gospel was
written when this belief, the basis and *raison d'être*
of Christianity, was in process of formation.   See
Matt. xxii. 29-32; Mark xii. 24-27; Luke xvi. 22-31;
xx. 34-37; John v. 24-29; vi. 40, 54, 58; viii. 51; xi. 25, 56;
xiv. 2, 19.   And, above all, that passage in Matt. xxvii. 52,
which tells how at the resurrection of Christ "many
bodies of the saints which slept arose."

And this was not a natural resurrection.   No; the
Christian faith was born of the faith that Jesus did not
remain dead, but that God raised him up again, and
that this resurrection was a fact; but this did not presuppose a mere immortality of the soul in the philosophical sense (see Harnack, *Dogmengeschichte*, Pro-
legomena, v. 4).   For the first Fathers of the Church
themselves the immortality of the soul was not a thing
pertaining to the natural order; the teaching of the
Divine Scriptures, as Nimesius said, sufficed for its
demonstration, and it was, according to Lactantius, a
gift—and as such gratuitous—of God.   But more of this
later.

Christianity sprang, as we have said, from two great
spiritual streams—the Judaic and the Hellenic—each one
of which had arrived on its account, if not at a precise
definition of, at any rate at a definite yearning for,
another life.   Among the Jews faith in another life was
neither general nor clear; but they were led to it by faith
in a personal and living God, the formation of which
faith comprises all their spiritual history.

Jahwé, the Judaic God, began by being one god among many others—the God of the people of Israel, revealed among the thunders of the tempest on Mount Sinai. But he was so jealous that he demanded that worship should be paid to him alone, and it was by way of mono-cultism that the Jews arrived at monotheism. He was adored as a living force, not as a metaphysical entity, and he was the god of battles. But this God of social and martial origin, to whose genesis we shall have to return later, became more inward and personal in the prophets, and in becoming more inward and personal he thereby became more individual and more universal. He is the Jahwé who, instead of loving Israel because Israel is his son, takes Israel for a son because he loves him (Hosea xi. 1). And faith in the personal God, in the Father of men, carries with it faith in the eternalization of the individual man—a faith which had already dawned in Pharisaism even before Christ.

Hellenic culture, on its side, ended by discovering death; and to discover death is to discover the hunger of immortality. This longing does not appear in the Homeric poems, which are not initial, but final, in their character, marking not the start but the close of a civilization. They indicate the transition from the old religion of Nature, of Zeus, to the more spiritual religion of Apollo—of redemption. But the popular and inward religion of the Eleusinian mysteries, the worship of souls and ancestors, always persisted underneath. " In so far as it is possible to speak of a Delphic theology, among its more important elements must be counted the belief in the continuation of the life of souls after death in its popular forms, and in the worship of the souls of the dead."[1] There were the Titanic and the Dionysiac

[1] Erwin Rohde, *Psyche*, " Seelencult und Unsterblichkeitsglaube der Griechen." Tubingen, 1907. Up to the present this is the leading work dealing with the belief of the Greeks in the immortality of the soul.

elements, and it was the duty of man, according to the Orphic doctrine, to free himself from the fetters of the body, in which the soul was like a captive in a prison (see Rohde, *Psyche*, "Die Orphiker," 4). The Nietzschean idea of eternal recurrence is an Orphic idea. But the idea of the immortality of the soul was not a philosophical principle. The attempt of Empedocles to harmonize a hylozoistic system with spiritualism proved that a philosophical natural science cannot by itself lead to a corroboration of the axiom of the perpetuity of the individual soul; it could only serve as a support to a theological speculation. It was by a contradiction that the first Greek philosophers affirmed immortality, by abandoning natural philosophy and intruding into theology, by formulating not an Apollonian but a Dionysiac and Orphic dogma. But "an immortality of the soul as such, in virtue of its own nature and condition as an imperishable divine force in the mortal body, was never an object of popular Hellenic belief" (Rohde, *op. cit.*).

Recall the *Phædo* of Plato and the neo-platonic lucubrations. In them the yearning for personal immortality already shows itself—a yearning which, as it was left totally unsatisfied by reason, produced the Hellenic pessimism. For, as Pfleiderer very well observes (*Religionsphilosophie auf geschichtliche Grundlage*, 3. Berlin, 1896), " no people ever came upon the earth so serene and sunny as the Greeks in the youthful days of their historical existence . . . but no people changed so completely their idea of the value of life. The Hellenism which ended in the religious speculations of neo-pythagorism and neo-platonism viewed this world, which had once appeared to it so joyous and radiant, as an abode of darkness and error, and earthly existence as a period of trial which could never be too quickly traversed." Nirvana is an Hellenic idea.

Thus Jews and Greeks each arrived independently at

the real discovery of death—a discovery which occasions, in peoples as in men, the entrance into spiritual puberty, the realization of the tragic sense of life, and it is then that the living God is begotten by humanity. The discovery of death is that which reveals God to us, and the death of the perfect man, Christ, was the supreme revelation of death, being the death of the man who ought not to have died yet did die.

Such a discovery—that of immortality—prepared as it was by the Judaic and Hellenic religious processes, was a specifically Christian discovery. And its full achievement was due above all to Paul of Tarsus, the hellenizing Jew and Pharisee. Paul had not personally known Jesus, and hence he discovered him as Christ. " It may be said that the theology of the Apostle Paul is, in general, the first Christian theology. For him it was a necessity; it was, in a certain sense, his substitution for the lack of a personal knowledge of Jesus," says Weizsäcker (*Das apostolische Zeitalter der christlichen Kirche.* Freiburg-i.-B., 1892). He did not know Jesus, but he felt him born again in himself, and thus he could say, " Nevertheless I live, yet not I, but Christ liveth in me."[1] And he preached the Cross, unto the Jews a stumblingblock, and unto the Greeks foolishness (1 Cor. i. 23), and the central doctrine for the converted Apostle was that of the resurrection of Christ. The important thing for him was that Christ had been made man and had died and had risen again, and not what he did in his life—not his ethical work as a teacher, but his religious work as a giver of immortality. And he it was who wrote those immortal words : " Now if Christ be preached that He rose from the dead, how say some among you that there is no resurrection from the dead? But if there be no resurrection of the dead, then is Christ not risen ; and if Christ be not risen, then is our preaching vain, and your faith is also vain. . . .   Then they also which are fallen

---

[1] Gal. ii. 20.

asleep in Christ are perished. If in this life only we have hope in Christ, we are of all men most miserable" (1 Cor. xv. 12-19).

And it is possible to affirm that thenceforward he who does not believe in the bodily resurrection of Christ may be Christophile but cannot be specifically Christian. It is true that a Justin Martyr could say that "all those are Christians who live in accordance with reason, even though they may be deemed to be atheists, as, among the Greeks, Socrates and Heraclitus and other such"; but this martyr, is he a martyr—that is to say a witness—of Christianity? No.

And it was around this dogma, inwardly experienced by Paul, the dogma of the resurrection and immortality of Christ, the guarantee of the resurrection and immortality of each believer, that the whole of Christology was built up. The God-man, the incarnate Word, came in order that man, according to his mode, might be made God—that is, immortal. And the Christian God, the Father of Christ, a God necessarily anthropomorphic, is He who—as the Catechism of Christian Doctrine which we were made to learn by heart at school says—created the world for man, for each man. And the end of redemption, in spite of appearances due to an ethical deflection of a dogma properly religious, was to save us from death rather than from sin, or from sin in so far as sin implies death. And Christ died, or rather rose again, for *me,* for each one of us. And a certain solidarity was established between God and His creature. Malebranche said that the first man fell *in order that* Christ might redeem us, rather than that Christ redeemed us *because* man had fallen.

After the death of Paul years passed, and generations of Christianity wrought upon this central dogma and its consequences in order to safeguard faith in the immortality of the individual soul, and the Council of Nicæa came, and with it the formidable Athanasius, whose

name is still a battle-cry, an incarnation of the popular
faith.  Athanasius was a man of little learning but of
great faith, and above all of popular faith, devoured by
the hunger of immortality.  And he opposed Arianism,
which, like Unitarian and Socinian Protestantism,
threatened, although unknowingly and unintentionally,
the foundation of that belief.  For the Arians, Christ
was first and foremost a teacher—a teacher of morality,
the wholly perfect man, and therefore the guarantee that
we may all attain to supreme perfection; but Athanasius
felt that Christ cannot make us gods if he has not first
made himself God; if his Divinity had been communicated, he could not have communicated it to us.  "He
was not, therefore," he said, "first man and then
became God; but He was first God and then became man
in order that He might the better deify us (θεοποιήσῃ)"
(Orat. i. 39).  It was not the Logos of the philosophers,
the cosmological Logos, that Athanasius knew and
adored;[1] and thus he instituted a separation between
nature and revelation.  The Athanasian or Nicene
Christ, who is the Catholic Christ, is not the cosmological, nor even, strictly, the ethical Christ; he is the
eternalizing, the deifying, the religious Christ.  Harnack
says of this Christ, the Christ of Nicene or Catholic
Christology, that he is essentially docetic—that is,
apparential—because the process of the divinization of
the man in Christ was made in the interests of eschatology.  But which is the real Christ?  Is it, indeed, that
so-called historical Christ of rationalist exegesis who is
diluted for us in a myth or in a social atom?

This same Harnack, a Protestant rationalist, tells us
that Arianism or Unitarianism would have been the
death of Christianity, reducing it to cosmology and
ethics, and that it served only as a bridge whereby the

[1] On all relating to this question see, among others, Harnack, _Dogmen-
geschichte_, ii., Teil i., Buch vii., cap i.

learned might pass over to Catholicism—that is to say, from reason to faith. To this same learned historian of dogmas it appears to be an indication of a perverse state of things that the man Athanasius, who saved Christianity as the religion of a living communion with God, should have obliterated the Jesus of Nazareth, the historical Jesus, whom neither Paul nor Athanasius knew personally, nor yet Harnack himself. Among Protestants, this historical Jesus is subjected to the scalpel of criticism, while the Catholic Christ lives, the really historical Christ, he who lives throughout the centuries guaranteeing the faith in personal immortality and personal salvation.

And Athanasius had the supreme audacity of faith, that of asserting things mutually contradictory : "The complete contradiction that exists in the ὁμοούσιος carried in its train a whole army of contradictions which increased as thought advanced," says Harnack. Yes, so it was, and so it had to be. And he adds : "Dogma took leave for ever of clear thinking and tenable concepts, and habituated itself to the contra-rational." In truth, it drew closer to life, which is contra-rational and opposed to clear thinking. Not only are judgements of worth never rationalizable—they are anti-rational.

At Nicæa, then, as afterwards at the Vatican, victory rested with the idiots—taking this word in its proper, primitive, and etymological sense—the simple-minded, the rude and headstrong bishops, the representatives of the genuine human spirit, the popular spirit, the spirit that does not want to die, in spite of whatever reason may say, and that seeks a guarantee, the most material possible, for this desire.

*Quid ad æternitatem?* This is the capital question. And the Creed ends with that phrase, *resurrectionem mortuorum et vitam venturi sæculi*—the resurrection of the dead and the life of the world to come. In the ceme-

5

tery of Mallona, in my native town of Bilbao, there is a
tombstone on which this verse is carved :

> *Aunque estamos en polvo convertidos,*
> *en Ti, Señor, nuestra esperanza fía,*
> *que tornaremos a vivir vestidos*
> *con la carne y la piel que nos cubria.*[1]

" With the same bodies and souls that they had," as the
Catechism says. So much so, that it is orthodox Catholic
doctrine that the happiness of the blessed is not perfectly
complete until they recover their bodies. They lament
in heaven, says our Brother Pedro Malón de Chaide of
the Order of St. Augustine, a Spaniard and a Basque,[2]
and " this lament springs from their not being perfectly
whole in heaven, for only the soul is there; and although
they cannot suffer, because they see God, in whom they
unspeakably delight, yet with all this it appears that they
are not wholly content. They will be so when they are
clothed with their own bodies."

And to this central dogma of the resurrection in Christ
and by Christ corresponds likewise a central sacrament,
the axis of popular Catholic piety—the Sacrament of the
Eucharist. In it is administered the body of Christ,
which is the bread of immortality.

This sacrament is genuinely realist—*dinglich*, as the
Germans would say—which may without great violence
be translated " material." It is the sacrament most
genuinely *ex opere operato*, for which is substituted
among Protestants the idealistic sacrament of the word.
Fundamentally it is concerned with—and I say it with
all possible respect, but without wishing to sacrifice the
expressiveness of the phrase—the eating and drinking of
God, the Eternalizer, the feeding upon Him. Little

---

[1] Though we are become dust,
In thee, O Lord, our hope confides,
That we shall live again clad
In the flesh and skin that once covered us.

[2] *Libro de la Conversión de la Magdelena*, part iv., chap. ix.

wonder then if St. Teresa tells us that when she was communicating in the monastery of the Incarnation and in the second year of her being Prioress there, on the octave of St. Martin, and the Father, Fr. Juan de la Cruz, divided the Host between her and another sister, she thought that it was done not because there was any want of Hosts, but because he wished to mortify her, "for I had told him how much I delighted in Hosts of a large size. Yet I was not ignorant that the size of the Host is of no moment, for I knew that our Lord is whole and entire in the smallest particle." Here reason pulls one way, feeling another. And what importance for this feeling have the thousand and one difficulties that arise from reflecting rationally upon the mystery of this sacrament? What is a divine body? And the body, in so far as it is the body of Christ, is it divine? What is an immortal and immortalizing body? What is substance separated from the accidents? Nowadays we have greatly refined our notion of materiality and substantiality; but there were even some among the Fathers of the Church to whom the immateriality of God Himself was not a thing so clear and definite as it is for us. And this sacrament of the Eucharist is the immortalizing sacrament *par excellence*, and therefore the axis of popular Catholic piety, and if it may be so said, the most specifically religious of sacraments.

For what is specific in the Catholic religion is immortalization and not justification, in the Protestant sense. Rather is this latter ethical. It was from Kant, in spite of what orthodox Protestants may think of him, that Protestantism derived its penultimate conclusions—namely, that religion rests upon morality, and not morality upon religion, as in Catholicism.

The preoccupation of sin has never been such a matter of anguish, or at any rate has never displayed itself with such an appearance of anguish, among Catholics. The sacrament of Confession contributes to this. And there persists, perhaps, among Catholics more than among Protestants the substance of the primitive Judaic and pagan conception of sin as something material and infectious and hereditary, which is cured by baptism and absolution. In Adam all his posterity sinned, almost materially, and his sin was transmitted as a material disease is transmitted. Renan, whose education was Catholic, was right, therefore, in calling to account the Protestant Amiel who accused him of not giving due importance to sin. And, on the other hand, Protestantism, absorbed in this preoccupation with justification, which in spite of its religious guise was taken more in an ethical sense than anything else, ends by neutralizing and almost obliterating eschatology; it abandons the Nicene symbol, falls into an anarchy of creeds, into pure religious individualism and a vague esthetic, ethical, or cultured religiosity. What we may call "other-worldliness" (*Jenseitigkeit*) was obliterated little by little by "this-worldliness" (*Diesseitigkeit*); and this in spite of Kant, who wished to save it, but by destroying it. To its earthly vocation and passive trust in God is due the religious coarseness of Lutheranism, which was almost at the point of expiring in the age of the Enlightenment, of the *Aufklärung*, and which pietism, infusing into it something of the religious sap of Catholicism, barely succeeded in galvanizing a little. Hence the exactness of the remarks of Oliveira Martins in his magnificent *History of Iberian Civilization*, in which he says (book iv, chap. iii.) that "Catholicism produced heroes and Protestantism produced societies that are sensible, happy, wealthy, free, as far as their outer institutions go, but incapable of any great action, because their religion has begun by destroying in the heart of man all that made him capable of daring and noble self-sacrifice."

Take any of the dogmatic systems that have resulted from the latest Protestant dissolvent analysis—that of Kaftan, the follower of Ritschl, for example—and note the extent to which eschatology is reduced.   And his master, Albrecht Ritschl, himself says : " The question regarding the necessity of justification or forgiveness can only be solved by conceiving eternal life as the direct end and aim of that divine operation.   But if the idea of eternal life be applied merely to our state in the next life, then its content, too, lies beyond all experience, and cannot form the basis of knowledge of a scientific kind. Hopes and desires, though marked by the strongest subjective certainty, are not any the clearer for that, and contain in themselves no guarantee of the completeness of what one hopes or desires.   Clearness and completeness of idea, however, are the conditions of comprehending anything—*i.e.*, of understanding the necessary connection between the various elements of a thing, and between the thing and its given presuppositions.   The Evangelical article of belief, therefore, that justification by faith establishes or brings with it assurance of eternal life, is of no use theologically, so long as this purposive aspect of justification cannot be verified in such experience as is possible now " (*Rechtfertigung und Versöhnung,* vol. iii., chap. vii., 52).   All this is very rational, but . . .

In the first edition of Melanchthon's *Loci Communes,* that of 1521, the first Lutheran theological work, its author omits all Trinitarian and Christological speculations, the dogmatic basis of eschatology.   And Dr. Hermann, professor at Marburg, the author of a book on the Christian's commerce with God (*Der Verkehr des Christen mit Gott*)—a book the first chapter of which treats of the opposition between mysticism and the Christian religion, and which is, according to Harnack, the most perfect Lutheran manual—tells us in another place,[1] referring to this Christological (or Athanasian) specula-

---

[1] In his exposition of Protestant dogma in *Systematische christliche Religion,* Berlin, 1909, one of the series entitled *Die Kultur der Gegenwart,* published by P Hinneberg

tion, that "the effective knowledge of God and of Christ, in which knowledge faith lives, is something entirely different. Nothing ought to find a place in Christian doctrine that is not capable of helping man to recognize his sins, to obtain the grace of God, and to serve Him in truth. Until that time—that is to say, until Luther—the Church had accepted much as *doctrina sacra* which cannot absolutely contribute to confer upon man liberty of heart and tranquillity of conscience." For my part, I cannot conceive the liberty of a heart or the tranquillity of a conscience that are not sure of their perdurability after death. "The desire for the soul's salvation," Hermann continues, "must at last have led men to the knowledge and understanding of the effective doctrine of salvation." And in his book on the Christian's commerce with God, this eminent Lutheran doctor is continually discoursing upon trust in God, peace of conscience, and an assurance of salvation that is not strictly and precisely certainty of everlasting life, but rather certainty of the forgiveness of sins.

And I have read in a Protestant theologian, Ernst Troeltsch, that in the conceptual order Protestantism has attained its highest reach in music, in which art Bach has given it its mightiest artistic expression. This, then, is what Protestantism dissolves into—celestial music![1] On the other hand we may say that the highest artistic expression of Catholicism, or at least of Spanish Catholicism, is in the art that is most material, tangible, and permanent—for the vehicle of sounds is air—in sculpture and painting, in the Christ of Velasquez, that Christ who is for ever dying, yet never finishes dying, in order that he may give us life.

And yet Catholicism does not abandon ethics. No! No modern religion can leave ethics on one side. But

---

[1] The common use of the expression *música celestial* to denote "nonsense, something not worth listening to," lends it a satirical byplay which disappears in the English rendering.—J. E. C. F.

our religion—although its doctors may protest against this—is fundamentally and for the most part a compromise between eschatology and ethics; it is eschatology pressed into the service of ethics. What else but this is that atrocity of the eternal pains of hell, which agrees so ill with the Pauline apocatastasis? Let us bear in mind those words which the *Theologica Germanica,* the manual of mysticism that Luther read, puts into the mouth of God: "If I must recompense your evil, I must recompense it with good, for I am and have none other." And Christ said: "Father, forgive them, for they know not what they do," and there is no man who perhaps knows what he does. But it has been necessary, for the benefit of the social order, to convert religion into a kind of police system, and hence hell. Oriental or Greek Christianity is predominantly eschatological, Protestantism predominantly ethical, and Catholicism is a compromise between the two, although with the eschatological element preponderating. The most authentic Catholic ethic, monastic asceticism, is an ethic of eschatology, directed to the salvation of the individual soul rather than to the maintenance of society. And in the cult of virginity may there not perhaps be a certain obscure idea that to perpetuate ourselves in others hinders our own personal perpetuation? The ascetic morality is a negative morality. And, strictly, what is important for a man is not to die, whether he sins or not. It is not necessary to take very literally, but as a lyrical, or rather rhetorical, effusion, the words of our famous sonnet—

> *No me mueve, mi Dios, para quererte*
> *el cielo que me tienes prometido,*[1]

and the rest that follows.

The real sin—perhaps it is the sin against the Holy Ghost for which there is no remission—is the sin of

[1] It is not Thy promised heaven, my God, that moves me to love Thee. (Anonymous, sixteenth or seventeenth century. See *Oxford Book of Spanish Verse,* No 106.)

heresy, the sin of thinking for oneself. The saying has been heard before now, here in Spain, that to be a liberal —that is, a heretic—is worse than being an assassin, a thief, or an adulterer. The gravest sin is not to obey the Church, whose infallibility protects us from reason.

And why be scandalized by the infallibility of a man, of the Pope? What difference does it make whether it be a book that is infallible—the Bible, or a society of men—the Church, or a single man? Does it make any essential change in the rational difficulty? And since the infallibility of a book or of a society of men is not more rational than that of a single man, this supreme offence in the eyes of reason had to be posited.

It is the vital asserting itself, and in order to assert itself it creates, with the help of its enemy, the rational, a complete dogmatic structure, and this the Church defends against rationalism, against Protestantism, and against Modernism. The Church defends life. It stood up against Galileo, and it did right; for his discovery, in its inception and until it became assimilated to the general body of human knowledge, tended to shatter the anthropomorphic belief that the universe was created for man. It opposed Darwin, and it did right, for Darwinism tends to shatter our belief that man is an exceptional animal, created expressly to be eternalized. And lastly, Pius IX., the first Pontiff to be proclaimed infallible, declared that he was irreconcilable with the so-called modern civilization. And he did right.

Loisy, the Catholic ex-abbé, said : " I say simply this, that the Church and theology have not looked with favour upon the scientific movement, and that on certain decisive occasions, so far as it lay in their power, they have hindered it. I say, above all, that Catholic teaching has not associated itself with, or accommodated itself to, this movement. Theology has conducted itself, and conducts itself still, as if it were self-possessed of a science of nature and a science of history, together with that general philosophy of nature and history which results from a scientific knowledge of them. It might be supposed that the domain of theology and that of science, distinct in principle and even as defined by the Vatican Council, must not be distinct in practice. Everything proceeds almost as if theology had nothing to learn from modern science, natural or historical, and as if by itself it had the power and the right to exercise a direct and absolute control over all the activities of the human mind " (*Autour d'un Petit Livre*, 1903, p. 211).

And such must needs be, and such in fact is, the Church's attitude in its struggle with Modernism, of which Loisy was the learned and leading exponent.

The recent struggle against Kantian and fideist Modernism is a struggle for life. Is it indeed possible for life, life that seeks assurance of survival, to tolerate that a Loisy, a Catholic priest, should affirm that the resurrection of the Saviour is not a fact of the historical order, demonstrable and demonstrated by the testimony of history alone? Read, moreover, the exposition of the central dogma, that of the resurrection of Jesus, in E. Le Roy's excellent work, *Dogme et Critique*, and tell me if any solid ground is left for our hope to build on. Do not the Modernists see that the question at issue is not so much that of the immortal life of Christ, reduced, perhaps, to a life in the collective Christian consciousness, as that of a guarantee of our own personal resurrection of body as well as soul? This new psychological apologetic appeals to the moral miracle, and we, like the Jews, seek for a sign, something that can be taken hold of with all the powers of the soul and with all the senses of the body. And with the hands and the feet and the mouth, if it be possible.

But alas! we do not get it. Reason attacks, and faith, which does not feel itself secure without reason, has to come to terms with it. And hence come those tragic con-

tradictions and lacerations of consciousness.   We need
security, certainty, signs, and they give us *motiva credi-
bilitatis*—motives of credibility—upon which to establish
the *rationale obsequium*, and although faith precedes
reason (*fides præcedit rationem*), according to St. Augustine, this same learned doctor and bishop sought to
travel by faith to understanding (*per fidem ad intel-
lectum*), and to believe in order to understand (*credo ut
intelligam*).   How far is this from that superb expression
of Tertullian—*et sepultus resurrexit, certum est quia
impossibile est!*—"and he was buried and rose again; it
is certain because it is impossible!" and his sublime
*credo quia absurdum!*—the scandal of the rationalists.
How far from the *il faut s'abêtir* of Pascal and from the
"human reason loves the absurd" of our Donoso
Cortés, which he must have learned from the great
Joseph de Maistre!

And a first foundation-stone was sought in the
authority of tradition and the revelation of the word of
God, and the principle of unanimous consent was
arrived at.   *Quod apud multos unum invenitur, non est
erratum, sed traditum*, said Tertullian; and Lamennais
added, centuries later, that "certitude, the principle of
life and intelligence . . . is, if I may be allowed the
expression, a social product."[1]   But here, as in so many
cases, the supreme formula was given by that great
Catholic, whose Catholicism was of the popular and vital
order, Count Joseph de Maistre, when he wrote: "I do
not believe that it is possible to show a single opinion
of universal utility that is not true."[2]   Here you have the
Catholic hall-mark—the deduction of the truth of a principle from its supreme goodness or utility.   And what
is there of greater, of more sovereign utility, than the
immortality of the soul?   "As all is uncertain, either
we must believe all men or none," said Lactantius; but

[1] *Essai sur l'indifférence en matière de religion*, part iii , chap i
[2] *Les Soirées de Saint-Petersbourg*, xⁱᵐᵉ entretien

that great mystic and ascetic, Blessed Heinrich Seuse, the Dominican, implored the Eternal Wisdom for one word affirming that He was love, and when the answer came, " All creatures proclaim that I am love," Seuse replied, " Alas ! Lord, that does not suffice for a yearning soul." Faith feels itself secure neither with universal consent, nor with tradition, nor with authority. It seeks the support of its enemy, reason.

And thus scholastic theology was devised, and with it its handmaiden—*ancilla theologiæ* — scholastic philosophy, and this handmaiden turned against her mistress. Scholasticism, a magnificent cathedral, in which all the problems of architectonic mechanism were resolved for future ages, but a cathedral constructed of unbaked bricks, gave place little by little to what is called natural theology and is merely Christianity depotentialized. The attempt was even made, where it was possible, to base dogmas upon reason, to show at least that if they were indeed super-rational they were not contra-rational, and they were reinforced with a philosophical foundation of Aristotelian-Neoplatonic thirteenth-century philosophy. And such is the Thomism recommended by Leo XIII. And now the question is not one of the enforcement of dogma but of its philosophical, medieval, and Thomist interpretation. It is not enough to believe that in receiving the consecrated Host we receive the body and blood of our Lord Jesus Christ ; we must needs negotiate all those difficulties of transubstantiation and substance separated from accidents, and so break with the whole of the modern rational conception of substantiality.

But for this, implicit faith suffices—the faith of the coalheaver,[1] the faith of those who, like St. Teresa (*Vida*, cap. xxv. 2), do not wish to avail themselves of theology.

---

[1] The allusion is to the traditional story of the coalheaver whom the devil sought to convince of the irrationality of belief in the Trinity. The coalheaver took the cloak that he was wearing and folded it in three folds. "Here are three folds," he said, "and the cloak though threefold is yet one " And the devil departed baffled.—J. E. C. F.

" Do not ask me the reason of that, for I am ignorant;
Holy Mother Church possesses doctors who will know
how to answer you," as we were made to learn in the
Catechism. It was for this, among other things, that
the priesthood was instituted, that the teaching Church
might be the depositary—" reservoir instead of river,"
as Phillips Brooks said—of theological secrets. " The
work of the Nicene Creed," says Harnack (*Dogmengeschichte*, ii. 1, cap. vii. 3), " was a victory of the priesthood over the faith of the Christian people. The doctrine
of the Logos had already become unintelligible to those
who were not theologians. The setting up of the Niceno-
Cappadocian formula as the fundamental confession of
the Church made it perfectly impossible for the Catholic
laity to get an inner comprehension of the Christian
Faith, taking as their guide the form in which it was
presented in the doctrine of the Church. The idea
became more and more deeply implanted in men's minds
that Christianity was the revelation of the unintelligible."
And so, in truth, it is.

And why was this ? Because faith—that is, Life—no
longer felt sure of itself. Neither traditionalism nor the
theological positivism of Duns Scotus sufficed for it; it
sought to rationalize itself. And it sought to establish
its foundation—not, indeed, over against reason, where it
really is, but upon reason—that is to say, within reason—
itself. The nominalist or positivist or voluntarist position of Scotus—that which maintains that law and truth
depend, not so much upon the essence as upon the free
and inscrutable will of God—by accentuating its supreme
irrationality, placed religion in danger among the
majority of believers endowed with mature reason and
not mere coalheavers. Hence the triumph of the
Thomist theological rationalism. It is no longer enough
to believe in the existence of God; but the sentence of
anathema falls on him who, though believing in it, does
not believe that His existence is demonstrable by

rational arguments, or who believes that up to the present nobody by means of these rational arguments has ever demonstrated it irrefutably.   However, in this connection the remark of Pohle is perhaps capable of application : " If eternal salvation depended upon mathematical axioms, we should have to expect that the most odious human sophistry would attack their universal validity as violently as it now attacks God, the soul, and Christ."[1]

The truth is, Catholicism oscillates between mysticism, which is the inward experience of the living God in Christ, an intransmittible experience, the danger of which, however, is that it absorbs our own personality in God, and so does not save our vital longing—between mysticism and the rationalism which it fights against (see Weizsäcker, *op. cit.*); it oscillates between religionized science and scientificized religion.   The apocalyptic enthusiasm changed little by little into neo-platonic mysticism, which theology thrust further into the background.   It feared the excesses of the imagination which was supplanting faith and creating gnostic extravagances.   But it had to sign a kind of pact with gnosticism and another with rationalism; neither imagination nor reason allowed itself to be completely vanquished.   And thus the body of Catholic dogma became a system of contradictions, more or less successfully harmonized.   The Trinity was a kind of pact between monotheism and polytheism, and humanity and divinity sealed a peace in Christ, nature covenanted with grace, grace with free will, free will with the Divine prescience, and so on.   And it is perhaps true, as Hermann says (*loc. cit.*), that " as soon as we develop religious thought to its logical conclusions, it enters into conflict with other ideas which belong equally to the life of religion."   And this it is that gives to Catholicism its profound vital dialectic.   But at what a cost ?

[1] Joseph Pohle, "Christlich Katolische Dogmatik," in *Systematische Christliche Religion*, Berlin, 1909.   *Die Kultur der Gegenwart* series

At the cost, it must needs be said, of doing violence to
the mental exigencies of those believers in possession
of an adult reason.  It demands from them that they
shall believe all or nothing, that they shall accept the
complete totality of dogma or that they shall forfeit all
merit if the least part of it be rejected.  And hence the
result, as the great Unitarian preacher Channing pointed
out,[1] that in France and Spain there are multitudes who
have proceeded from rejecting Popery to absolute
atheism, because "the fact is, that false and absurd
doctrines, when exposed, have a natural tendency to
beget scepticism in those who received them without
reflection.  None are so likely to believe too little as those
who have begun by believing too much."  Here is,
indeed, the terrible danger of believing too much.  But
no! the terrible danger comes from another quarter—
from seeking to believe with the reason and not with life.

The Catholic solution of our problem, of our unique
vital problem, the problem of the immortality and eternal
salvation of the individual soul, satisfies the will, and
therefore satisfies life; but the attempt to rationalize it
by means of dogmatic theology fails to satisfy the reason.
And reason has its exigencies as imperious as those of
life.  It is no use seeking to force ourselves to consider
as super-rational what clearly appears to us to be contra-
rational, neither is it any good wishing to become coalheavers when we are not coalheavers.  Infallibility, a
notion of Hellenic origin, is in its essence a rationalistic
category.

Let us now consider the rationalist or scientific solution—or, more properly, dissolution—of our problem.

---

[1] "Objections to Unitarian Christianity Considered," 1816, in *The Complete Works of William Ellery Channing, D D.*, London, 1884.

# THE RATIONALIST DISSOLUTION

THE great master of rationalist phenomenalism, David Hume, begins his essay "On the Immortality of the Soul" with these decisive words: "It appears difficult by the mere light of reason to prove the immortality of the soul. The arguments in favour of it are commonly derived from metaphysical, moral, or physical considerations. But it is really the Gospel, and only the Gospel, that has brought to light life and immortality." Which is equivalent to denying the rationality of the belief that the soul of each one of us is immortal.

Kant, whose criticism found its point of departure in Hume, attempted to establish the rationality of this longing for immortality and the belief that it imports; and this is the real origin, the inward origin, of his *Critique of Practical Reason*, and of his categorical imperative and of his God. But in spite of all this, the sceptical affirmation of Hume holds good. There is no way of proving the immortality of the soul rationally. There are, on the other hand, ways of proving rationally its mortality.

It would be not merely superfluous but ridiculous to enlarge here upon the extent to which the individual human consciousness is dependent upon the physical organism, pointing out how it comes to birth by slow degrees according as the brain receives impressions from the outside world, how it is temporarily suspended during sleep, swoons, and other accidents, and how everything leads us to the rational conjecture that death carries with it the loss of consciousness. And just as before our

birth we were not, nor have we any personal pre-natal
memory, so after our death we shall cease to be. This
is the rational position.

The designation "soul" is merely a term used to
denote the individual consciousness in its integrity and
continuity; and that this soul undergoes change, that
in like manner as it is integrated so it is disintegrated, is
a thing very evident. For Aristotle it was the substantial form of the body—the entelechy, but not a
substance. And more than one modern has called it an
epiphenomenon — an absurd term. The appellation
phenomenon suffices.

Rationalism—and by rationalism I mean the doctrine
that abides solely by reason, by objective truth—is
necessarily materialist. And let not idealists be scandalized thereby.

The truth is—it is necessary to be perfectly explicit in
this matter—that what we call materialism means for us
nothing else but the doctrine which denies the immortality of the individual soul, the persistence of personal
consciousness after death.

In another sense it may be said that, as we know what
matter is no more than we know what spirit is, and as
matter is for us merely an idea, materialism is idealism.
In fact, and as regards our problem—the most vital, the
only really vital problem—it is all the same to say that
everything is matter as to say that everything is idea, or
that everything is energy, or whatever you please.
Every monist system will always seem to us materialist.
The immortality of the soul is saved only by the dualist
systems—those which teach that human consciousness is
something substantially distinct and different from the
other manifestations of phenomena. And reason is
naturally monist. For it is the function of reason to
understand and explain the universe, and in order to
understand and explain it, it is in no way necessary for the
soul to be an imperishable substance. For the purpose

of explaining and understanding our psychic life, for psychology, the hypothesis of the soul is unnecessary. What was formerly called rational psychology, in opposition to empirical psychology, is not psychology but metaphysics, and very muddy metaphysics; neither is it rational, but profoundly irrational, or rather contra-rational.

The pretended rational doctrine of the substantiality and spirituality of the soul, with all the apparatus that accompanies it, is born simply of the necessity which men feel of grounding upon reason their inexpugnable longing for immortality and the subsequent belief in it. All the sophistries which aim at proving that the soul is substance, simple and incorruptible, proceed from this source. And further, the very concept of substance, as it was fixed and defined by scholasticism, a concept which does not bear criticism, is a theological concept, designed expressly to sustain faith in the immortality of the soul.

William James, in the third of the lectures which he devoted to pragmatism in the Lowell Institute in Boston, in December, 1906, and January, 1907[1]—the weakest thing in all the work of the famous American thinker, an extremely weak thing indeed—speaks as follows : "Scholasticism has taken the notion of substance from common sense and made it very technical and articulate. Few things would seem to have fewer pragmatic consequences for us than substances, cut off as we are from every contact with them. Yet in one case scholasticism has proved the importance of the substance-idea by treating it pragmatically. I refer to certain disputes about the mystery of the Eucharist. Substance here would appear to have momentous pragmatic value. Since the accidents of the wafer do not change in the Lord's Supper, and yet it has become the very body of

[1] *Pragmatism, a New Name for some Old Ways of Thinking* Popular lectures on philosophy by William James, 1907.

Christ, it must be that the change is in the substance
solely.   The bread-substance must have been withdrawn
and the Divine substance substituted miraculously without altering the immediate sensible properties.   But
though these do not alter, a tremendous difference has
been made—no less a one than this, that we who take the
sacrament now feed upon the very substance of Divinity.
The substance-notion breaks into life, with tremendous
effect, if once you allow that substances can separate
from their accidents and exchange these latter.   This is
the only pragmatic application of the substance-idea
with which I am acquainted ; and it is obvious that it will
only be treated seriously by those who already believe in
the ' real presence ' on independent grounds.''

Now, leaving on one side the question as to whether it
is good theology—and I do not say good reasoning
because all this lies outside the sphere of reason—to confound the substance of the body—the body, not the soul
—of Christ with the very substance of Divinity—that is
to say, with God Himself—it would appear impossible
that one so ardently desirous of the immortality of the
soul as William James, a man whose whole philosophy
aims simply at establishing this belief on rational
grounds, should not have perceived that the pragmatic
application of the concept of substance to the doctrine of the
Eucharistic transubstantiation is merely a consequence of
its anterior application to the doctrine of the immortality
of the soul.   As I explained in the preceding chapter,
the Sacrament of the Eucharist is simply the reflection
of the belief in immortality ; it is, for the believer, the
proof, by a mystical experience, that the soul is immortal
and will enjoy God eternally.   And the concept of substance was born, above all and before all, of the concept
of the substantiality of the soul, and the latter was
affirmed in order to confirm faith in the persistence of
the soul after its separation from the body.   Such was at
the same time its first pragmatic application and its

origin. And subsequently we have transferred this concept to external things. It is because I feel myself to be
substance—that is to say, permanent in the midst of my
changes—that I attribute substantiality to those agents
exterior to me, which are also permanent in the midst of
their changes—just as the concept of force is born of my
sensation of personal effort in putting a thing in motion.

Read carefully in the first part of the *Summa Theologica* of St. Thomas Aquinas the first six articles of
question lxxv., which discuss whether the human soul is
body, whether it is something self-subsistent, whether
such also is the soul of the lower animals, whether the soul
is the man, whether the soul is composed of matter and
form, and whether it is incorruptible, and then say if all
this is not subtly intended to support the belief that this
incorruptible substantiality of the soul renders it capable
of receiving from God immortality, for it is clear that as
He created it when He implanted it in the body, as St.
Thomas says, so at its separation from the body He could
annihilate it. And as the criticism of these proofs has
been undertaken a hundred times, it is unnecessary to
repeat it here.

Is it possible for the unforewarned reason to conclude
that our soul is a substance from the fact that our consciousness of our identity—and this within very narrow
and variable limits—persists through all the changes of
our body? We might as well say of a ship that put out
to sea and lost first one piece of timber, which was replaced by another of the same shape and dimensions, then
lost another, and so on with all her timbers, and finally
returned to port the same ship, with the same build, the
same sea-going qualities, recognizable by everybody as
the same—we might as well say of such a ship that it
had a substantial soul. Is it possible for the unforewarned reason to infer the simplicity of the soul from the
fact that we have to judge and unify our thoughts?
Thought is not one but complex, and for the reason the

soul is nothing but the succession of co-ordinated states of consciousness.

In books of psychology written from the spiritualist point of view, it is customary to begin the discussion of the existence of the soul as a simple substance, separable from the body, after this style : There is in me a principle which thinks, wills, and feels. . . . Now this implies a begging of the question. For it is far from being an immediate truth that there is in me such a principle; the immediate truth is that I think, will, and feel. And I —the I that thinks, wills, and feels—am immediately my living body with the states of consciousness which it sustains. It is my living body that thinks, wills, and feels. How? How you please.

And they proceed to seek to establish the substantiality of the soul, hypostatizing the states of consciousness, and they begin by saying that this substance must be simple —that is, by opposing thought to extension, after the manner of the Cartesian dualism. And as Balmes was one of the spiritualist writers who have given the clearest and most concise form to the argument, I will present it as he expounds it in the second chapter of his *Curso de Filosofía Elemental.* "The human soul is simple," he says, and adds : "Simplicity consists in the absence of parts, and the soul has none. Let us suppose that it has three parts—A, B, C. I ask, Where, then, does thought reside? If in A only, then B and C are superfluous; and consequently the simple subject A will be the soul. If thought resides in A, B, and C, it follows that thought is divided into parts, which is absurd. What sort of a thing is a perception, a comparison, a judgement, a ratiocination, distributed among three subjects?" A more obvious begging of the question cannot be conceived. Balmes begins by taking it for granted that the whole, as a whole, is incapable of making a judgement. He continues : "The unity of consciousness is opposed to the division of the soul. When we think, there is a subject which knows everything that it thinks, and this is impossible if parts be attributed to it. Of the thought that is in A, B and C will know nothing, and so in the other cases respectively. There will not, therefore, be *one* consciousness of the whole thought : each part will have its special consciousness, and there will be within us as many thinking beings as there are parts." The begging of the question continues; it is assumed without any proof that a whole, as a whole, cannot perceive as a unit. Balmes then proceeds to ask if these parts A, B, and C are simple or compound, and repeats his argument until he arrives at the conclusion that the thinking subject must be a part which is not a whole—that is, simple. The argument is based, as will be seen, upon the unity of apperception and of judgement. Subsequently he endeavours to refute the hypothesis of a communication of the parts among themselves.

Balmes—and with him the *a priori* spiritualists who seek to rationalize faith in the immortality of the soul— ignore the only rational explanation, which is that apperception and judgement are a resultant, that perceptions or ideas themselves are components which agree. They begin by supposing something external to and distinct from the states of consciousness, something that is not the living body which supports these states, something that is not I but is within me.

The soul is simple, others say, because it reflects upon itself as a complete whole. No; the state of consciousness A, in which I think of my previous state of consciousness B, is not the same as its predecessor. Or if I think of my soul, I think of an idea distinct from the act by which I think of it. To think that one thinks and nothing more, is not to think.

The soul is the principle of life, it is said. Yes; and similarly the category of force or energy has been conceived as the principle of movement. But these are concepts, not phenomena, not external realities. Does the principle of movement move? And only that which moves has external reality. Does the principle of life live? Hume was right when he said that he never encountered this idea of himself—that he only observed himself desiring or performing or feeling something.[1] The idea of some individual thing—of this inkstand in front of me, of that horse standing at my gate, of these two and not of any other individuals of the same class—is the fact, the phenomenon itself. The idea of myself is myself.

All the efforts to substantivate consciousness, making it independent of extension—remember that Descartes opposed thought to extension — are but sophistical subtilties intended to establish the rationality of faith in the immortality of the soul. It is sought to give the value of objective reality to that which does not possess it—to that whose reality exists only in thought. And the immortality that we crave is a phenomenal immortality—it is the continuation of this present life.

The unity of consciousness is for scientific psychology —the only rational psychology—simply a phenomenal unity. No one can say what a substantial unity is. And, what is more, no one can say what a substance is. For the notion of substance is a non-phenomenal category. It is a noumenon and belongs properly to the unknowable—that is to say, according to the sense in which it is understood. But in its transcendental sense it is something really unknowable and strictly irrational. It is precisely this concept of substance that an unforewarned mind reduces to a use that is very far from that pragmatic application to which William James referred.

And this application is not saved by understanding it in an idealistic sense, according to the Berkeleyan principle that to be is to be perceived (*esse est percipi*). To

[1] *Treatise of Human Nature*, book 1., part iv., sect. vi., "Of Personal Identity": "I never can catch *myself* at any time without a perception, and never can observe anything but the perception."

say that everything is idea or that everything is spirit, is the same as saying that everything is matter or that everything is energy, for if everything is idea or everything spirit, and if, therefore, this diamond is idea or spirit, just as my consciousness is, it is not plain why the diamond should not endure for ever, if my consciousness, because it is idea or spirit, endures for ever.

George Berkeley, Anglican Bishop of Cloyne and brother in spirit to the Anglican bishop Joseph Butler, was equally as anxious to save the belief in the immortality of the soul. In the first words of the Preface to his *Treatise concerning the Principles of Human Knowledge,* he tells us that he considers that this treatise will be useful, "particularly to those who are tainted with scepticism, or want a demonstration of the existence and immateriality of God, or the natural immortality of the soul." In paragraph cxl. he lays it down that we have an idea, or rather a notion, of spirit, and that we know other spirits by means of our own, from which follows— so in the next paragraph he roundly affirms—the natural immortality of the soul. And here he enters upon a series of confusions arising from the ambiguity with which he invests the term notion. And after having established the immortality of the soul, almost as it were *per saltum,* on the ground that the soul is not passive like the body, he proceeds to tell us in paragraph cxlvii. that the existence of God is more evident than that of man. And yet, in spite of this, there are still some who are doubtful !

The question was complicated by making consciousness a property of the soul, consciousness being something more than soul—that is to say, a substantial form of the body, the originator of all the organic functions of the body. The soul not only thinks, feels, and wills, but moves the body and prompts its vital functions ; in the human soul are united the vegetative, animal, and rational functions. Such is the theory. But the soul separated from the body can have neither vegetative nor animal functions.

A theory, in short, which for the reason is a veritable contexture of confusions.

After the Renaissance and the restoration of purely rational thought, emancipated from all theology, the doctrine of the mortality of the soul was re-established by the newly published writings of the second-century philosopher Alexander of Aphrodisias and by Pietro Pomponazzi and others. And in point of fact, little or nothing can be added to what Pomponazzi has written in his *Tractatus de immortalitate animæ*. It is reason itself, and it serves nothing to reiterate his arguments.

Attempts have not been wanting, however, to find an empirical support for belief in the immortality of the soul, and among these may be counted the work of Frederic W. H. Myers on *Human Personality and its Survival of Bodily Death*. No one ever approached more eagerly than myself the two thick volumes of this work in which the leading spirit of the Society for Psychical Research resumed that formidable mass of data relating to presentiments, apparitions of the dead, the phenomena of dreams, telepathy, hypnotism, sensorial automatism, ecstasy, and all the rest that goes to furnish the spiritualist arsenal. I entered upon the reading of it not only without that temper of cautious suspicion which men of science maintain in investigations of this character, but even with a predisposition in its favour, as one who comes to seek the confirmation of his innermost longings; but for this reason was my disillusion all the greater. In spite of its critical apparatus it does not differ in any respect from medieval miracle-mongering. There is a fundamental defect of method, of logic.

And if the belief in the immortality of the soul has been unable to find vindication in rational empiricism, neither is it satisfied with pantheism. To say that everything is God, and that when we die we return to God, or, more accurately, continue in Him, avails our longing nothing; for if this indeed be so, then we were in God before we were born, and if when we die we return to where we were before being born, then the human soul, the individual consciousness, is perishable. And since we know very well that God, the personal and conscious God of Christian monotheism, is simply the provider, and above all the guarantor, of our immortality, pantheism is said, and rightly said, to be merely atheism disguised; and, in my opinion, undisguised. And they were right in calling Spinoza an atheist, for his is the most logical, the most rational, system of pantheism.

Neither is the longing for immortality saved, but rather dissolved and submerged, by agnosticism, or the doctrine of the unknowable, which, when it has professed to wish to leave religious feelings scathless, has always been inspired by the most refined hypocrisy. The whole of the first part of Spencer's *First Principles*, and especially the fifth chapter entitled "Reconciliation "—that between reason and faith or science and religion being understood —is a model at the same time of philosophical superficiality and religious insincerity, of the most refined British cant. The unknowable, if it is something more than the merely hitherto unknown, is but a purely negative concept, a concept of limitation. And upon this foundation no human feeling can be built up.

The science of religion, on the other hand, of religion considered as an individual and social psychic phenomenon irrespective of the transcendental objective validity of religious affirmations, is a science which, in explaining the origin of the belief that the soul is something that can live disjoined from the body, has destroyed the rationality of this belief. However much the religious man may repeat with Schleiermacher, "Science can teach thee nothing; it is for science to learn from thee," inwardly he thinks otherwise.

From whatever side the matter is regarded, it is always

found that reason confronts our longing for personal immortality and contradicts it. And the truth is, in all strictness, that reason is the enemy of life.

A terrible thing is intelligence. It tends to death as memory tends to stability. The living, the absolutely unstable, the absolutely individual, is, strictly, unintelligible. Logic tends to reduce everything to identities and genera, to each representation having no more than one single and self-same content in whatever place, time, or relation it may occur to us. And there is nothing that remains the same for two successive moments of its existence. My idea of God is different each time that I conceive it. Identity, which is death, is the goal of the intellect. The mind seeks what is dead, for what is living escapes it; it seeks to congeal the flowing stream in blocks of ice; it seeks to arrest it. In order to analyze a body it is necessary to extenuate or destroy it. In order to understand anything it is necessary to kill it, to lay it out rigid in the mind. Science is a cemetery of dead ideas, even though life may issue from them. Worms also feed upon corpses. My own thoughts, tumultuous and agitated in the innermost recesses of my soul, once they are torn from their roots in the heart, poured out on to this paper and there fixed in unalterable shape, are already only the corpses of thoughts. How, then, shall reason open its portals to the revelation of life? It is a tragic combat—it is the very essence of tragedy—this combat of life with reason. And truth? Is truth something that is lived or that is comprehended?

It is only necessary to read the terrible *Parmenides* of Plato to arrive at his tragic conclusion that "the one is and is not, and both itself and others, in relation to themselves and one another, are and are not, and appear to be and appear not to be." All that is vital is irrational, and all that is rational is anti-vital, for reason is essentially sceptical.

The rational, in effect, is simply the relational; reason

is limited to relating irrational elements. Mathematics is the only perfect science, inasmuch as it adds, subtracts, multiplies, and divides numbers, but not real and substantial things, inasmuch as it is the most formal of the sciences. Who can extract the cube root of an ash-tree?

Nevertheless we need logic, this terrible power, in order to communicate thoughts and perceptions and even in order to think and perceive, for we think with words, we perceive with forms. To think is to converse with oneself; and speech is social, and social are thought and logic. But may they not perhaps possess a content, an individual matter, incommunicable and untranslatable? And may not this be the source of their power?

The truth is that man, the prisoner of logic, without which he cannot think, has always sought to make logic subservient to his desires, and principally to his fundamental desire. He has always sought to hold fast to logic, and especially in the Middle Ages, in the interests of theology and jurisprudence, both of which based themselves on what was established by authority. It was not until very much later that logic propounded the problem of knowledge, the problem of its own validity, the scrutiny of the metalogical foundations.

"The Western theology," Dean Stanley wrote, "is essentially logical in form and based on law. The Eastern theology is rhetorical in form and based on philosophy. The Latin divine succeeded to the Roman advocate. The Oriental divine succeeded to the Grecian sophist."[1]

And all the laboured arguments in support of our hunger of immortality, which pretend to be grounded on reason or logic, are merely advocacy and sophistry.

The property and characteristic of advocacy is, in effect, to make use of logic in the interests of a thesis that is to be defended, while, on the other hand, the strictly

[1] Arthur Penrhyn Stanley, *Lectures on the History of the Eastern Church*, lecture i., sect. iii.

scientific method proceeds from the facts, the data, presented to us by reality, in order that it may arrive, or not arrive, as the case may be, at a certain conclusion. What is important is to define the problem clearly, whence it follows that progress consists not seldom in undoing what has been done. Advocacy always supposes a *petitio principii*, and its arguments are *ad probandum*. And theology that pretends to be rational is nothing but advocacy.

Theology proceeds from dogma, and dogma, δόγμα, in its primitive and most direct sense, signifies a decree, something akin to the Latin *placitum*, that which has seemed to the legislative authority fitting to be law. This juridical concept is the starting-point of theology. For the theologian, as for the advocate, dogma, law, is something given—a starting-point which admits of discussion only in respect of its application and its most exact interpretation. Hence it follows that the theological or advocatory spirit is in its principle dogmatical, while the strictly scientific and purely rational spirit is sceptical, σκεπτικός—that is, investigative. It is so at least in its principle, for there is the other sense of the term scepticism, that which is most usual to-day, that of a system of doubt, suspicion, and uncertainty, and this has arisen from the theological or advocatory use of reason, from the abuse of dogmatism. The endeavour to apply the law of authority, the *placitum*, the dogma, to different and sometimes contraposed practical necessities, is what has engendered the scepticism of doubt. It is advocacy, or what amounts to the same thing, theology, that teaches the distrust of reason—not true science, not the science of investigation, sceptical in the primitive and direct meaning of the word, which hastens towards no predetermined solution nor proceeds save by the testing of hypotheses.

Take the *Summa Theologica* of St. Thomas, the classical monument of the theology—that is, of the advocacy—of Catholicism, and open it where you please. First comes the thesis—*utrum* . . . whether such a thing be thus or otherwise; then the objections—*ad primum sic proceditur;* next the answers to these objections—*sed contra est* . . . or *respondeo dicendum.* . . . Pure advocacy! And underlying many, perhaps most, of its arguments you will find a logical fallacy which may be expressed *more scholastico* by this syllogism: I do not understand this fact save by giving it this explanation; it is thus that I must understand it, therefore this must be its explanation. The alternative being that I am left without any understanding of it at all. True science teaches, above all, to doubt and to be ignorant; advocacy neither doubts nor believes that it does not know. It requires a solution.

To the mentality that assumes, more or less consciously, that we must of necessity find a solution to every problem, belongs the argument based on the disastrous consequences of a thing. Take any book of apologetics—that is to say, of theological advocacy—and you will see how many times you will meet with this phrase—" the disastrous consequences of this doctrine." Now the disastrous consequences of a doctrine prove at most that the doctrine is disastrous, but not that it is false, for there is no proof that the true is necessarily that which suits us best. The identification of the true and the good is but a pious wish. In his *Études sur Blaise Pascal,* A. Vinet says: " Of the two needs that unceasingly belabour human nature, that of happiness is not only the more universally felt and the more constantly experienced, but it is also the more imperious. And this need is not only of the senses; it is intellectual. It is not only for the *soul;* it is for the *mind* that happiness is a necessity. Happiness forms a part of truth." This last proposition—*le bonheur fait partie de la verité*—is a proposition of pure advocacy, but not of science or of pure reason. It would be better to say that truth forms

a part of happiness in a Tertullianesque sense, in the
sense of *credo quia absurdum*, which means actually
*credo quia consolans*—I believe because it is a thing consoling to me.

No, for reason, truth is that of which it can be proved
that it is, that it exists, whether it console us or not. And
reason is certainly not a consoling faculty. That terrible
Latin poet Lucretius, whose apparent serenity and
Epicurean *ataraxia* conceal so much despair, said that
piety consists in the power to contemplate all things with
a serene soul—*pacata posse mente omnia tueri*. And it
was the same Lucretius who wrote that religion can persuade us into so great evils—*tantum religio potuit
suadere malorum*. And it is true that religion—above
all the Christian religion—has been, as the Apostle says,
to the Jews a stumbling-block, and to the intellectuals
foolishness.[1]  The Christian religion, the religion of the
immortality of the soul, was called by Tacitus a pernicious superstition (*exitialis superstitio*), and he asserted
that it involved a hatred of mankind (*odium generis
humani*).

Speaking of the age in which these men lived, the
most genuinely rationalistic age in the world's history,
Flaubert, writing to Madame Roger des Genettes,
uttered these pregnant words : " You are right; we must
speak with respect of Lucretius; I see no one who can
compare with him except Byron, and Byron has not his
gravity nor the sincerity of his sadness. The melancholy
of the ancients seems to me more profound than that of
the moderns, who all more or less presuppose an immortality on the yonder side of the *black hole*. But for the
ancients this black hole was the infinite itself; the procession of their dreams is imaged against a background
of immutable ebony. The gods being no more and
Christ being not yet, there was between Cicero and Marcus
Aurelius a unique moment in which man stood alone.

[1] 1 Cor. i. 23.

Nowhere else do I find this grandeur; but what renders Lucretius intolerable is his physics, which he gives as if positive. If he is weak, it is because he did not doubt enough; he wished to explain, to arrive at a conclusion!"[1]

Yes, Lucretius wished to arrive at a conclusion, a solution, and, what is worse, he wished to find consolation in reason. For there is also an anti-theological advocacy, and an *odium anti-theologicum*.

Many, very many, men of science, the majority of those who call themselves rationalists, are afflicted by it.

The rationalist acts rationally—that is to say, he does not speak out of his part—so long as he confines himself to denying that reason satisfies our vital hunger for immortality; but, furious at not being able to believe, he soon becomes a prey to the vindictiveness of the *odium anti-theologicum*, and exclaims with the Pharisees : "This people who knoweth not the law are cursed." There is much truth in these words of Soloviev : "I have a foreboding of the near approach of a time when Christians will gather together again in the Catacombs, because of the persecution of the faith—a persecution less brutal, perhaps, than that of Nero's day, but not less refined in its severity, consummated by mendacity, derision, and all the hypocrisies."

The anti-theological hate, the scientificist—I do not say scientific—fury, is manifest. Consider, not the more detached scientific investigators, those who know how to doubt, but the fanatics of rationalism, and observe with what gross brutality they speak of faith. Vogt considered it probable that the cranial structure of the Apostles was of a pronounced simian character; of the indecencies of Haeckel, that supreme incomprehender, there is no need to speak, nor yet of those of Buchner; even Virchow is not free from them. And others work with more subtlty. There are people who seem not to

[1] Gustave Flaubert, *Correspondance*, troisième série (1854-1869). Paris, 1910.

be content with not believing that there is another life,
or rather, with believing that there is none, but who are
vexed and hurt that others should believe in it or even
should wish that it might exist.    And this attitude is as
contemptible as that is worthy of respect which characterizes those who, though urged by the need they have of
it to believe in another life, are unable to believe.    But
of this most noble attitude of the spirit, the most profound, the most human, and the most fruitful, the attitude
of despair, we will speak later on.

And the rationalists who do not succumb to the anti-
theological fury are bent on convincing men that there
are motives for living and consolations for having been
born, even though there shall come a time, at the end of
some tens or hundreds or millions of centuries, when all
human consciousness shall have ceased to exist.    And
these motives for living and working, this thing which
some call humanism, are the amazing products of the
affective and emotional hollowness of rationalism and of
its stupendous hypocrisy—a hypocrisy bent on sacrificing
sincerity to veracity, and sworn not to confess that reason
is a dissolvent and disconsolatory power.

Must I repeat again what I have already said about all
this business of manufacturing culture, of progressing,
of realizing good, truth, and beauty, of establishing
justice on earth, of ameliorating life for those who shall
come after us, of subserving I know not what destiny,
and all this without our taking thought for the ultimate
end of each one of us?    Must I again declare to you the
supreme vacuity of culture, of science, of art, of good, of
truth, of beauty, of justice . . . of all these beautiful conceptions, if at the last, in four days or in four millions of
centuries—it matters not which—no human consciousness shall exist to appropriate this civilization, this
science, art, good, truth, beauty, justice, and all the rest?

Many and very various have been the rationalist
devices—more or less rational—by means of which from

the days of the Epicureans and the Stoics it has been sought to discover rational consolation in truth and to convince men, although those who sought so to do remained themselves unconvinced, that there are motives for working and lures for living, even though the human consciousness be destined some day to disappear.

The Epicurean attitude, the extreme and grossest expression of which is " Let us eat and drink, for to-morrow we die," or the Horatian *carpe diem*, which may be rendered by " Live for the day," does not differ in its essence from the Stoic attitude with its " Accomplish what the moral conscience dictates to thee, and afterward let it be as it may be." Both attitudes have a common base ; and pleasure for pleasure's sake comes to the same as duty for duty's sake.

Spinoza, the most logical and consistent of atheists— I mean of those who deny the persistence of individual consciousness through indefinite future time—and at the same time the most pious, Spinoza devoted the fifth and last part of his *Ethic* to elucidating the path that leads to liberty and to determining the concept of happiness. The concept ! Concept, not feeling ! For Spinoza, who was a terrible intellectualist, happiness (*beatitudo*) is a concept, and the love of God an intellectual love. After establishing in proposition xxi. of the fifth part that " the mind can imagine nothing, neither can it remember anything that is past, save during the continuance of the body "—which is equivalent to denying the immortality of the soul, since a soul which, disjoined from the body in which it lived, does not remember its past, is neither immortal nor is it a soul—he goes on to affirm in proposition xxiii. that "the human mind cannot be absolutely destroyed with the body, but there remains of it something which is *eternal*," and this eternity of the mind is a certain mode of thinking. But do not let yourselves be deceived ; there is no such eternity of the individual mind. Everything is *sub æternitatis specie*—that is to

7

say, pure illusion. Nothing could be more dreary, nothing more desolating, nothing more anti-vital than this happiness, this *beatitudo*, of Spinoza, that consists in the intellectual love of the mind towards God, which is nothing else but the very love with which God loves Himself (prop. xxxvi.). Our happiness—that is to say, our liberty—consists in the constant and eternal love of God towards men. So affirms the corollary to this thirty-sixth proposition. And all this in order to arrive at the conclusion, which is the final and crowning proposition of the whole *Ethic*, that happiness is not the reward of virtue, but virtue itself. The everlasting refrain! Or, to put it plainly, we proceed from God and to God we return, which, translated into concrete language, the language of life and feeling, means that my personal consciousness sprang from nothingness, from my unconsciousness, and to nothingness it will return.

And this most dreary and desolating voice of Spinoza is the very voice of reason. And the liberty of which he tells us is a terrible liberty. And against Spinoza and his doctrine of happiness there is only one irresistible argument, the argument *ad hominem*. Was he happy, Benedict Spinoza, while, to allay his inner unhappiness, he was discoursing of happiness? Was he free?

In the corollary to proposition xli. of this same final and most tragic part of that tremendous tragedy of his *Ethic*, the poor desperate Jew of Amsterdam discourses of the common persuasion of the vulgar of the truth of eternal life. Let us hear what he says : "It would appear that they esteem piety and religion—and, indeed, all that is referred to fortitude or strength of mind—as burdens which they expect to lay down after death, when they hope to receive a reward for their servitude, not for their piety and religion in this life. Nor is it even this hope alone that leads them; the fear of frightful punishments with which they are menaced after death also influences them to live—in so far as their impotence and poverty of spirit permits—in conformity with the prescription of the Divine law. And were not this hope and this fear infused into the minds of men—but, on the contrary, did they believe that the soul perished with the body, and that, beyond the grave, there was no other life prepared for the wretched who had borne the burden *of piety* in this—they would return to their natural inclinations, preferring to accommodate everything to their own liking, and would follow fortune rather than reason. But all this appears no less absurd than it would be to suppose that a man, because he did not believe that he could nourish his body eternally with wholesome food, would saturate himself with deadly poisons ; or than if because believing that his soul was not eternal and immortal, he should therefore prefer to be without a soul (*amens*) and to live without reason ; all of which is so absurd as to be scarcely worth refuting (*quæ adeo absurda sunt, ut vix recenseri mereantur*)."

When a thing is said to be not worth refuting you may be sure that either it is flagrantly stupid—in which case all comment is superfluous—or it is something formidable, the very crux of the problem. And this it is in this case. Yes ! poor Portuguese Jew exiled in Holland, yes ! that he who is convinced without a vestige of doubt, without the faintest hope of any saving uncertainty, that his soul is not immortal, should prefer to be without a soul (*amens*), or irrational, or idiot, that he should prefer not to have been born, is a supposition that has nothing, absolutely nothing, absurd in it. Was he happy, the poor Jewish intellectualist definer of intellectual love and of happiness? For that and no other is the problem. " What does it profit thee to know the definition of compunction if thou dost not feel it?" says à Kempis. And what profits it to discuss or to define happiness if you cannot thereby achieve happiness? Not inapposite in this connection is that terrible story that Diderot tells of a eunuch who desired to take lessons in esthetics from

a native of Marseilles in order that he might be better
qualified to select the slaves destined for the harem of
the Sultan, his master. At the end of the first lesson, a
physiological lesson, brutally and carnally physiological,
the eunuch exclaimed bitterly, "It is evident that I shall
never know esthetics!" Even so, and just as eunuchs
will never know esthetics as applied to the selection of
beautiful women, so neither will pure rationalists ever
know ethics, nor will they ever succeed in defining happiness, for happiness is a thing that is lived and felt, not a
thing that is reasoned about or defined.

And you have another rationalist, one not sad or sub-
missive, like Spinoza, but rebellious, and though con-
cealing a despair not less bitter, making a hypocritical
pretence of light-heartedness, you have Nietzsche, who
discovered *mathematically* (!!!) that counterfeit of the
immortality of the soul which is called "eternal recurrence," and which is in fact the most stupendous tragicomedy or comi-tragedy. The number of atoms or
irreducible primary elements being finite and the universe
eternal, a combination identical with that which at present
exists must at some future time be reproduced, and therefore that which now is must be repeated an infinite number of times. This is evident, and just as I shall live
again the life that I am now living, so I have already
lived it before an infinite number of times, for there is an
eternity that stretches into the past—*a parte ante*—just
as there will be one stretching into the future—*a parte
post*. But, unfortunately, it happens that I remember
none of my previous existences, and perhaps it is impossible that I should remember them, for two things absolutely and completely identical are but one. Instead of
supposing that we live in a finite universe, composed of a
finite number of irreducible primary elements, suppose
that we live in an infinite universe, without limits in
space—which concrete infinity is not less inconceivable
than the concrete eternity in time—then it will follow that

this system of ours, that of the Milky Way, is repeated an infinite number of times in the infinite of space, and that therefore I am now living an infinite number of lives, all exactly identical. A jest, as you see, but one not less comic—that is to say, not less tragic—than that of Nietzsche, that of the laughing lion. And why does the lion laugh? I think he laughs with rage, because he can never succeed in finding consolation in the thought that he has been the same lion before and is destined to be the same lion again.

But if Spinoza and Nietzsche were indeed both rationalists, each after his own manner, they were not spiritual eunuchs; they had heart, feeling, and, above all, hunger, a mad hunger for eternity, for immortality. The physical eunuch does not feel the need of reproducing himself carnally, in the body, and neither does the spiritual eunuch feel the hunger for self-perpetuation.

Certain it is that there are some who assert that reason suffices them, and they counsel us to desist from seeking to penetrate into the impenetrable. But of those who say that they have no need of any faith in an eternal personal life to furnish them with incentives to living and motives for action, I know not well how to think. A man blind from birth may also assure us that he feels no great longing to enjoy the world of sight nor suffers any great anguish from not having enjoyed it, and we must needs believe him, for what is wholly unknown cannot be the object of desire—*nihil volitum quin præcognitum,* there can be no volition save of things already known. But I cannot be persuaded that he who has once in his life, either in his youth or for some other brief space of time, cherished the belief in the immortality of the soul, will ever find peace without it. And of this sort of blindness from birth there are but few instances among us, and then only by a kind of strange aberration. For the merely and exclusively rational man is an aberration and nothing but an aberration.

More sincere, much more sincere, are those who say :
"We must not talk about it, for in talking about it we
only waste our time and weaken our will; let us do our
duty here and hereafter let come what may." But this
sincerity hides a yet deeper insincerity. May it perhaps
be that by saying "We must not talk about it," they
succeed in not thinking about it? Our will is weakened?
And what then? We lose the capacity for human
action? And what then? It is very convenient to tell
a man whom a fatal disease condemns to an early death,
and who knows it, not to think about it.

> *Meglio oprando obliar, senzá indagarlo,*
> *Questo enorme mister del universo !*

"Better to work and to forget and not to probe into
this vast mystery of the universe !" Carducci wrote in his
*Idilio Maremmano,* the same Carducci who at the close
of his ode *Sul Monte Mario* tells us how the earth, the
mother of the fugitive soul, must roll its burden of glory
and sorrow round the sun " until, worn out beneath the
equator, mocked by the last flames of dying heat, the
exhausted human race is reduced to a single man and
woman, who, standing in the midst of dead woods, surrounded by sheer mountains, livid, with glassy eyes
watch thee, O sun, set across the immense frozen waste."

But is it possible for us to give ourselves to any serious
and lasting work, forgetting the vast mystery of the
universe and abandoning all attempt to understand it?
Is it possible to contemplate the vast All with a serene
soul, in the spirit of the Lucretian piety, if we are conscious of the thought that a time must come when this All
will no longer be reflected in any human consciousness?

Cain, in Byron's poem, asks of Lucifer, the prince of
the intellectuals, " Are ye happy ?" and Lucifer replies,
" We are mighty." Cain questions again, " Are ye
happy ?" and then the great Intellectual says to him :
" No; art thou?" And further on, this same Lucifer
says to Adah, the sister and wife of Cain : "Choose

betwixt love and knowledge—since there is no other choice." And in the same stupendous poem, when Cain says that the tree of the knowledge of good and evil was a lying tree, for " we know nothing; at least it promised knowledge at the price of death," Lucifer answers him : " It may be death leads to the highest knowledge "—that is to say, to nothingness.

To this word *knowledge* which Lord Byron uses in the above quotations, the Spanish *ciencia*, the French *science*, the German *Wissenschaft*, is often opposed the word *wisdom, sabiduria, sagesse, Weisheit.*

> Knowledge comes, but Wisdom lingers, and he bears a laden breast,
> Full of sad experience, moving toward the stillness of his rest,

says another lord, Tennyson, in his *Locksley Hall.* And what is this wisdom which we have to seek chiefly in the poets, leaving knowledge on one side? It is well enough to say with Matthew Arnold in his Introduction to Wordsworth's poems, that poetry is reality and philosophy illusion; but reason is always reason and reality is always reality, that which can be proved to exist externally to us, whether we find in it consolation or despair.

I do not know why so many people were scandalized, or pretended to be scandalized, when Brunetière proclaimed again the bankruptcy of science. For science as a substitute for religion and reason as a substitute for faith have always fallen to pieces. Science will be able to satisfy, and in fact does satisfy in an increasing measure, our increasing logical or intellectual needs, our desire to know and understand the truth; but science does not satisfy the needs of our heart and our will, and far from satisfying our hunger for immortality it contradicts it. Rational truth and life stand in opposition to one another. And is it possible that there is any other truth than rational truth?

It must remain established, therefore, that reason—human reason—within its limits, not only does not prove

rationally that the soul is immortal or that the human
consciousness shall preserve its indestructibility through
the tracts of time to come, but that it proves rather—
within its limits, I repeat—that the individual consciousness cannot persist after the death of the physical
organism upon which it depends. And these limits,
within which I say that human reason proves this, are
the limits of rationality, of what is known by demonstration. Beyond these limits is the irrational, which,
whether it be called the super-rational or the infra-
rational or the contra-rational, is all the same thing.
Beyond these limits is the absurd of Tertullian, the
impossibile of the *certum est, quia impossibile est*. And
this absurd can only base itself upon the most absolute
uncertainty.

The rational dissolution ends in dissolving reason
itself; it ends in the most absolute scepticism, in the
phenomenalism of Hume or in the doctrine of absolute
contingencies of Stuart Mill, the most consistent and
logical of the positivists. The supreme triumph of
reason, the analytical—that is, the destructive and dissolvent—faculty, is to cast doubt upon its own validity.
The stomach that contains an ulcer ends by digesting
itself; and reason ends by destroying the immediate and
absolute validity of the concept of truth and of the concept of necessity. Both concepts are relative; there is
no absolute truth, no absolute necessity. We call a
concept true which agrees with the general system of all
our concepts; and we call a perception true which does
not contradict the system of our perceptions. Truth is
coherence. But as regards the whole system, the aggre-
gate, as there is nothing outside of it of which we have
knowledge, we cannot say whether it is true or not. It
is conceivable that the universe, as it exists in itself, outside of our consciousness, may be quite other than it
appears to us, although this is a supposition that has no
meaning for reason. And as regards necessity, is there

an absolute necessity? By necessary we mean merely that which is, and in so far as it is, for in another more transcendental sense, what absolute necessity, logical and independent of the fact that the universe exists, is there that there should be a universe or anything else at all?

Absolute relativism, which is neither more nor less than scepticism, in the most modern sense of the term, is the supreme triumph of the reasoning reason.

Feeling does not succeed in converting consolation into truth, nor does reason succeed in converting truth into consolation. But reason going beyond truth itself, beyond the concept of reality itself, succeeds in plunging itself into the depths of scepticism. And in this abyss the scepticism of the reason encounters the despair of the heart, and this encounter leads to the discovery of a basis—a terrible basis!—for consolation to build on.

Let us examine it.

# VI

## IN THE DEPTHS OF THE ABYSS

*Parce unicæ spes totius orbis.*—TERTULLIANUS, Adversus Marcionem, 5.

WE have seen that the vital longing for human immortality finds no consolation in reason and that reason leaves us without incentive or consolation in life and life itself without real finality. But here, in the depths of the abyss, the despair of the heart and of the will and the scepticism of reason meet face to face and embrace like brothers. And we shall see it is from this embrace, a tragic—that is to say, an intimately loving—embrace, that the wellspring of life will flow, a life serious and terrible. Scepticism, uncertainty—the position to which reason, by practising its analysis upon itself, upon its own validity, at last arrives—is the foundation upon which the heart's despair must build up its hope.

Disillusioned, we had to abandon the position of those who seek to give consolation the force of rational and logical truth, pretending to prove the rationality, or at any rate the non-irrationality, of consolation; and we had to abandon likewise the position of those who seek to give rational truth the force of consolation and of a motive for life. Neither the one nor the other of these positions satisfied us. The one is at variance with our reason, the other with our feeling. These two powers can never conclude peace and we must needs live by their war. We must make of this war, of war itself, the very condition of our spiritual life.

Neither does this high debate admit of that indecent and repugnant expedient which the more or less parliamentary type of politician has devised and dubbed "a formula of agreement," the property of which is to render it impossible for either side to claim to be victorious. There is no place here for a time-serving compromise. Perhaps a degenerate and cowardly reason might bring itself to propose some such formula of agreement, for in truth reason lives by formulas; but life, which cannot be formulated, life which lives and seeks to live for ever, does not submit to formulas. Its sole formula is : all or nothing. Feeling does not compound its differences with middle terms.

*Initium sapientiæ timor Domini*, it is said, meaning perhaps *timor mortis*, or it may be, *timor vitæ*, which is the same thing. Always it comes about that the beginning of wisdom is a fear.

Is it true to say of this saving scepticism which I am now going to discuss, that it is doubt? It is doubt, yes, but it is much more than doubt. Doubt is commonly something very cold, of very little vitalizing force, and above all something rather artificial, especially since Descartes degraded it to the function of a method. The conflict between reason and life is something more than a doubt. For doubt is easily resolved into a comic element.

The methodical doubt of Descartes is a comic doubt, a doubt purely theoretical and provisional—that is to say, the doubt of a man who acts as if he doubted without really doubting. And because it was a stove-excogitated doubt, the man who deduced that he existed from the fact that he thought did not approve of " those turbulent (*brouillonnes*) and restless persons who, being called neither by birth nor by fortune to the management of public affairs, are perpetually devising some new reformation," and he was pained by the suspicion that there might be something of this kind in his own writings. No, he, Descartes, proposed only to " reform his own thoughts and to build upon ground that was wholly his." And he resolved not to accept anything as true when he did not recognize it clearly to be so, and to make a clean sweep of

all prejudices and received ideas, to the end that he might
construct his intellectual habitation anew.    But " as it is
not enough, before beginning to rebuild one's dwelling-
house, to pull it down and to furnish materials and archi-
tects, or to study architecture oneself . . . but it is also
necessary to be provided with some other wherein to lodge
conveniently while the work is in progress," he framed for
himself a provisional ethic—*une morale de provision*—
the first law of which was to observe the customs of his
country and to keep always to the religion in which, by the
grace of God, he had been instructed from his infancy,
governing himself in all things according to the most
moderate opinions.    Yes, exactly, a provisional religion
and even a provisional God!    And he chose the most
moderate opinions " because these are always the most
convenient for practice."    But it is best to proceed no
further.

This methodical or theoretical Cartesian doubt, this
philosophical doubt excogitated in a stove, is not the
doubt, is not the scepticism, is not the incertitude, that I
am talking about here.    No!    This other doubt is a passionate doubt, it is the eternal conflict between reason and
feeling, science and life, logic and biotic.    For science
destroys the concept of personality by reducing it to a
complex in continual flux from moment to moment—that
is to say, it destroys the very foundation of the spiritual
and emotional life, which ranges itself unyieldingly
against reason.

And this doubt cannot avail itself of any provisional
ethic, but has to found its ethic, as we shall see, on the conflict itself, an ethic of battle, and itself has to serve as the
foundation of religion.    And it inhabits a house which is
continually being demolished and which continually it
has to rebuild.    Without ceasing the will, I mean the will
never to die, the spirit of unsubmissiveness to death,
labours to build up the house of life, and without ceasing
the keen blasts and stormy assaults of reason beat it down.

And more than this, in the concrete vital problem that concerns us, reason takes up no position whatever. In truth, it does something worse than deny the immortality of the soul—for that at any rate would be one solution—it refuses even to recognize the problem as our vital desire presents it to us. In the rational and logical sense of the term problem, there is no such problem. This question of the immortality of the soul, of the persistence of the individual consciousness, is not rational, it falls outside reason. As a problem, and whatever solution it may receive, it is irrational. Rationally even the very propounding of the problem lacks sense. The immortality of the soul is as unconceivable as, in all strictness, is its absolute mortality. For the purpose of explaining the world and existence—and such is the task of reason—it is not necessary that we should suppose that our soul is either mortal or immortal. The mere enunciation of the problem is, therefore, an irrationality.

Let us hear what our brother Kierkegaard has to say. "The danger of abstract thought is seen precisely in respect of the problem of existence, the difficulty of which it solves by going round it, afterwards boasting that it has completely explained it. It explains immortality in general, and it does so in a remarkable way by identifying it with eternity—with the eternity which is essentially the medium of thought. But with the immortality of each individually existing man, wherein precisely the difficulty lies, abstraction does not concern itself, is not interested in it. And yet the difficulty of existence lies just in the interest of the existing being—the man who exists is infinitely interested in existing. Abstract thought besteads immortality only in order that it may kill me as an individual being with an individual existence, and so make me immortal, pretty much in the same way as that famous physician in one of Holberg's plays, whose medicine, while it took away the patient's fever, took away his life at the same time. An abstract thinker, who

refuses to disclose and admit the relation that exists
between his abstract thought and the fact that he is an
existing being, produces a comic impression upon us,
however accomplished and distinguished he may be, for
he runs the risk of ceasing to be a man. While an
effective man, compounded of infinitude and finitude,
owes his effectiveness precisely to the conjunction of these
two elements and is infinitely interested in existing, an
abstract thinker, similarly compounded, is a double
being, a fantastical being, who lives in the pure being of
abstraction, and at times presents the sorry figure of a
professor who lays aside this abstract essence as he lays
aside his walking-stick. When one reads the Life of a
thinker of this kind—whose writings may be excellent—
one trembles at the thought of what it is to be a man.
And when one reads in his writings that thinking and
being are the same thing, one thinks, remembering his
life, that that being, which is identical with thinking,
is not precisely the same thing as being a man "
(*Afsluttende uvidenskabelig Efterskrift*, chap. iii.).

What intense passion—that is to say, what truth—there
is in this bitter invective against Hegel, prototype of the
rationalist !—for the rationalist takes away our fever by
taking away our life, and promises us, instead of a concrete, an abstract immortality, as if the hunger for
immortality that consumes us were an abstract and not a
concrete hunger !

It may indeed be said that when once the dog is dead
there is an end to the rabies, and that after I have died I
shall no more be tortured by this rage of not dying, and
that the fear of death, or more properly, of nothingness,
is an irrational fear, but . . . Yes, but . . . *Eppur si
muove!* And it will go on moving. For it is the source
of all movement !

I doubt, however, whether our brother Kierkegaard is
altogether in the right, for this same abstract thinker,
or thinker of abstractions, thinks *in order that* he may

exist, that he may not cease to exist, or thinks perhaps in order to forget that he will have to cease to exist. This is the root of the passion for abstract thought. And possibly Hegel was as infinitely interested as Kierkegaard in his own concrete, individual existence, although the professional decorum of the state-philosopher compelled him to conceal the fact.

Faith in immortality is irrational. And, notwithstanding, faith, life, and reason have mutual need of one another. This vital longing is not properly a problem, cannot assume a logical status, cannot be formulated in propositions susceptible of rational discussion; but it announces itself in us as hunger announces itself. Neither can the wolf that throws itself with the fury of hunger upon its prey or with the fury of instinct upon the she-wolf, enunciate its impulse rationally and as a logical problem. Reason and faith are two enemies, neither of which can maintain itself without the other. The irrational demands to be rationalized and reason only can operate on the irrational. They are compelled to seek mutual support and association. But association in struggle, for struggle is a mode of association.

In the world of living beings the struggle for life establishes an association, and a very close one, not only between those who unite together in combat against a common foe, but between the combatants themselves. And is there any possible association more intimate than that uniting the animal that eats another and the animal that is eaten, between the devourer and the devoured? And if this is clearly seen in the struggle between individuals, it is still more evident in the struggle between peoples. War has always been the most effective factor of progress, even more than commerce. It is through war that conquerors and conquered learn to know each other and in consequence to love each other.

Christianity, the foolishness of the Cross, the irrational faith that Christ rose from the dead in order to raise us

from the dead, was saved by the rationalistic Hellenic
culture, and this in its turn was saved by Christianity.
Without Christianity the Renaissance would have been
impossible. Without the Gospel, without St. Paul, the
peoples who had traversed the Middle Ages would have
understood neither Plato nor Aristotle. A purely
rationalist tradition is as impossible as a tradition purely
religious. It is frequently disputed whether the Reformation was born as the child of the Renaissance or as a protest against it, and both propositions may be said to be
true, for the son is always born as a protest against the
father. It is also said that it was the revived Greek
classics that led men like Erasmus back to St. Paul and to
primitive Christianity, which is the most irrational form
of Christianity; but it may be retorted that it was St. Paul,
that it was the Christian irrationality underlying his
Catholic theology, that led them back to the classics.
"Christianity is what it has come to be," it has been
said, "only through its alliance with antiquity, while
with the Copts and Ethiopians it is but a kind of
buffoonery. Islam developed under the influence of Persian and Greek culture, and under that of the Turks it
has been transformed into a destructive barbarism."[1]

We have emerged from the Middle Ages, from the
medieval faith as ardent as it was at heart despairing, and
not without its inward and abysmal incertitudes, and we
have entered upon the age of rationalism, likewise not
without its incertitudes. Faith in reason is exposed to
the same rational indefensibility as all other faith. And
we may say with Robert Browning,

> All we have gained, then, by our unbelief
> Is a life of doubt diversified by faith
> For one of faith diversified by doubt.
> (*Bishop Blougram's Apology*)

---

[1] See Troeltsch, *Systematische christliche Religion* in *Die Kultur der
Gegenwart* series.

And if, as I have said, faith, life, can only sustain itself by leaning upon reason, which renders it transmissible—and above all transmissible from myself to myself—that is to say, reflective and conscious—it is none the less true that reason in its turn can only sustain itself by leaning upon faith, upon life, even if only upon faith in reason, faith in its availability for something more than mere knowing, faith in its availability for living. Nevertheless, neither is faith transmissible or rational, nor is reason vital.

The will and the intelligence have need of one another, and the reverse of that old aphorism, *nihil volitum quin præcognitum*, nothing is willed but what is previously known, is not so paradoxical as at first sight it may appear—*nihil cognitum quin prævolitum*, nothing is known but what is previously willed. Vinet, in his study of Cousin's book on the *Pensées* of Pascal, says : " The very knowledge of the mind as such has need of the heart. Without the desire to see there is no seeing; in a great materialization of life and of thought there is no believing in the things of the spirit." We shall see presently that to believe is, in the first instance, to wish to believe.

The will and the intelligence seek opposite ends : that we may absorb the world into ourselves, appropriate it to ourselves, is the aim of the will; that we may be absorbed into the world, that of the intelligence. Opposite ends ?—are they not rather one and the same? No, they are not, although they may seem to be so. The intelligence is monist or pantheist, the will monotheist or egoist. The intelligence has no need of anything outside it to exercise itself upon ; it builds its foundation with ideas themselves, while the will requires matter. To know something is to make this something that I know myself ; but to avail myself of it, to dominate it, it has to remain distinct from myself.

Philosophy and religion are enemies, and because they are enemies they have need of one another. There is no

8

religion without some philosophic basis, no philosophy
without roots in religion.  Each lives by its contrary.
The history of philosophy is, strictly speaking, a history
of religion.  And the attacks which are directed against
religion from a presumed scientific or philosophical point
of view are merely attacks from another but opposing religious point of view.  " The opposition which professedly
exists between natural science and Christianity really
exists between an impulse derived from natural religion
blended with the scientific investigation of nature, and
the validity of the Christian view of the world,
which assures to spirit its pre-eminence over the entire
world of nature," says Ritschl (*Rechtfertgung und
Versohnung*, iii. chap. iv. § 28).  Now this instinct is
the instinct of rationality itself.  And the critical
idealism of Kant is of religious origin, and it is
in order to save religion that Kant enlarged the limits
of reason after having in a certain sense dissolved it
in scepticism.  The system of antitheses, contradictions,
and antinomies, upon which Hegel constructed his absolute idealism, has its root and germ in Kant himself, and
this root is an irrational root.

We shall see later on, when we come to deal with faith,
that faith is in its essence simply a matter of will, not of
reason, that to believe is to wish to believe, and to believe
in God is, before all and above all, to wish that there may
be a God.  In the same way, to believe in the immortality
of the soul is to wish that the soul may be immortal, but
to wish it with such force that this volition shall trample
reason under foot and pass beyond it.  But reason has
its revenge.

The instinct of knowing and the instinct of living, or
rather of surviving, come into conflict.  In his work on
the *Analysis of the Sensations and the Relation of the
Physical to the Psychical*,[1] Dr. E. Mach tells us that not

[1] *Die Analyse der Empfindigungen und das Verhältniss des Physischen
zum Psychischen*, i , § 12, note.

even the investigator, the savant, *der Forscher*, is exempted from taking his part in the struggle for existence, that even the roads of science lead mouth-wards, and that in the actual conditions of the society in which we live the pure instinct of knowing, *der reine Erkenntnisstrieb*, is still no more than an ideal.   And so it always will be.   *Primum vivere, deinde philosophari*, or perhaps better, *primum supervivere* or *superesse*.

Every position of permanent agreement or harmony between reason and life, between philosophy and religion, becomes impossible.   And the tragic history of human thought is simply the history of a struggle between reason and life—reason bent on rationalizing life and forcing it to submit to the inevitable, to mortality; life bent on vitalizing reason and forcing it to serve as a support for its own vital desires.   And this is the history of philosophy, inseparable from the history of religion.

Our sense of the world of objective reality is necessarily subjective, human, anthropomorphic.   And vitalism will always rise up against rationalism; reason will always find itself confronted by will.   Hence the rhythm of the history of philosophy and the alternation of periods in which life imposes itself, giving birth to spiritual forms, with those in which reason imposes itself, giving birth to materialist forms, although both of these classes of forms of belief may be disguised by other names.   Neither reason nor life ever acknowledges itself vanquished.   But we will return to this in the next chapter.

The vital consequence of rationalism would be suicide. Kierkegaard puts it very well : " The consequence for existence[1] of pure thought is suicide. . . .   We do not praise suicide but passion.   The thinker, on the contrary, is a curious animal—for a few spells during the day he is very intelligent, but, for the rest, he has nothing in

[1] I have left the original expression here, almost without translating it—*Existents-Consequents*.   It means the existential or practical, not the purely rational or logical, consequence.   (Author's note )

common with man " (*Afsluttende uvidenskabelig Efter-skrift,* chap iii., § 1).

As the thinker, in spite of all, does not cease to be a man, he employs reason in the interests of life, whether he knows it or not. Life cheats reason and reason cheats life. Scholastic-Aristotelian philosophy fabricated in the interest of life a teleologic-evolutionist system, rational in appearance, which might serve as a support for our vital longing. This philosophy, the basis of the orthodox Christian supernaturalism, whether Catholic or Protestant, was, in its essence, merely a trick on the part of life to force reason to lend it its support. But reason supported it with such pressure that it ended by pulverizing it.

I have read that the ex-Carmelite, Hyacinthe Loyson, declared that he could present himself before God with tranquillity, for he was at peace with his conscience and with his reason. With what conscience? If with his religious conscience, then I do not understand. For it is a truth that no man can serve two masters, and least of all when, though they may sign truces and armistices and compromises, these two are enemies because of their conflicting interests.

To all this someone is sure to object that life ought to subject itself to reason, to which we will reply that nobody ought to do what he is unable to do, and life cannot subject itself to reason. " Ought, therefore can," some Kantian will retort. To which we shall demur: " Cannot, therefore ought not." And life cannot submit itself to reason, because the end of life is living and not understanding.

Again, there are those who talk of the religious duty of resignation to mortality. This is indeed the very summit of aberration and insincerity. But someone is sure to oppose the idea of veracity to that of sincerity. Granted, and yet the two may very well be reconciled. Veracity, the homage I owe to what I believe to be rational, to what logically we call truth, moves me to affirm, in this case, that the immortality of the individual soul is a contradiction in terms, that it is something, not only irrational, but contra-rational; but sincerity leads me to affirm also my refusal to resign myself to this previous affirmation and my protest against its validity.   What I feel is a truth, at any rate as much a truth as what I see, touch, hear, or what is demonstrated to me—nay, I believe it is more of a truth—and sincerity obliges me not to hide what I feel.

And life, quick to defend itself, searches for the weak point in reason and finds it in scepticism, which it straightway fastens upon, seeking to save itself by means of this stranglehold.   It needs the weakness of its adversary.

Nothing is sure.   Everything is elusive and in the air. In an outburst of passion Lamennais exclaims: " But what ! Shall we, losing all hope, shut our eyes and plunge into the voiceless depths of a universal scepticism ?   Shall we doubt that we think, that we feel, that we are ?   Nature does not allow it ; she forces us to believe even when our reason is not convinced.   Absolute certainty and absolute doubt are both alike forbidden to us.   We hover in a vague mean between these two extremes, as between being and nothingness; for complete scepticism would be the extinction of the intelligence and the total death of man. But it is not given to man to annihilate himself; there is in him something which invincibly resists destruction, I know not what vital faith, indomitable even by his will. Whether he likes it or not, he must believe, because he must act, because he must preserve himself.   His reason, if he listened only to that, teaching him to doubt everything, itself included, would reduce him to a state of absolute inaction; he would perish before even he had been able to prove to himself that he existed " (*Essai sur l'indifférence en matière de religion*, iiie partie, chap. lxvii.).

Reason, however, does not actually lead us to absolute scepticism. No! Reason does not lead me and cannot lead me to doubt that I exist. Whither reason does lead me is to vital scepticism, or more properly, to vital nega- tion—not merely to doubt, but to deny, that my con- sciousness survives my death. Scepticism is produced by the clash between reason and desire. And from this clash, from this embrace between despair and scepticism, is born that holy, that sweet, that saving incertitude, which is our supreme consolation.

The absolute and complete certainty, on the one hand, that death is a complete, definite, irrevocable annihilation of personal consciousness, a certainty of the same order as the certainty that the three angles of a triangle are equal to two right angles, or, on the other hand, the absolute and complete certainty that our personal con- sciousness is prolonged beyond death in these present or in other conditions, and above all including in itself that strange and adventitious addition of eternal rewards and punishments—both of these certainties alike would make life impossible for us. In the most secret chamber of the spirit of him who believes himself convinced that death puts an end to his personal consciousness, his memory, for ever, and all unknown to him perhaps, there lurks a shadow, a vague shadow, a shadow of shadow, of uncertainty, and while he says within himself, " Well, let us live this life that passes away, for there is no other !" the silence of this secret chamber speaks to him and murmurs, " Who knows ! . . ." He may not think he hears it, but he hears it nevertheless. And likewise in some secret place of the soul of the believer who most firmly holds the belief in a future life, there is a muffled voice, a voice of uncertainty, which whispers in the ear of his spirit, " Who knows ! . . ." These voices are like the humming of a mosquito when the south-west wind roars through the trees in the wood; we cannot dis- tinguish this faint humming, yet nevertheless, merged in the clamour of the storm, it reaches the ear.    Otherwise, without this uncertainty, how could we live?

"*Is there?*"    "*Is there not?*"—these are the bases of our inner life.    There may be a rationalist who has never wavered in his conviction of the mortality of the soul, and there may be a vitalist who has never wavered in his faith in immortality; but at the most this would only prove that just as there are natural monstrosities, so there are those who are stupid as regards heart and feeling, however great their intelligence, and those who are stupid intellectually, however great their virtue.    But, in normal cases, I cannot believe those who assure me that never, not in a fleeting moment, not in the hours of direst loneliness and grief, has this murmur of uncertainty breathed upon their consciousness.    I do not understand those men who tell me that the prospect of the yonder side of death has never tormented them, that the thought of their own annihilation never disquiets them.    For my part I do not wish to make peace between my heart and my head, between my faith and my reason—I wish rather that there should be war between them!

In the ninth chapter of the Gospel according to Mark it is related how a man brought unto Jesus his son who was possessed by a dumb spirit, and wheresoever the spirit took him it tore him, causing him to foam and gnash his teeth and pine away, wherefore he sought to bring him to Jesus that he might cure him.    And the Master, impatient of those who sought only for signs and wonders, exclaimed : " O faithless generation, how long shall I be with you ? how long shall I suffer you ? bring him unto me " (ver. 19), and they brought him unto him.    And when the Master saw him wallowing on the ground, he asked his father how long it was ago since this had come unto him and the father replied that it was since he was a child.    And Jesus said unto him : " If thou canst believe, all things are possible to him that believeth " (ver. 23).    And then the father of the epileptic or

demoniac uttered these pregnant and immortal words:
" Lord, I believe; help thou mine unbelief !"—Πιστεύω,
κύριε, βοήθει τῇ ἀπιστίᾳ μου (ver. 24).

" Lord, I believe; help thou mine unbelief !"   A contradiction seemingly, for if he believes, if he trusts, how
is it that he beseeches the Lord to help his lack of trust?
Nevertheless, it is this contradiction that gives to the
heart's cry of the father of the demoniac its most profound
human value.   His faith is a faith that is based upon
incertitude.   Because he believes—that is to say, because
he wishes to believe, because he has need that his son
should be cured—he beseeches the Lord to help his unbelief, his doubt that such a cure could be effected.   Of
such kind is human faith; of such kind was the heroic
faith that Sancho Panza had in his master, the knight
Don Quijote de la Mancha, as I think I have shown in
my *Vida de Don Quijote y Sancho;* a faith based upon
incertitude, upon doubt.   Sancho Panza was indeed a
man, a whole and a true man, and he was not stupid, for
only if he had been stupid would he have believed, without a shadow of doubt, in the follies of his master.   And
his master himself did not believe in them without a
shadow of doubt, for neither was Don Quixote, though
mad, stupid.   He was at heart a man of despair, as I
think I have shown in my above-mentioned book.   And
because he was a man of an heroical despair, the hero
of that inward and resigned despair, he stands as the
eternal exemplar of every man whose soul is the battle-
ground of reason and immortal desire.   Our Lord Don
Quixote is the prototype of the vitalist whose faith is
based upon uncertainty, and Sancho is the prototype of
the rationalist who doubts his own reason.

Tormented by torturing doubts, August Hermann
Francke resolved to call upon God, a God in whom he
did not believe, or rather in whom he believed that he
did not believe, imploring Him to take pity upon him,
upon the poor pietist Francke, if perchance He really

existed.[1] And from a similar state of mind came the
inspiration of the sonnet entitled "The Atheist's
Prayer," which is included in my *Rosario de Sonetos
Líricos,* and closes with these lines :

> *Sufro yo a tu costa,*
> *Dios no existiente, pues si tú existieras*
> *existiería yo también de veras.*[2]

Yes, if God the guarantor of our personal immortality
existed, then should we ourselves really exist.   And if
He exists not, neither do we exist.

That terrible secret, that hidden will of God which,
translated into the language of theology, is known as
predestination, that idea which dictated to Luther his
*servum arbitrium,* and which gives to Calvinism its tragic
sense, that doubt of our own salvation, is in its essence
nothing but uncertainty, and this uncertainty, allied
with despair, forms the basis of faith.   Faith, some say,
consists in not thinking about it, in surrendering ourselves trustingly to the arms of God, the secrets of whose
providence are inscrutable.   Yes, but infidelity also
consists in not thinking about it.   This absurd faith, this
faith that knows no shadow of uncertainty, this faith of
the stupid coalheaver, joins hands with an absurd
incredulity, the incredulity that knows no shadow of
uncertainty, the incredulity of the intellectuals who are
afflicted with affective stupidity in order that they may
not think about it.

And what but uncertainty, doubt, the voice of reason,
was that abyss, that terrible *gouffre,* before which Pascal
trembled ?   And it was that which led him to pronounce
his terrible sentence, *il faut s'abêtir*—need is that we
become fools !

All Jansenism, the Catholic adaptation of Calvinism,

---

[1] Albrecht Ritschl : *Geschichte des Pietismus,* ii., Abt. i., Bonn, 1884,
p. 251.

[2] Thou art the cause of my suffering, O non-existing God, for if Thou
didst exist, then should I also really exist.

bears the same impress.  Port-Royal, which owed its
existence to a Basque, the Abbé de Saint-Cyran, a man
of the same race as Iñigo de Loyola and as he who writes
these lines, always preserved deep down a sediment of
religious despair, of the suicide of reason.  Loyola also
slew his reason in obedience.

Our affirmation is despair, our negation is despair,
and from despair we abstain from affirming and denying.
Note the greater part of our atheists and you will see
that they are atheists from a kind of rage, rage at not
being able to believe that there is a God.  They are the
personal enemies of God.  They have invested Nothingness with substance and personality, and their No-God
is an Anti-God.

And concerning that abject and ignoble saying, " If
there were not a God it would be necessary to invent
Him," we shall say nothing.  It is the expression of the
unclean scepticism of those conservatives who look upon
religion merely as a means of government and whose
interest it is that in the other life there shall be a hell for
those who oppose their worldly interests in this life.
This repugnant and Sadducean phrase is worthy of the
time-serving sceptic to whom it is attributed.

No, with all this the deep vital sense has nothing to
do.  It has nothing to do with a transcendental police
regimen, or with securing order—and what an order!—
upon earth by means of promises and threats of eternal
rewards and punishments after death.  All this belongs
to a lower plane—that is to say, it is merely politics, or
if you like, ethics.  The vital sense has to do with living.

But it is in our endeavour to represent to ourselves
what the life of the soul after death really means that
uncertainty finds its surest foundation.  This it is that
most shakes our vital desire and most intensifies the
dissolvent efficacy of reason.  For even if by a mighty
effort of faith we overcome that reason which tells and
teaches us that the soul is only a function of the physical

organism, it yet remains for our imagination to conceive an image of the immortal and eternal life of the soul. This conception involves us in contradictions and absurdities, and it may be that we shall arrive with Kierkegaard at the conclusion that if the mortality of the soul is terrible, not less terrible is its immortality.

But when we have overcome the first, the only real difficulty, when we have overcome the impediment of reason, when we have achieved the faith, however painful and involved in uncertainty it may be, that our personal consciousness shall continue after death, what difficulty, what impediment, lies in the way of our imagining to ourselves this persistence of self in harmony with our desire? Yes, we can imagine it as an eternal rejuvenescence, as an eternal growth of ourselves, and as a journeying towards God, towards the Universal Consciousness, without ever an arrival, we can imagine it as . . . But who shall put fetters upon the imagination, once it has broken the chain of the rational?

I know that all this is dull reading, tiresome, perhaps tedious, but it is all necessary. And I must repeat once again that we have nothing to do with a transcendental police system or with the conversion of God into a great Judge or Policeman—that is to say, we are not concerned with heaven or hell considered as buttresses to shore up our poor earthly morality, nor are we concerned with anything egoistic or personal. It is not I myself alone, it is the whole human race that is involved, it is the ultimate finality of all our civilization. I am but one, but all men are I's.

Do you remember the end of that *Song of the Wild Cock* which Leopardi wrote in prose?—the despairing Leopardi, the victim of reason, who never succeeded in achieving belief. " A time will come," he says, " when this Universe and Nature itself will be extinguished. And just as of the grandest kingdoms and empires of mankind and the marvellous things achieved therein,

very famous in their own time, no vestige or memory
remains to-day, so, in like manner, of the entire world
and of the vicissitudes and calamities of all created things
there will remain not a single trace, but a naked silence
and a most profound stillness will fill the immensity of
space.   And so before ever it has been uttered or understood, this admirable and fearful secret of universal
existence will be obliterated and lost." And this they
now describe by a scientific and very rationalistic term—
namely, *entropia*.   Very pretty, is it not?   Spencer
invented the notion of a primordial homogeneity, from
which it is impossible to conceive how any heterogeneity
could originate.   Well now, this *entropia* is a kind of
ultimate homogeneity, a state of perfect equilibrium.
For a soul avid of life, it is the most like nothingness
that the mind can conceive.

To this point, through a series of dolorous reflections,
I have brought the reader who has had the patience to
follow me, endeavouring always to do equal justice to
the claims of reason and of feeling.   I have not wished
to keep silence on matters about which others are silent;
I have sought to strip naked, not only my own soul, but
the human soul, be its nature what it may, its destiny to
disappear or not to disappear.   And we have arrived at
the bottom of the abyss, at the irreconcilable conflict
between reason and vital feeling.   And having arrived
here, I have told you that it is necessary to accept the
conflict as such and to live by it.   Now it remains for me
to explain to you how, according to my way of feeling,
and even according to my way of thinking, this despair
may be the basis of a vigorous life, of an efficacious
activity, of an ethic, of an esthetic, of a religion and even
of a logic.   But in what follows there will be as much of
imagination as of ratiocination, or rather, much more.
I do not wish to deceive anyone, or to offer as
philosophy what it may be is only poetry or phantasma-

goria, in any case a kind of mythology. The divine Plato, after having discussed the immortality of the soul in his dialogue *Phædo* (an ideal—that is to say, a lying—immortality), embarked upon an interpretation of the myths which treat of the other life, remarking that it was also necessary to mythologize. Let us, then, mythologize.

He who looks for reasons, strictly so called, scientific arguments, technically logical reflections, may refuse to follow me further. Throughout the remainder of these reflections upon the tragic sense, I am going to fish for the attention of the reader with the naked, unbaited hook; whoever wishes to bite, let him bite, but I deceive no one. Only in the conclusion I hope to gather everything together and to show that this religious despair which I have been talking about, and which is nothing other than the tragic sense of life itself, is, though more or less hidden, the very foundation of the consciousness of civilized individuals and peoples to-day—that is to say, of those individuals and those peoples who do not suffer from stupidity of intellect or stupidity of feeling.

And this tragic sense is the spring of heroic achievements.

If in that which follows you shall meet with arbitrary apothegms, brusque transitions, inconsecutive statements, veritable somersaults of thought, do not cry out that you have been deceived. We are about to enter—if it be that you wish to accompany me—upon a field of contradictions between feeling and reasoning, and we shall have to avail ourselves of the one as well as of the other.

That which follows is not the outcome of reason but of life, although in order that I may transmit it to you I shall have to rationalize it after a fashion. The greater part of it can be reduced to no logical theory or system; but like that tremendous Yankee poet, Walt Whitman, " I charge that there be no theory or school founded out of me " (*Myself and Mine*).

Neither am I the only begetter of the fancies I am about to set forth. By no means. They have also been conceived by other men, if not precisely by other thinkers, who have preceded me in this vale of tears, and who have exhibited their life and given expression to it. Their life, I repeat, not their thought, save in so far as it was thought inspired by life, thought with a basis of irrationality.

Does this mean that in all that follows, in the efforts of the irrational to express itself, there is a total lack of rationality, of all objective value? No; the absolutely, the irrevocably irrational, is inexpressible, is intransmissible. But not the contra-rational. Perhaps there is no way of rationalizing the irrational; but there is a way of rationalizing the contra-rational, and that is by trying to explain it. Since only the rational is intelligible, really intelligible, and since the absurd, being devoid of sense, is condemned to be incommunicable, you will find that whenever we succeed in giving expression and intelligibility to anything apparently irrational or absurd we invariably resolve it into something rational, even though it be into the negation of that which we affirm.

The maddest dreams of the fancy have some ground of reason, and who knows if everything that the imagination of man can conceive either has not already happened, or is not now happening or will not happen some time, in some world or another? The possible combinations are perhaps infinite. It only remains to know whether all that is imaginable is possible.

It may also be said, and with justice, that much of what I am about to set forth is merely a repetition of ideas which have been expressed a hundred times before and a hundred times refuted; but the repetition of an idea really implies that its refutation has not been final. And as I do not pretend that the majority of these fancies are new, so neither do I pretend, obviously, that other voices before mine have not spoken to the winds the same laments. But when yet another voice echoes the same eternal lament it can only be inferred that the same grief still dwells in the heart.

And it comes not amiss to repeat yet once again the same eternal lamentations that were already old in the days of Job and Ecclesiastes, and even to repeat them in the same words, to the end that the devotees of progress may see that there is something that never dies. Whosoever repeats the " Vanity of vanities " of Ecclesiastes or the lamentations of Job, even though without changing a letter, having first experienced them in his soul, performs a work of admonition. Need is to repeat without ceasing the *memento mori*.

" But to what end ?" you will ask. Even though it be only to the end that some people should be irritated and should see that these things are not dead and, so long as men exist, cannot die; to the end that they should be convinced that to-day, in the twentieth century, all the bygone centuries and all of them alive, are still subsisting. When a supposed error reappears, it must be, believe me, that it has not ceased to be true in part, just as when one who was dead reappears, it must be that he was not wholly dead.

Yes, I know well that others before me have felt what I feel and express; that many others feel it to-day, although they keep silence about it. Why do I not keep silence about it too? Well, for the very reason that most of those who feel it are silent about it; and yet, though they are silent, they obey in silence that inner voice. And I do not keep silence about it because it is for many the thing which must not be spoken, the abomination of abominations—*infandum*—and I believe that it is necessary now and again to speak the thing which must not be spoken. But if it leads to nothing ? Even if it should lead only to irritating the devotees of progress, those who believe that truth is consolation, it would lead to not a little. To irritating them and making

them say : Poor fellow ! if he would only use his intelligence to better purpose ! . . . Someone perhaps will
add that I do not know what I say, to which I shall reply
that perhaps he may be right—and being right is such a
little thing !—but that I feel what I say and I know what
I feel and that suffices me.   And that it is better to be
lacking in reason than to have too much of it.

And the reader who perseveres in reading me will also
see how out of this abyss of despair hope may arise, and
how this critical position may be the well-spring of
human, profoundly human, action and effort, and of
solidarity and even of progress.   He will see its pragmatic justification.   And he will see how, in order to
work, and to work efficaciously and morally, there is no
need of either of these two conflicting certainties, either
that of faith or that of reason, and how still less is there
any need—this never under any circumstances—to shirk
the problem of the immortality of the soul, or to distort
it idealistically—that is to say, hypocritically.   The
reader will see how this uncertainty, with the suffering
that accompanies it, and the fruitless struggle to escape
from it, may be and is a basis for action and morals.

And in the fact that it serves as a basis for action and
morals, this feeling of uncertainty and the inward
struggle between reason on the one hand and faith and
the passionate longing for eternal life on the other, should
find their justification in the eyes of the pragmatist.   But
it must be clearly stated that I do not adduce this practical consequence in order to justify the feeling, but
merely because I encounter it in my inward experience.
I neither desire to seek, nor ought I to seek, any justification for this state of inward struggle and uncertainty and
longing; it is a fact and that suffices.   And if anyone
finding himself in this state, in the depth of the abyss,
fails to find there motives for and incentives to life and
action, and concludes by committing bodily or spiritual
suicide, whether he kills himself or he abandons all

co-operation with his fellows in human endeavour, it will not be I who will pass censure upon him.   And apart from the fact that the evil consequences of a doctrine, or rather those which we call evil, only prove, I repeat, that the doctrine is disastrous for our desires, but not that it is false in itself, the consequences themselves depend not so much upon the doctrine as upon him who deduces them.   The same principle may furnish one man with grounds for action and another man with grounds for abstaining from action, it may lead one man to direct his effort towards a certain end and another man towards a directly opposite end.   For the truth is that our doctrines are usually only the justification *a posteriori* of our conduct, or else they are our way of trying to explain that conduct to ourselves.

Man, in effect, is unwilling to remain in ignorance of the motives of his own conduct.   And just as a man who has been led to perform a certain action by hypnotic suggestion will afterwards invent reasons which would justify it and make it appear logical to himself and others, being unaware all the time of the real cause of his action, so every man—for since " life is a dream " every man is in a condition of hypnotism—seeks to find reasons for his conduct.   And if the pieces on a chessboard were endowed with consciousness, they would probably have little difficulty in ascribing their moves to freewill—that is to say, they would claim for them a finalist rationality. And thus it comes about that every philosophic theory serves to explain and justify an ethic, a doctrine of conduct, which has its real origin in the inward moral feeling of the author of the theory.   But he who harbours this feeling may possibly himself have no clear consciousness of its true reason or cause.

Consequently, if my reason, which is in a certain sense a part of the reason of all my brothers in humanity in time and space, teaches me this absolute scepticism in respect of what concerns my longing for never-ending life, I think that I can assume that my feeling of life, which is the essence of life itself, my vitality, my boundless appetite for living and my abhorrence of dying, my refusal to submit to death—that it is this which suggests to me the doctrines with which I try to counter-check the working of the reason. Have these doctrines an objective value? someone will ask me, and I shall answer that I do not understand what this objective value of a doctrine is. I will not say that the more or less poetical and unphilosophical doctrines that I am about to set forth are those which make me live; but I will venture to say that it is my longing to live and to live for ever that inspires these doctrines within me. And if by means of them I succeed in strengthening and sustaining this same longing in another, perhaps when it was all but dead, then I shall have performed a man's work and, above all, I shall have lived. In a word, be it with reason or without reason or against reason, I am resolved not to die. And if, when at last I die out, I die out altogether, then I shall not have died out of myself—that is, I shall not have yielded myself to death, but my human destiny will have killed me. Unless I come to lose my head, or rather my heart, I will not abdicate from life—life will be wrested from me.

To have recourse to those ambiguous words, " optimism " and " pessimism," does not assist us in any way, for frequently they express the very contrary of what those who use them mean to express. To ticket a doctrine with the label of pessimism is not to impugn its validity, and the so-called optimists are not the most efficient in action. I believe, on the contrary, that many of the greatest heroes, perhaps the greatest of all, have been men of despair and that by despair they have accomplished their mighty works. Apart from this, however, and accepting in all their ambiguity these denominations of optimism and pessimism, that there exists a certain transcendental pessimism which may be the begetter of a temporal and terrestrial optimism, is a matter that I propose to develop in the following part of this treatise.

Very different, well I know, is the attitude of our progressives, the partisans of "the central current of contemporary European thought"; but I cannot bring myself to believe that these individuals do not voluntarily close their eyes to the grand problem of existence and that, in endeavouring to stifle this feeling of the tragedy of life, they themselves are not living a lie.

The foregoing reflections are a kind of practical summary of the criticism developed in the first six chapters of this treatise, a kind of definition of the practical position to which such a criticism is capable of leading whosoever will not renounce life and will not renounce reason and who is compelled to live and act between these upper and nether millstones which grind upon the soul. The reader who follows me further is now aware that I am about to carry him into the region of the imagination, of imagination not destitute of reason, for without reason nothing subsists, but of imagination founded on feeling. And as regards its truth, the real truth, that which is independent of ourselves, beyond the reach of our logic and of our heart—of this truth who knows aught?

# VII

## LOVE, SUFFERING, PITY, AND PERSONALITY

CAIN . Let me, or happy or unhappy, learn
　　　To anticipate my immortality.
LUCIFER ; Thou didst before I came upon thee.
CAIN ·　　　　　　　　　　　　　　　　How ?
LUCIFER : By suffering.

BYRON : *Cain*, Act II., Scene I

THE most tragic thing in the world and in life, readers
and brothers of mine, is love. Love is the child of
illusion and the parent of disillusion; love is consolation
in desolation; it is the sole medicine against death, for
it is death's brother.

*Fratelli, a un tempo stesso, Amore e Morte*
*Ingeneró la sorte,*

as Leopardi sang.

Love seeks with fury, through the medium of the
beloved, something beyond, and since it finds it not, it
despairs.

Whenever we speak of love there is always present in
our memory the idea of sexual love, the love between
man and woman, whose end is the perpetuation of the
human race upon the earth. Hence it is that we never
succeed in reducing love either to a purely intellectual
or to a purely volitional element, putting aside that part
in it which belongs to the feeling, or, if you like, to the
senses. For, in its essence, love is neither idea nor
volition; rather it is desire, feeling; it is something

132

carnal in spirit itself. Thanks to love, we feel all that spirit has of flesh in it.

Sexual love is the generative type of every other love. In love and by love we seek to perpetuate ourselves, and we perpetuate ourselves on the earth only on condition that we die, that we yield up our life to others. The humblest forms of animal life, the lowest of living beings, multiply by dividing themselves, by splitting into two, by ceasing to be the unit which they previously formed.

But when at last the vitality of the being that multiplies itself by division is exhausted, the species must renew the source of life from time to time by means of the union of two wasting individuals, by means of what is called, among protozoaria, conjugation. They unite in order to begin dividing again with more vigour. And every act of generation consists in a being's ceasing to be what it was, either wholly or in part, in a splitting up, in a partial death. To live is to give oneself, to perpetuate oneself, and to perpetuate oneself and to give oneself is to die. The supreme delight of begetting is perhaps nothing but a foretaste of death, the eradication of our own vital essence. We unite with another, but it is to divide ourselves; this most intimate embrace is only a most intimate sundering. In its essence, the delight of sexual love, the genetic spasm, is a sensation of resurrection, of renewing our life in another, for only in others can we renew our life and so perpetuate ourselves.

Without doubt there is something tragically destructive in the essence of love, as it presents itself to us in its primitive animal form, in the unconquerable instinct which impels the male and the female to mix their being in a fury of conjunction. The same impulse that joins their bodies, separates, in a certain sense, their souls; they hate one another, while they embrace, no less than they love, and above all they contend with one another, they contend for a third life, which as yet is without life. Love

is a contention, and there are animal species in which the
male maltreats the female in his union with her, and other
in which the female devours the male after being fertilized
by him.

It has been said that love is a mutual selfishness; and,
in fact, each one of the lovers seeks to possess the other,
and in seeking his own perpetuation through the instru-
mentality of the other, though without being at the time
conscious of it or purposing it, he thereby seeks his own
enjoyment. Each one of the lovers is an immediate
instrument of enjoyment and a mediate instrument of
perpetuation, for the other. And thus they are tyrants
and slaves, each one at once the tyrant and slave of the
other.

Is there really anything strange in the fact that the
deepest religious feeling has condemned carnal love and
exalted virginity? Avarice, said the Apostle, is the root
of all evil, and the reason is because avarice takes riches,
which are only a means, for an end; and therein lies the
essence of sin, in taking means for ends, in not recogniz-
ing or in disesteeming the end. And since it takes
enjoyment for the end, whereas it is only the means, and
not perpetuation, which is the true end, what is carnal
love but avarice? And it is possible that there are some
who preserve their virginity in order the better to perpetuate themselves, and in order to perpetuate something
more human than the flesh.

For it is the suffering flesh, it is suffering, it is death,
that lovers perpetuate upon the earth. Love is at once
the brother, son, and father of death, which is its sister,
mother, and daughter. And thus it is that in the depth
of love there is a depth of eternal despair, out of which
spring hope and consolation. For out of this carnal and
primitive love of which I have been speaking, out of this
love of the whole body with all its senses, which is the
animal origin of human society, out of this loving-fond-
ness, rises spiritual and sorrowful love.

This other form of love, this spiritual love, is born of sorrow, is born of the death of carnal love, is born also of the feeling of compassion and protection which parents feel in the presence of a stricken child. Lovers never attain to a love of self abandonment, of true fusion of soul and not merely of body, until the heavy pestle of sorrow has bruised their hearts and crushed them in the same mortar of suffering. Sensual love joined their bodies but disjoined their souls; it kept their souls strangers to one another; but of this love is begotten a fruit of their flesh—a child. And perchance this child, begotten in death, falls sick and dies. Then it comes to pass that over the fruit of their carnal fusion and spiritual separation and estrangement, their bodies now separated and cold with sorrow but united by sorrow their souls, the lovers, the parents, join in an embrace of despair, and then is born, of the death of the child of their flesh, the true spiritual love. Or rather, when the bond of flesh which united them is broken, they breathe with a sigh of relief. For men love one another with a spiritual love only when they have suffered the same sorrow together, when through long days they have ploughed the stony ground bowed beneath the common yoke of a common grief. It is then that they know one another and feel one another, and feel with one another in their common anguish, they pity one another and love one another. For to love is to pity; and if bodies are united by pleasure, souls are united by pain.

And this is felt with still more clearness and force in the seeding, the taking root, and the blossoming of one of those tragic loves which are doomed to contend with the diamond-hard laws of Destiny—one of those loves which are born out of due time and season, before or after the moment, or out of the normal mode in which the world, which is custom, would have been willing to welcome them. The more barriers Destiny and the world and its law interpose between the lovers, the

stronger is the impulse that urges them towards one
another, and their happiness in loving one another turns
to bitterness, and their unhappiness in not being able to
love freely and openly grows heavier, and they pity one
another from the bottom of their hearts; and this common pity, which is their common misery and their
common happiness, gives fire and fuel to their love.
And they suffer their joy, enjoying their suffering.    And
they establish their love beyond the confines of the world,
and the strength of this poor love suffering beneath the
yoke of Destiny gives them intuition of another world
where there is no other law than the liberty of love—
another world where there are no barriers because there
is no flesh.    For nothing inspires us more with hope and
faith in another world than the impossibility of our love
truly fructifying in this world of flesh and of appearances.

And what is maternal love but compassion for the
weak, helpless, defenceless infant that craves the mother's
milk and the comfort of her breast?    And woman's love
is all maternal.

To love with the spirit is to pity, and he who pities
most loves most.    Men aflame with a burning charity
towards their neighbours are thus enkindled because they
have touched the depth of their own misery, their own
apparentiality, their own nothingness, and then, turning
their newly opened eyes upon their fellows, they have
seen that they also are miserable, apparential, condemned
to nothingness, and they have pitied them and loved
them.

Man yearns to be loved, or, what is the same thing, to
be pitied.    Man wishes others to feel and share his hardships and his sorrows.    The roadside beggar's exhibition
of his sores and gangrened mutilations is something more
than a device to extort alms from the passer-by.    True
alms is pity rather than the pittance that alleviates the
material hardships of life.    The beggar shows little
gratitude for alms thrown to him by one who hurries past

with averted face; he is more grateful to him who pities him but does not help than to him who helps but does not pity, although from another point of view he may prefer the latter. Observe with what satisfaction he relates his woes to one who is moved by the story of them. He desires to be pitied, to be loved.

Woman's love, above all, as I have remarked, is always compassionate in its essence—maternal. Woman yields herself to the lover because she feels that his desire makes him suffer. Isabel had compassion upon Lorenzo, Juliet upon Romeo, Francesca upon Paolo. Woman seems to say: "Come, poor one, thou shalt not suffer so for my sake!" And therefore is her love more loving and purer than that of man, braver and more enduring.

Pity, then, is the essence of human spiritual love, of the love that is conscious of being love, of the love that is not purely animal, of the love, in a word, of a rational person. Love pities, and pities most when it loves most.

Reversing the terms of the adage *nihil volitum quin præcognitum*, I have told you that *nihil cognitum quin prævolitum*, that we know nothing save what we have first, in one way or another, desired; and it may even be added that we can know nothing well save what we love, save what we pity.

As love grows, this restless yearning to pierce to the uttermost and to the innermost, so it continually embraces all that it sees, and pities all that it embraces. According as you turn inwards and penetrate more deeply into yourself, you will discover more and more your own emptiness, that you are not all that you are not, that you are not what you would wish to be, that you are, in a word, only a nonentity. And in touching your own nothingness, in not feeling your permanent base, in not reaching your own infinity, still less your own eternity, you will have a whole-hearted pity for yourself, and you will burn with a sorrowful love for yourself—a love that will consume your so-called self-

love, which is merely a species of sensual self-delecta-
tion, the self-enjoyment, as it were, of the flesh of your
soul.

Spiritual self-love, the pity that one feels for oneself,
may perhaps be called egotism; but nothing could be
more opposed to ordinary egoism. For this love or pity
for yourself, this intense despair, bred of the consciousness that just as before you were born you were not, so
after your death you will cease to be, will lead you to pity
—that is, to love—all your fellows and brothers in this
world of appearance, these unhappy shadows who pass
from nothingness to nothingness, these sparks of consciousness which shine for a moment in the infinite and
eternal darkness. And this compassionate feeling for
other men, for your fellows, beginning with those most
akin to you, those with whom you live, will expand into
a universal pity for all living things, and perhaps even
for things that have not life but merely existence. That
distant star which shines up there in the night will some
day be quenched and will turn to dust and will cease to
shine and cease to exist. And so, too, it will be with the
whole of the star-strewn heavens. Unhappy heavens!

And if it is grievous to be doomed one day to cease to
be, perhaps it would be more grievous still to go on
being always oneself, and no more than oneself, without
being able to be at the same time other, without being
able to be at the same time everything else, without
being able to be all.

If you look at the universe as closely and as inwardly
as you are able to look—that is to say, if you look within
yourself; if you not only contemplate but feel all things
in your own consciousness, upon which all things have
traced their painful impression—you will arrive at the
abyss of the tedium, not merely of life, but of something
more: at the tedium of existence, at the bottomless pit
of the vanity of vanities. And thus you will come to
pity all things; you will arrive at universal love.

In order to love everything, in order to pity everything, human and extra-human, living and non-living,
you must feel everything within yourself, you must personalize everything.  For everything that it loves, everything that it pities, love personalizes.  We only pity—
that is to say, we only love—that which is like ourselves
and in so far as it is like ourselves, and the more like it
is the more we love; and thus our pity for things, and
with it our love, grows in proportion as we discover in
them the likenesses which they have with ourselves.  Or,
rather, it is love itself, which of itself tends to grow, that
reveals these resemblances to us.  If I am moved to pity
and love the luckless star that one day will vanish from
the face of heaven, it is because love, pity, makes me feel
that it has a consciousness, more or less dim, which
makes it suffer because it is no more than a star, and a
star that is doomed one day to cease to be.  For all consciousness is consciousness of death and of suffering.

Consciousness (*conscientia*) is participated knowledge,
is co-feeling, and co-feeling is com-passion.  Love personalizes all that it loves.  Only by personalizing it can
we fall in love with an idea.  And when love is so great
and so vital, so strong and so overflowing, that it loves
everything, then it personalizes everything and discovers
that the total All, that the Universe, is also a Person
possessing a Consciousness, a Consciousness which in its
turn suffers, pities, and loves, and therefore is consciousness.  And this Consciousness of the Universe, which
love, personalizing all that it loves, discovers, is what we
call God.  And thus the soul pities God and feels itself
pitied by Him; loves Him and feels itself loved by Him,
sheltering its misery in the bosom of the eternal and
infinite misery, which, in eternalizing itself and infinitiz-
ing itself, is the supreme happiness itself.

God is, then, the personalization of the All; He is the
eternal and infinite Consciousness of the Universe—
Consciousness taken captive by matter and struggling to

free himself from it. We personalize the All in order to save ourselves from Nothingness; and the only mystery really mysterious is the mystery of suffering.

Suffering is the path of consciousness, and by it living beings arrive at the possession of self-consciousness. For to possess consciousness of oneself, to possess personality, is to know oneself and to feel oneself distinct from other beings, and this feeling of distinction is only reached through an act of collision, through suffering more or less severe, through the sense of one's own limits. Consciousness of oneself is simply consciousness of one's own limitation. I feel myself when I feel that I am not others; to know and to feel the extent of my being is to know at what point I cease to be, the point beyond which I no longer am.

And how do we know that we exist if we do not suffer, little or much? How can we turn upon ourselves, acquire reflective consciousness, save by suffering? When we enjoy ourselves we forget ourselves, forget that we exist; we pass over into another, an alien being, we alienate ourselves. And we become centred in ourselves again, we return to ourselves, only by suffering.

> *Nessun maggior dolore*
> *che ricordarsi del tempo felice*
> *nella miseria*

are the words that Dante puts into the mouth of Francesca da Rimini (*Inferno*, v., 121-123); but if there is no greater sorrow than the recollection in adversity of happy bygone days, there is, on the other hand, no pleasure in remembering adversity in days of prosperity.

" The bitterest sorrow that man can know is to aspire to do much and to achieve nothing " (πολλὰ φρονέοιτα μηδενὸς χρατέειν)—so Herodotus relates that a Persian said to a Theban at a banquet (book ix., chap. xvi.). And it is true. With knowledge and desire we can embrace everything, or almost everything; with the will nothing,

or almost nothing.   And contemplation is not happiness
—no ! not if this contemplation implies impotence.   And
out of this collision between our knowledge and our
power pity arises.

We pity what is like ourselves, and the greater and
clearer our sense of its likeness with ourselves, the greater
our pity.   And if we may say that this likeness provokes
our pity, it may also be maintained that it is our reservoir
of pity, eager to diffuse itself over everything, that makes
us discover the likeness of things with ourselves, the
common bond that unites us with them in suffering.

Our own struggle to acquire, preserve, and increase
our own consciousness makes us discover in the endeavours and movements and revolutions of all things a
struggle to acquire, preserve, and increase consciousness,
to which everything tends.   Beneath the actions of those
most akin to myself, of my fellow-men, I feel—or, rather,
I co-feel—a state of consciousness similar to that which
lies beneath my own actions.   On hearing my brother
give a cry of pain, my own pain awakes and cries in the
depth of my consciousness.   And in the same way I feel
the pain of animals, and the pain of a tree when one of its
branches is being cut off, and I feel it most when my
imagination is alive, for the imagination is the faculty of
intuition, of inward vision.

Proceeding from ourselves, from our own human consciousness, the only consciousness which we feel from
within and in which feeling is identical with being, we
attribute some sort of consciousness, more or less dim,
to all living things, and even to the stones themselves, for
they also live.   And the evolution of organic beings is
simply a struggle to realize fullness of consciousness
through suffering, a continual aspiration to be others
without ceasing to be themselves, to break and yet to
preserve their proper limits.

And this process of personalization or subjectivization
of everything external, phenomenal, or objective, is none

other than the vital process of philosophy in the contest
of life against reason and of reason against life. We
have already indicated it in the preceding chapter, and
we must now confirm it by developing it further.

Giovanni Baptista Vico, with his profound esthetic
penetration into the soul of antiquity, saw that the spontaneous philosophy of man was to make of himself the
norm of the universe, guided by the *instinto d'animazione*.
Language, necessarily anthropomorphic, mythopeic,
engenders thought. "Poetic wisdom, which was the
primitive wisdom of paganism," says Vico in his *Scienza
Nuova*, "must have begun with a metaphysic, not
reasoned and abstract, like that of modern educated men,
but felt and imagined, such as must have been that of
primitive men. This was their own poetry, which with
them was inborn, an innate faculty, for nature had
furnished them with such feelings and such imaginations,
a faculty born of the ignorance of causes, and therefore
begetting a universal sense of wonder, for knowing
nothing they marvelled greatly at everything. This
poetry had a divine origin, for, while they invented the
causes of things out of their own imagination, at the same
time they regarded these causes with feelings of wonder
as gods. In this way the first men of the pagan peoples,
as children of the growing human race, fashioned things
out of their ideas. . . . This nature of human things
has bequeathed that eternal property which Tacitus
elucidated with a fine phrase when he said, not without
reason, that men in their terror *fingunt simul creduntque*.

And then, passing from the age of imagination, Vico
proceeds to show us the age of reason, this age of ours
in which the mind, even the popular mind, is too remote
from the senses, "with so many abstractions of which all
languages are full," an age in which "the ability to conceive an immense image of such a personage as we call
sympathetic Nature is denied to us, for though the phrase
'Dame Nature' may be on our lips, there is nothing in our

minds that corresponds with it, our minds being occupied
with the false, the non-existent." "To-day," Vico continues, "it is naturally impossible for us to enter into the
vast imagination of these primitive men." But is this
certain ? Do not we continue to live by the creations of
their imagination, embodied for ever in the language
with which we think, or, rather, the language which
thinks in us ?

It was in vain that Kant declared that human thought
had already emerged from the age of theology and was
now emerging from the age of metaphysics into the age
of positivism; the three ages coexist, and although
antagonistic they lend one another mutual support.
High-sounding positivism, whenever it ceases to deny
and begins to affirm something, whenever it becomes
really positive, is nothing but metaphysics; and metaphysics, in its essence, is always theology, and theology
is born of imagination yoked to the service of life, of life
with its craving for immortality.

Our feeling of the world, upon which is based our
understanding of it, is necessarily anthropomorphic and
mythopeic. When rationalism dawned with Thales of
Miletus, this philosopher abandoned Oceanus and Thetis,
gods and the progenitors of gods, and attributed the
origin of things to water; but this water was a god
in disguise. Beneath nature ($\phi\acute{v}\sigma\iota\varsigma$) and the world
($\kappa\acute{o}\sigma\mu o\varsigma$), mythical and anthropomorphic creations
throbbed with life. They were implicated in the structure
of language itself. Xenophon tells us (Memorabilia,
i , i., 6-9) that among phenomena Socrates distinguished
between those which were within the scope of human
study and those which the gods had reserved for themselves, and that he execrated the attempt of Anaxagoras
to explain everything rationally. His contemporary,
Hippocrates, regarded diseases as of divine origin, and
Plato believed that the sun and stars were animated gods
with their souls (Philebus, cap. xvi., Laws, x.), and

only permitted astronomical investigation so long as it abstained from blasphemy against these gods. And Aristotle in his *Physics* tells us that Zeus rains not in order that the corn may grow, but by necessity (ἐξ ἀνάρχης). They tried to mechanize and rationalize God, but God rebelled against them.

And what is the concept of God, a concept continually renewed because springing out of the eternal feeling of God in man, but the eternal protest of life against reason, the unconquerable instinct of personalization? And what is the notion of substance itself but the objectivization of that which is most subjective—that is, of the will or consciousness? For consciousness, even before it knows itself as reason, feels itself, is palpable to itself, is most in harmony with itself, as will, and as will not to die. Hence that rhythm, of which we spoke, in the history of thought. Positivism inducted us into an age of rationalism—that is to say, of materialism, mechanism, or mortalism; and behold now the return of vitalism, of spiritualism. What was the effort of pragmatism but an effort to restore faith in the human finality of the universe? What is the effort of a Bergson, for example, especially in his work on creative evolution, but an attempt to redintegrate the personal God and eternal consciousness? Life never surrenders.

And it avails us nothing to seek to repress this mythopeic or anthropomorphic process and to rationalize our thought, as if we thought only for the sake of thinking and knowing, and not for the sake of living. The very language with which we think prevents us from so doing. Language, the substance of thought, is a system of metaphors with a mythic and anthropomorphic base. And to construct a purely rational philosophy it would be necessary to construct it by means of algebraic formulas or to create a new language for it, an inhuman language—that is to say, one inapt for the needs of life—as indeed Dr. Richard Avenarius, professor of philosophy at

Zürich, attempted to do in his *Critique of Pure Experience (Kritik der reinen Erfahrung)*, in order to avoid preconceptions. And this rigorous attempt of Avenarius, the chief of the critics of experience, ends strictly in pure scepticism. He himself says at the end of the Prologue to the work above mentioned : " The childish confidence that it is granted to us to discover truth has long since disappeared; as we progress we become aware of the difficulties that lie in the way of its discovery and of the limitation of our powers. And what is the end? . . . If we could only succeed in seeing clearly into ourselves !"

Seeing clearly ! seeing clearly ! Clear vision would be only attainable by a pure thinker who used algebra instead of language and was able to divest himself of his own humanity—that is to say, by an unsubstantial, merely objective being : a no-being, in short. In spite of reason we are compelled to think with life, and in spite of life we are compelled to rationalize thought.

This animation, this personification, interpenetrates our very knowledge. "Who is it that sends the rain ? Who is it that thunders?" old Strepsiades asks of Socrates in *The Clouds* of Aristophanes, and the philosopher replies : " Not Zeus, but the clouds." " But," questions Strepsiades, "who but Zeus makes the clouds sweep along ?" to which Socrates answers : "Not a bit of it; it is atmospheric whirligig." " Whirligig ?" muses Strepsiades ; " I never thought of that—that Zeus is gone and that Son Whirligig rules now in his stead." And so the old man goes on personifying and animating the whirlwind, as if the whirlwind were now a king, not without consciousness of his kingship. And in exchanging a Zeus for a whirlwind—God for matter, for example —we all do the same thing. And the reason is because philosophy does not work upon the objective reality which we perceive with the senses, but upon the complex of ideas, images, notions, perceptions, etc., embodied in language and transmitted to us with our language by our

ancestors. That which we call the world, the objective
world, is a social tradition. It is given to us ready made.

Man does not submit to being, as consciousness, alone
in the Universe, nor to being merely one objective
phenomenon the more. He wishes to save his vital or
passional subjectivity by attributing life, personality,
spirit, to the whole Universe. In order to realize his
wish he has discovered God and substance; God and
substance continually reappear in his thought cloaked in
different disguises. Because we are conscious, we feel
that we exist, which is quite another thing from knowing
that we exist, and we wish to feel the existence of everything else; we wish that of all the other individual things
each one should also be an " I."

The most consistent, although the most incongruous
and vacillating, idealism, that of Berkeley, who denied
the existence of matter, of something inert and extended
and passive, as the cause of our sensations and the substratum of external phenomena, is in its essence nothing
but an absolute spiritualism or dynamism, the supposition that every sensation comes to us, causatively, from
another spirit—that is, from another consciousness. And
his doctrine has a certain affinity with those of Schopenhauer and Hartmann. The former's doctrine of the Will
and the latter's doctrine of the Unconscious are already
implied in the Berkeleyan theory that to be is to be perceived. To which must be added : and to cause others
to perceive what is. Thus the old adage *operari sequitur
esse* (action follows being) must be modified by saying
that to be is to act, and only that which acts—the active—
exists, and in so far as it acts.

As regards Schopenhauer, there is no need to endeavour
to show that the will, which he posits as the essence of
things, proceeds from consciousness. And it is only
necessary to read his book on the Will in Nature to see
how he attributed a certain spirit and even a certain personality to the plants themselves. And this doctrine of

his carried him logically to pessimism, for the true
property and most inward function of the will is to suffer.
The will is a force which feels itself—that is, which
suffers. And, someone will add, which enjoys. But
the capacity to enjoy is impossible without the capacity
to suffer; and the faculty of enjoyment is one with that
of pain. Whosoever does not suffer does not enjoy, just
as whosoever is insensible to cold is insensible to heat.

And it is also quite logical that Schopenhauer, who
deduced pessimism from the voluntarist doctrine or
doctrine of universal personalization, should have
deduced from both of these that the foundation of morals
is compassion. Only his lack of the social and historical
sense, his inability to feel that humanity also is a person,
although a collective one, his egoism, in short, prevented
him from feeling God, prevented him from individualizing and personalizing the total and collective Will—the
Will of the Universe.

On the other hand, it is easy to understand his aver-
sion from purely empirical, evolutionist, or transformist
doctrines, such as those set forth in the works of Lamarck
and Darwin which came to his notice. Judging Darwin's
theory solely by an extensive extract in *The Times*, he
described it, in a letter to Adam Louis von Doss (March 1,
1860), as " downright empiricism " (*platter Empirismus*).
In fact, for a voluntarist like Schopenhauer, a theory so
sanely and cautiously empirical and rational as that of
Darwin left out of account the inward force, the essential
motive, of evolution. For what is, in effect, the hidden
force, the ultimate agent, which impels organisms to
perpetuate themselves and to fight for their persistence
and propagation? Selection, adaptation, heredity, these
are only external conditions. This inner, essential force
has been called will on the supposition that there exists
also in other beings that which we feel in ourselves as a
feeling of will, the impulse to be everything, to be others
as well as ourselves yet without ceasing to be what we are.

And it may be said that this force is the divine in us, that it is God Himself who works in us because He suffers in us.

And sympathy teaches us to discover this force, this aspiration towards consciousness, in all things. It moves and activates the most minute living creatures; it moves and activates, perhaps, the very cells of our own bodily organism, which is a confederation, more or less solidary, of living beings; it moves the very globules of our blood. Our life is composed of lives, our vital aspiration of aspirations existing perhaps in the limbo of subconsciousness. Not more absurd than so many other dreams which pass as valid theories is the belief that our cells, our globules, may possess something akin to a rudimentary cellular, globular consciousness or basis of consciousness. Or that they may arrive at possessing such consciousness. And since we have given a loose rein to the fancy, we may fancy that these cells may communicate with one another, and that some of them may express their belief that they form part of a superior organism endowed with a collective personal consciousness. And more than once in the history of human feeling this fancy has been expressed in the surmisal of some philosopher or poet that we men are a kind of globules in the blood of a Supreme Being, who possesses his own personal collective consciousness, the consciousness of the Universe.

Perhaps the immense Milky Way which on clear nights we behold stretching across the heavens, this vast encircling ring in which our planetary system is itself but a molecule, is in its turn but a cell in the Universe, in the Body of God. All the cells of our body combine and co-operate in maintaining and kindling by their activity our consciousness, our soul; and if the consciousness or the souls of all these cells entered completely into our consciousness, into the composite whole, if I possessed consciousness of all that happens in my bodily organism, I should feel the universe happening within myself, and perhaps the painful sense of my limitedness would disappear. And if all the consciousness of all beings unite in their entirety in the universal consciousness, this consciousness—that is to say, God—is all.

In every instant obscure consciousnesses, elementary souls, are born and die within us, and their birth and death constitute our life. And their sudden and violent death constitutes our pain. And in like manner, in the heart of God consciousnesses are born and die—but do they die?—and their births and deaths constitute His life.

If there is a Universal and Supreme Consciousness, I am an idea in it; and is it possible for any idea in this Supreme Consciousness to be completely blotted out? After I have died, God will go on remembering me, and to be remembered by God, to have my consciousness sustained by the Supreme Consciousness, is not that, perhaps, to be?

And if anyone should say that God has made the universe, it may be rejoined that so also our soul has made our body as much as, if not more than, it has been made by it—if, indeed, there be a soul.

When pity, love, reveals to us the whole universe striving to gain, to preserve, and to enlarge its consciousness, striving more and more to saturate itself with consciousness, feeling the pain of the discords which are produced within it, pity reveals to us the likeness of the whole universe with ourselves; it reveals to us that it is human, and it leads us to discover our Father in it, of whose flesh we are flesh; love leads us to personalize the whole of which we form a part.

To say that God is eternally producing things is fundamentally the same as saying that things are eternally producing God. And the belief in a personal and spiritual God is based on the belief in our own personality and spirituality. Because we feel ourselves to be consciousness, we feel God to be consciousness—that is to say, a person; and because we desire ardently that our consciousness shall live and be independently of the body, we believe that the divine person lives and exists independently of the universe, that his state of consciousness is *ad extra*.

No doubt logicians will come forward and confront us with the evident rational difficulties which this involves; but we have already stated that, although presented under logical forms, the content of all this is not strictly rational. Every rational conception of God is in itself contradictory. Faith in God is born of love for God— we believe that God exists by force of wishing that He may exist, and it is born also, perhaps, of God's love for us. Reason does not prove to us that God exists, but neither does it prove that He cannot exist.

But of this conception of faith in God as the personalization of the universe we shall have more to say presently.

And recalling what has been said in another part of this work, we may say that material things, in so far as they are known to us, issue into knowledge through the agency of hunger, and out of hunger issues the sensible or material universe in which we conglomerate these things; and that ideal things issue out of love, and out of love issues God, in whom we conglomerate these ideal things as in the Consciousness of the Universe. It is social consciousness, the child of love, of the instinct of perpetuation, that leads us to socialize everything, to see society in everything, and that shows us at last that all Nature is really an infinite Society. For my part, the feeling that Nature is a society has taken hold of me hundreds of times in walking through the woods, possessed with a sense of solidarity with the oaks, a sense of their dim awareness of my presence.

Imagination, which is the social sense, animates the inanimate and anthropomorphizes everything; it humanizes everything and even makes everything identical with man.[1]   And the work of man is to supernaturalize Nature—that is to say, to make it divine by making it human, to help it to become conscious of itself, in short.   The action of reason, on the other hand, is to mechanize or materialize.

And just as a fruitful union is consummated between the individual—who is, in a certain sense, a society—and society, which is also an individual—the two being so inseparable from one another that it is impossible to say where the one begins and the other ends, for they are rather two aspects of a single essence—so also the spirit, the social element, which by relating us to others makes us conscious, unites with matter, the individual and individualizing element; similarly, reason or intelligence and imagination embrace in a mutually fruitful union, and the Universe merges into one with God.

Is all this true?   And what is truth?  I in my turn will ask, as Pilate asked—not, however, only to turn away and wash my hands, without waiting for an answer.

Is truth in reason, or above reason, or beneath reason, or outside of reason, in some way or another?   Is only the rational true?   May there not be a reality, by its very nature, unattainable by reason, and perhaps, by its very nature, opposed to reason?   And how can we know this reality if reason alone holds the key to knowledge?

Our desire of living, our need of life, asks that that may be true which urges us to self-preservation and self-perpetuation, which sustains man and society; it asks that the true water may be that which assuages our thirst, and because it assuages it, that the true bread may be that which satisfies our hunger, because it satisfies it.

The senses are devoted to the service of the instinct of preservation, and everything that satisfies this need of preserving ourselves, even though it does not pass

---

[1] *Todo lo humaniza, y aun lo humana*

through the senses, is nevertheless a kind of intimate penetration of reality in us. Is the process of assimilating nutriment perhaps less real than the process of knowing the nutritive substance? It may be said that to eat a loaf of bread is not the same thing as seeing, touching, or tasting it; that in the one case it enters into our body, but not therefore into our consciousness. Is this true? Does not the loaf of bread that I have converted into my flesh and blood enter more into my consciousness than the other loaf which I see and touch, and of which I say : "This is mine"? And must I refuse objective reality to the bread that I have thus converted into my flesh and blood and made mine when I only touch it?

There are some who live by air without knowing it. In the same way, it may be, we live by God and in God —in God the spirit and consciousness of society and of the whole Universe, in so far as the Universe is also a society.

God is felt only in so far as He is lived; and man does not live by bread alone, but by every word that proceedeth out of the mouth of God (Matt. iv. 4; Deut. viii. 3).

And this personalization of the all, of the Universe, to which we are led by love, by pity, is the personalization of a person who embraces and comprehends within himself the other persons of which he is composed.

The only way to give finality to the world is to give it consciousness. For where there is no consciousness there is no finality, finality presupposing a purpose. And, as we shall see, faith in God is based simply upon the vital need of giving finality to existence, of making it answer to a purpose. We need God, not in order to understand the *why*, but in order to feel and sustain the ultimate *wherefore*, to give a meaning to the Universe.

And neither ought we to be surprised by the affirmation that this consciousness of the Universe is composed and integrated by the consciousnesses of the beings which form the Universe, by the consciousnesses of all the beings that exist, and that nevertheless it remains a personal consciousness distinct from those which compose it.   Only thus is it possible to understand how in God we live, move, and have our being.   That great visionary, Emanuel Swedenborg, saw or caught a glimpse of this in his book on Heaven and Hell (*De Cœlo et Inferno*, lii.), when he tells us: "An entire angelic society appears sometimes in the form of a single angel, which also it hath been granted me by the Lord to see.   When the Lord Himself appears in the midst of the angels, He doth not appear as encompassed by a multitude, but as a single being in angelic form.   Hence it is that the Lord in the Word is called an angel, and likewise that an entire society is so called.   Michael, Gabriel, and Raphael are nothing but angelical societies, which are so named from their functions."

May we not perhaps live and love—that is, suffer and pity—in this all-enveloping Supreme Person—we, all the persons who suffer and pity and all the beings that strive to achieve personality, to acquire consciousness of their suffering and their limitation ?   And are we not, perhaps, ideas of this total Grand Consciousness, which by thinking of us as existing confers existence upon us ?   Does not our existence consist in being perceived and felt by God ?   And, further on, this same visionary tells us, under the form of images, that each angel, each society of angels, and the whole of heaven comprehensively surveyed, appear in human form, and in virtue of this human form the Lord rules them as one man.

" God does not think, He creates ; He does not exist, He is eternal," wrote Kierkegaard (*Afslutende uvidenskabelige Efterskrift*) ; but perhaps it is more exact to say with Mazzini, the mystic of the Italian city, that "God is great because His thought is action " (*Ai giovani d'Italia*), because with Him to think is to create, and He gives existence to that which exists in His thought by the mere fact of thinking it, and the impossible is the unthinkable by God. Is it not written in the Scriptures that God creates with His word—that is to say, with His thought—and that by this, by His Word, He made every-thing that exists? And what God has once made does He ever forget? May it not be that all the thoughts that have ever passed through the Supreme Consciousness still subsist therein? In Him, who is eternal, is not all existence eternalized?

Our longing to save consciousness, to give personal and human finality to the Universe and to existence, is such that even in the midst of a supreme, an agonizing and lacerating sacrifice, we should still hear the voice that assured us that if our consciousness disappears, it is that the infinite and eternal Consciousness may be en-riched thereby, that our souls may serve as nutriment to the Universal Soul. Yes, I enrich God, because before I existed He did not think of me as existing, because I am one more—one more even though among an infinity of others—who, having really lived, really suffered, and really loved, abide in His bosom. It is the furious long-ing to give finality to the Universe, to make it conscious and personal, that has brought us to believe in God, to wish that God may exist, to create God, in a word. To create Him, yes! This saying ought not to scandalize even the most devout theist. For to believe in God is, in a certain sense, to create Him, although He first creates us.[1] It is He who in us is continually creating Himself.

We have created God in order to save the Universe from nothingness, for all that is not consciousness and eternal consciousness, conscious of its eternity and eternally conscious, is nothing more than appearance. There is nothing truly real save that which feels, suffers, pities, loves, and desires, save consciousness; there is nothing substantial but consciousness. And we need

---

[1] In the translation it is impossible to retain the play upon the verbs *crear*, to create, and *creer*, to believe : " *Porque creer en Dios es en cierto modo crearle, aunque El nos cree antes.*"—J E. C. F.

God in order to save consciousness; not in order to think existence, but in order to live it; not in order to know the why and how of it, but in order to feel the wherefore of it. Love is a contradiction if there is no God.

Let us now consider this idea of God, of the logical God or the Supreme Reason, and of the vital God or the God of the heart—that is, Supreme Love.

# VIII

## FROM GOD TO GOD

To affirm that the religious sense is a sense of divinity and that it is impossible without some abuse of the ordinary usages of human language to speak of an atheistic religion, is not, I think, to do violence to the truth; although it is clear that everything will depend upon the concept that we form of God, a concept which in its turn depends upon the concept of divinity.

Our proper procedure, in effect, will be to begin with this sense of divinity, before prefixing to the concept of this quality the definite article and the capital letter and so converting it into "the Divinity"—that is, into God. For man has not deduced the divine from God, but rather he has reached God through the divine.

In the course of these somewhat wandering but at the same time urgent reflections upon the tragic sense of life, I have already alluded to the *timor fecit deos* of Statius with the object of limiting and correcting it. It is not my intention to trace yet once again the historical processes by which peoples have arrived at the consciousness and concept of a personal God like the God of Christianity. And I say peoples and not isolated individuals, for if there is any feeling or concept that is truly collective and social it is the feeling and concept of God, although the individual subsequently individualizes it. Philosophy may, and in fact does, possess an individual origin; theology is necessarily collective.

Schleiermacher's theory, which attributes the origin, or rather the essence, of the religious sense to the

immediate and simple feeling of dependency, appears to
be the most profound and exact explanation. Primitive
man, living in society, feels himself to be dependent
upon the mysterious forces invisibly environing him; he
feels himself to be in social communion, not only with
beings like himself, his fellow-men, but with the whole
of Nature, animate and inanimate, which simply means,
in other words, that he personalizes everything. Not
only does he possess a consciousness of the world, but
he imagines that the world, like himself, possesses consciousness also. Just as a child talks to his doll or his
dog as if it understood what he was saying, so the
savage believes that his fetich hears him when he speaks
to it, and that the angry storm-cloud is aware of him and
deliberately pursues him. For the newly born mind of
the primitive natural man has not yet wholly severed
itself from the cords which still bind it to the womb of
Nature, neither has it clearly marked out the boundary
that separates dreaming from waking, imagination from
reality.

The divine, therefore, was not originally something
objective, but was rather the subjectivity of consciousness projected exteriorly, the personalization of the
world. The concept of divinity arose out of the feeling
of divinity, and the feeling of divinity is simply the dim
and nascent feeling of personality vented upon the outside world. And strictly speaking it is not possible to
speak of outside and inside, objective and subjective,
when no such distinction was actually felt; indeed it is
precisely from this lack of distinction that the feeling and
concept of divinity proceed. The clearer our consciousness of the distinction between the objective and the subjective, the more obscure is the feeling of divinity in us.

It has been said, and very justly so it would appear,
that Hellenic paganism was not so much polytheistic as
pantheistic. I do not know that the belief in a multitude
of gods, taking the concept of God in the sense in which

we understand it to-day, has ever really existed in any human mind. And if by pantheism is understood the doctrine, not that everything and each individual thing is God—a proposition which I find unthinkable—but that everything is divine, then it may be said without any great abuse of language that paganism was pantheistic. Its gods not only mixed among men but intermixed with them; they begat gods upon mortal women and upon goddesses mortal men begat demi-gods. And if demi-gods, that is, demi-men, were believed to exist, it was because the divine and the human were viewed as different aspects of the same reality. The divinization of everything was simply its humanization. To say that the sun was a god was equivalent to saying that it was a man, a human consciousness, more or less, aggrandized and sublimated. And this is true of all beliefs from fetichism to Hellenic paganism.

The real distinction between gods and men consisted in the fact that the former were immortal. A god came to be identical with an immortal man and a man was deified, reputed as a god, when it was deemed that at his death he had not really died. Of certain heroes it was believed that they were alive in the kingdom of the dead. And this is a point of great importance in estimating the value of the concept of the divine.

In those republics of gods there was always some predominating god, some real monarch. It was through the agency of this divine monarchy that primitive peoples were led from monocultism to monotheism. Hence monarchy and monotheism are twin brethren. Zeus, Jupiter, was in process of being converted into an only god, just as Jahwé, originally one god among many others, came to be converted into an only god, first the god of the people of Israel, then the god of humanity, and finally the god of the whole universe.

Like monarchy, monotheism had a martial origin. "It is only on the march and in time of war," says

Robertson Smith in *The Prophets of Israel*,[1] " that a nomad people feels any urgent need of a central authority, and so it came about that in the first beginnings of national organization, centring in the sanctuary of the ark, Israel was thought of mainly as the host of Jehovah. The very name of Israel is martial, and means ' God (*El*) fighteth,' and Jehovah in the Old Testament is Iahwè Çebâôth—the Jehovah of the armies of Israel. It was on the battlefield that Jehovah's presence was most clearly realized; but in primitive nations the leader in time of war is also the natural judge in time of peace."

God, the only God, issued, therefore, from man's sense of divinity as a warlike, monarchical and social God. He revealed himself to the people as a whole, not to the individual. He was the God of a people and he jealously exacted that worship should be rendered to him alone. The transition from this monocultism to monotheism was effected largely by the individual action, more philosophical perhaps than theological, of the prophets. It was, in fact, the individual activity of the prophets that individualized the divinity. And above all by making the divinity ethical.

Subsequently reason—that is, philosophy—took possession of this God who had arisen in the human consciousness as a consequence of the sense of divinity in man, and tended to define him and convert him into an idea. For to define a thing is to idealize it, a process which necessitates the abstraction from it of its incommensurable or irrational element, its vital essence. Thus the God of feeling, the divinity felt as a unique person and consciousness external to us, although at the same time enveloping and sustaining us, was converted into the idea of God.

The logical, rational God, the *ens summum,* the *primum movens,* the Supreme Being of theological philosophy, the God who is reached by the three famous

---

[1] Lecture I., p. 36. London, 1895, Black.

ways of negation, eminence and causality, *viæ negationis, eminentiæ, causalitatis*, is nothing but an idea of
God, a dead thing. The traditional and much debated
proofs of his existence are, at bottom, merely a vain
attempt to determine his essence; for as Vinet has very
well observed, existence is deduced from essence; and to
say that God exists, without saying what God is and how
he is, is equivalent to saying nothing at all.

And this God, arrived at by the methods of eminence
and negation or abstraction of finite qualities, ends by becoming an unthinkable God, a pure idea, a God of whom,
by the very fact of his ideal excellence, we can say that
he is nothing, as indeed he has been defined by Scotus
Erigena : *Deus propter excellentiam non inmerito nihil
vocatur.* Or in the words of the pseudo-Dionysius the
Areopagite, in his fifth Epistle, " The divine darkness is
the inaccessible light in which God is said to dwell."
The anthropomorphic God, the God who is felt, in being
purified of human, and as such finite, relative and temporal, attributes, evaporates into the God of deism or of
pantheism.

The traditional so-called proofs of the existence of God
all refer to this God-Idea, to this logical God, the God
by abstraction, and hence they really prove nothing, or
rather, they prove nothing more than the existence of this
idea of God.

In my early youth, when first I began to be puzzled
by these eternal problems, I read in a book, the author of
which I have no wish to recall,[1] this sentence : " God is
the great X placed over the ultimate barrier of human
knowledge; in the measure in which science advances,
the barrier recedes." And I wrote in the margin, " On
this side of the barrier, everything is explained without
Him; on the further side, nothing is explained, either

[1] *No quiero acordarme,* a phrase that is always associated in Spanish
literature with the opening sentence of *Don Quijote  En un lugar de la
Mancha de cuyo nombre no quiero acordarme.*—J  E. C. F.

with Him or without Him ; God therefore is superfluous."
And so far as concerns the God-Idea, the God of the
proofs, I continue to be of the same opinion.  Laplace
is said to have stated that he had not found the hypothesis
of God necessary in order to construct his scheme of the
origin of the Universe, and it is very true.  In no way
whatever does the idea of God help us to understand
better the existence, the essence and the finality of the
Universe.

That there is a Supreme Being, infinite, absolute and
eternal, whose existence is unknown to us, and who has
created the Universe, is not more conceivable than that
the material basis of the Universe itself, its matter, is
eternal and infinite and absolute.  We do not understand
the existence of the world one whit the better by telling
ourselves that God created it.  It is a begging of the
question, or a merely verbal solution, intended to cover
up our ignorance.  In strict truth, we deduce the existence of the Creator from the fact that the thing created
exists, a process which does not justify rationally His
existence.  You cannot deduce a necessity from a fact,
or else everything were necessary.

And if from the nature of the Universe we pass to
what is called its order, which is supposed to necessitate
an Ordainer, we may say that order is what there is, and
we do not conceive of any other.  This deduction of
God's existence from the order of the Universe implies a
transition from the ideal to the real order, an outward
projection of our mind, a supposition that the rational
explanation of a thing produces the thing itself.  Human
art, instructed by Nature, possesses a conscious creative
faculty, by means of which it apprehends the process of
creation, and we proceed to transfer this conscious and
artistic creative faculty to the consciousness of an artist-
creator, but from what nature he in his turn learnt his
art we cannot tell.

The traditional analogy of the watch and the watch-

maker is inapplicable to a Being absolute, infinite and
eternal. It is, moreover, only another way of explaining nothing. For to say that the world is as it is and not
otherwise because God made it so, while at the same time
we do not know for what reason He made it so, is to say
nothing. And if we knew for what reason God made it
so, then God is superfluous and the reason itself suffices.
If everything were mathematics, if there were no
irrational element, we should not have had recourse to
this explanatory theory of a Supreme Ordainer, who is
nothing but the reason of the irrational, and so merely
another cloak for our ignorance. And let us not discuss
here that absurd proposition that, if all the type in a
printing-press were printed at random, the result could
not possibly be the composition of *Don Quixote*. Something would be composed which would be as good as
*Don Quixote* for those who would have to be content
with it and would grow in it and would form part of it.

In effect, this traditional supposed proof of God's
existence resolves itself fundamentally into hypostatizing or substantivating the explanation or reason of a
phenomenon; it amounts to saying that Mechanics is the
cause of movement, Biology of life, Philology of language, Chemistry of bodies, by simply adding the capital
letter to the science and converting it into a force distinct from the phenomena from which we derive it and
distinct from our mind which effects the derivation. But
the God who is the result of this process, a God who is
nothing but reason hypostatized and projected towards
the infinite, cannot possibly be felt as something living
and real, nor yet be conceived of save as a mere idea
which will die with us.

The question arises, on the other hand, whether a thing
the idea of which has been conceived but which has no
real existence, does not exist because God wills that it
should not exist, or whether God does not will it to exist
because, in fact, it does not exist; and, with regard to the

impossible, whether a thing is impossible because God wills it so, or whether God wills it so because, in itself and by the very fact of its own inherent absurdity, it is impossible.  God has to submit to the logical law of contradiction, and He cannot, according to the theologians, cause two and two to make either more or less than four. Either the law of necessity is above Him or He Himself is the law of necessity.  And in the moral order the question arises whether falsehood, or homicide, or adultery, are wrong because IIe has so decreed it, or whether He has so decreed it because they are wrong.  If the former, then God is a capricious and unreasonable God, who decrees one law when He might equally well have decreed another, or, if the latter, He obeys an intrinsic nature and essence which exists in things themselves independently of Him—that is to say, independently of His sovereign will; and if this is the case, if He obeys the innate reason of things, this reason, if we could but know it, would suffice us without any further need of God, and since we do not know it, God explains nothing.  This reason would be above God.  Neither is it of any avail to say that this reason is God Himself, the supreme reason of things.  A reason of this kind, a necessary reason, is not a personal something.  It is will that gives personality.  And it is because of this problem of the relations between God's reason, necessarily necessary, and His will, necessarily free, that the logical and Aristotelian God will always be a contradictory God.

The scholastic theologians never succeeded in disentangling themselves from the difficulties in which they found themselves involved when they attempted to reconcile human liberty with divine prescience and with the knowledge that God possesses of the free and contingent future; and that is strictly the reason why the rational God is wholly inapplicable to the contingent, for the notion of contingency is fundamentally the same as the notion of irrationality.  The rational God is necessarily necessary in His being and in His working; in every single case He cannot do other than the best, and a number of different things cannot all equally be the best, for among infinite possibilities there is only one that is best accommodated to its end, just as among the infinite number of lines that can be drawn from one point to another, there is only one straight line. And the rational God, the God of reason, cannot but follow in each case the straight line, the line that leads most directly to the end proposed, a necessary end, just as the only straight line that leads to it is a necessary line. And thus for the divinity of God is substituted His necessity. And in the necessity of God, His free will—that is to say, His conscious personality—perishes. The God of our heart's desire, the God who shall save our soul from nothingness, must needs be an arbitrary God.

Not because He thinks can God be God, but because He works, because He creates; He is not a contemplative but an active God. A God-Reason, a theoretical or contemplative God, such as is this God of theological rationalism, is a God that is diluted in His own contemplation. With this God corresponds, as we shall see, the beatific vision, understood as the supreme expression of human felicity. A quietist God, in short, as reason, by its very essence, is quietist.

There remains the other famous proof of God's existence, that of the supposed unanimous consent in a belief in Him among all peoples. But this proof is not strictly rational, neither is it an argument in favour of the rational God who explains the Universe, but of the God of the heart, who makes us live. We should be justified in calling it a rational proof only on the supposition that we believed that reason was identical with a more or less unanimous agreement among all peoples, that it corresponded with the verdict of a universal suffrage, only on the supposition that we held that *vox populi,* which is said to be *vox Dei,* was actually the voice of reason.

Such was, indeed, the belief of Lamennais, that tragic and ardent spirit, who affirmed that life and truth were essentially one and the same thing—would that they were!—and that reason was one, universal, everlasting and holy (*Essai sur l'indifférence*, partie iv., chap. viii.). He invoked the *aut omnibus credendum est aut nemini* of Lactantius—we must believe all or none—and the saying of Heraclitus that every individual opinion is fallible, and that of Aristotle that the strongest proof consists in the general agreement of mankind, and above all that of Pliny (*Paneg. Trajani*, lxii.), to the effect that one man cannot deceive all men or be deceived by all—*nemo omnes, neminem omnes fefellerunt.* Would that it were so! And so he concludes with the dictum of Cicero (*De natura deorum*, lib. iii., cap. ii., 5 and 6), that we must believe the tradition of our ancestors even though they fail to render us a reason—*maioribus autem nostris, etiam nulla ratione reddita credere.*

Let us suppose that this belief of the ancients in the divine interpenetration of the whole of Nature is universal and constant, and that it is, as Aristotle calls it, an ancestral dogma (πάτριος δόξα) (*Metaphysica*, lib. vii., cap. vii.); this would prove only that there is a motive impelling peoples and individuals—that is to say, all or almost all or a majority of them—to believe in a God. But may it not be that there are illusions and fallacies rooted in human nature itself? Do not all peoples begin by believing that the sun turns round the earth? And do we not all naturally incline to believe that which satisfies our desires? Shall we say with Hermann[1] that, "if there is a God, He has not left us without some indication of Himself, and it is His will that we should find Him."

A pious desire, no doubt, but we cannot strictly call it a reason, unless we apply to it the Augustinian sentence,

---

[1] W. Hermann, *Christlich systematische Dogmatik*, in the volume entitled *Systematische christliche Religion. Die Kultur der Gegenwart* series, published by P. Hinneberg.

but which again is not a reason, "Since thou seekest Me,
it must be that thou hast found Me," believing that God
is the cause of our seeking Him.

This famous argument from the supposed unanimity
of mankind's belief in God, the argument which with a
sure instinct was seized upon by the ancients, is in its
essence identical with the so-called moral proof which
Kant employed in his *Critique of Practical Reason,*
transposing its application from mankind collectively to
the individual, the proof which he derives from our conscience, or rather from our feeling of divinity. It is not
a proof strictly or specifically rational, but vital; it cannot
be applied to the logical God, the *ens summum,* the essentially simple and abstract Being, the immobile and im-
passible prime mover, the God-Reason, in a word, but
to the biotic God, to the Being essentially complex and
concrete, to the suffering God who suffers and desires in
us and with us, to the Father of Christ who is only to be
approached through Man, through His Son (John xiv. 6),
and whose revelation is historical, or if you like,
anecdotical, but not philosophical or categorical.

The unanimous consent of mankind (let us suppose
the unanimity) or, in other words, this universal longing
of all human souls who have arrived at the consciousness
of their humanity, which desires to be the end and meaning of the Universe, this longing, which is nothing but
that very essence of the soul which consists in its effort
to persist eternally and without a break in the continuity
of consciousness, leads us to the human, anthropomorphic
God, the projection of our consciousness to the Consciousness of the Universe; it leads us to the God who confers
human meaning and finality upon the Universe and who
is not the *ens summum,* the *primum movens,* nor the
Creator of the Universe, nor merely the Idea-God. It
leads us to the living, subjective God, for He is simply
subjectivity objectified or personality universalized—He
is more than a mere idea, and He is will rather than

reason. God is Love—that is, Will. Reason, the Word, derives from Him, but He, the Father, is, above all, Will.

"There can be no doubt whatever," Ritschl says (*Rechtfertigung und Versöhnung*, iii., chap. v.), " that a very imperfect view was taken of God's spiritual personality in the older theology, when the functions of knowing and willing alone were employed to illustrate it. Religious thought plainly ascribes to God affections of feeling as well. The older theology, however, laboured under the impression that feeling and emotion were characteristic only of limited and created personality; it transformed, *e.g.*, the religious idea of the Divine blessedness into eternal self-knowledge, and that of the Divine wrath into a fixed purpose to punish sin." Yes, this logical God, arrived at by the *via negationis,* was a God who, strictly speaking, neither loved nor hated, because He neither enjoyed nor suffered, an inhuman God, and His justice was a rational or mathematical justice—that is, an injustice.

The attributes of the living God, of the Father of Christ, must be deduced from His historical revelation in the Gospel and in the conscience of every Christian believer, and not from metaphysical reasonings which lead only to the Nothing-God of Scotus Erigena, to the rational or pantheistic God, to the atheist God—in short, to the de-personalized Divinity.

Not by the way of reason, but only by the way of love and of suffering, do we come to the living God, the human God. Reason rather separates us from Him. We cannot first know Him in order that afterwards we may love Him; we must begin by loving Him, longing for Him, hungering after Him, before knowing Him. The knowledge of God proceeds from the love of God, and this knowledge has little or nothing of the rational in it. For God is indefinable. To seek to define Him is to seek to confine Him within the limits of our mind—that is to say, to kill Him. In so far as we attempt to define Him, there rises up before us—Nothingness.

The idea of God, formulated by a theodicy that claims to be rational, is simply an hypothesis, like the hypothesis of ether, for example.

Ether is, in effect, a merely hypothetical entity, valuable only in so far as it explains that which by means of it we endeavour to explain—light, electricity or universal gravitation—and only in so far as these facts cannot be explained in any other way. In like manner the idea of God is also an hypothesis, valuable only in so far as it enables us to explain that which by means of it we endeavour to explain—the essence and existence of the Universe—and only so long as these cannot be explained in any other way. And since in reality we explain the Universe neither better nor worse with this idea than without it, the idea of God, the supreme *petitio principii*, is valueless.

But if ether is nothing but an hypothesis explanatory of light, air, on the other hand, is a thing that is directly felt; and even though it did not enable us to explain the phenomenon of sound, we should nevertheless always be directly aware of it, and, above all, of the lack of it in moments of suffocation or air-hunger. And in the same way God Himself, not the idea of God, may become a reality that is immediately felt; and even though the idea of Him does not enable us to explain either the existence or the essence of the Universe, we have at times the direct feeling of God, above all in moments of spiritual suffocation. And this feeling—mark it well, for all that is tragic in it and the whole tragic sense of life is founded upon this—this feeling is a feeling of hunger for God, of the lack of God. To believe in God is, in the first instance, as we shall see, to wish that there may be a God, to be unable to live without Him.

So long as I pilgrimaged through the fields of reason in search of God, I could not find Him, for I was not

deluded by the idea of God, neither could I take an idea
for God, and it was then, as I wandered among the
wastes of rationalism, that I told myself that we ought
to seek no other consolation than the truth, meaning
thereby reason, and yet for all that I was not comforted.
But as I sank deeper and deeper into rational scepticism
on the one hand and into heart's despair on the other,
the hunger for God awoke within me, and the suffocation
of spirit made me feel the want of God, and with the want
of Him, His reality.  And I wished that there might be
a God, that God might exist.  And God does not exist,
but rather super-exists, and He is sustaining our existence, existing us (*existiéndonos*).

God, who is Love, the Father of Love, is the son of
love in us.  There are men of a facile and external habit
of mind, slaves of reason, that reason which externalizes
us, who think it a shrewd comment to say that so far
from God having made man in His image and likeness,
it is rather man who has made his gods or his God in his
own image and likeness,[1] and so superficial are they that
they do not pause to consider that if the second of these
propositions be true, as in fact it is, it is owing to the fact
that the first is not less true.  God and man, in effect,
mutually create one another; God creates or reveals Himself in man and man creates himself in God.  God is
His own maker, *Deus ipse se facit*, said Lactantius
(*Divinarum Institutionum*, ii., 8), and we may say that
He is making Himself continually both in man and by
man.  And if each of us, impelled by his love, by his
hunger for divinity, creates for himself an image of God
according to his own desire, and if according to His
desire God creates Himself for each of us, then there is
a collective, social, human God, the resultant of all the
human imaginations that imagine Him.  For God is

---

[1] *Dieu a fait l'homme à son image, mais l'homme le lui a bien rendu,*
Voltaire —J. E. C. F

and reveals Himself in collectivity. And God is the richest and most personal of human conceptions.

The Master of divinity has bidden us be perfect as our Father who is in heaven is perfect (Matt. v. 48), and in the sphere of thought and feeling our perfection consists in the zeal with which we endeavour to equate our imagination with the total imagination of the humanity of which in God we form a part.

The logical theory of the opposition between the extension and the comprehension of a concept, the one increasing in the ratio in which the other diminishes, is well known. The concept that is most extensive and at the same time least comprehensive is that of being or of thing, which embraces everything that exists and possesses no other distinguishing quality than that of being; while the concept that is most comprehensive and least extensive is that of the Universe, which is only applicable to itself and comprehends all existing qualities. And the logical or rational God, the God obtained by way of negation, the absolute entity, merges, like reality itself, into nothingness; for, as Hegel pointed out, pure being and pure nothingness are identical. And the God of the heart, the God who is felt, the God of living men, is the Universe itself conceived as personality, is the consciousness of the Universe. A God universal and personal, altogether different from the individual God of a rigid metaphysical monotheism.

I must advert here once again to my view of the opposition that exists between individuality and personality, notwithstanding the fact that the one demands the other. Individuality is, if I may so express it, the continent or thing which contains, personality the content or thing contained, or I might say that my personality is in a certain sense my comprehension, that which I comprehend or embrace within myself—which is in a certain way the whole Universe—and that my individuality is my extension; the one my infinite, the other

my finite. A hundred jars of hard earthenware are
strongly individualized, but it is possible for them to be
all equally empty or all equally full of the same homogeneous liquid, whereas two bladders of so delicate a
membrane as to admit of the action of osmosis and
exosmosis may be strongly differentiated and contain
liquids of a very mixed composition. And thus a man,
in so far as he is an individual, may be very sharply
detached from others, a sort of spiritual crustacean, and
yet be very poor in differentiating content. And further,
it is true on the other hand that the more personality a
man has and the greater his interior richness and the
more he is a society within himself, the less brusquely
he is divided from his fellows. In the same way the
rigid God of deism, of Aristotelian monotheism, the
*ens summum*, is a being in whom individuality, or rather
simplicity, stifles personality. Definition kills him, for
to define is to impose boundaries, it is to limit, and it is
impossible to define the absolutely indefinable. This
God lacks interior richness; he is not a society in himself. And this the vital revelation obviated by the
belief in the Trinity, which makes God a society and even
a family in himself and no longer a pure individual. The
God of faith is personal; He is a person because He
includes three persons, for personality is not sensible of
itself in isolation. An isolated person ceases to be a
person, for whom should he love? And if he does not
love, he is not a person. Nor can a simple being love
himself without his love expanding him into a compound
being.

It was because God was felt as a Father that the belief
in the Trinity arose. For a God-Father cannot be a
single, that is, a solitary, God. A father is always the
father of a family. And the fact that God was felt as a
father acted as a continual incentive to conceive Him not
merely anthropomorphically—that is to say, as a man,
ἄνθρωπος—but andromorphically, as a male, ἀνήρ. In the

popular Christian imagination, in effect, God the Father
is conceived of as a male.   And the reason is that man,
*homo, ἄνθρωπος*, as we know him, is necessarily either a
male, *vir, ἀνήρ*, or a female, *mulier, γυνή*.   And to these
may be added the child, who is neuter.   And hence in
order to satisfy imaginatively this necessity of feeling
God as a perfect man—that is, as a family—arose the cult
of the God-Mother, the Virgin Mary, and the cult of the
Child Jesus.

The cult of the Virgin, Mariolatry, which, by the
gradual elevation of the divine element in the Virgin has
led almost to her deification, answers merely to the
demand of the feeling that God should be a perfect man,
that God should include in His nature the feminine
element.   The progressive exaltation of the Virgin Mary,
the work of Catholic piety, having its beginning in the
expression Mother of God, *θεοτόκος, deipara,* has cul-
minated in attributing to her the status of co-redeemer
and in the dogmatic declaration of her conception without the stain of original sin.   Hence she now occupies a
position between Humanity and Divinity and nearer
Divinity than Humanity.   And it has been surmised that
in course of time she may perhaps even come to be
regarded as yet another personal manifestation of the
Godhead.

And yet this might not necessarily involve the conversion of the Trinity into a Quaternity.   If *πνεῦμα*, in
Greek, spirit, instead of being neuter had been feminine,
who can say that the Virgin Mary might not already
have become an incarnation or humanization of the Holy
Spirit?   That fervent piety which always knows how to
mould theological speculation in accordance with its own
desires would have found sufficient warranty for such a
doctrine in the text of the Gospel, in Luke's narrative
of the Annunciation where the angel Gabriel hails Mary
with the words, " The Holy Spirit shall come upon thee,"
*πνεῦμα ἅγιον ἐπελεύσεται ἐπί σε* (Luke i. 35).   And thus

a dogmatic evolution would have been effected parallel
to that of the divinization of Jesus, the Son, and his
identification with the Word.

In any case the cult of the Virgin, of the eternal
feminine, or rather of the divine feminine, of the divine
maternity, helps to complete the personalization of God
by constituting Him a family.

In one of my books (*Vida de Don Quijote y Sancho,*
part ii., chap. lxvii.) I have said that " God was and is,
in our mind, masculine. In His mode of judging and
condemning men, He acts as a male, not as a human
person above the limitation of sex; He acts as a father.
And to counterbalance this, the Mother element was
required, the Mother who always forgives, the Mother
whose arms are always open to the child when he flies
from the frowning brow or uplifted hand of the angry
father; the Mother in whose bosom we seek the dim,
comforting memory of that warmth and peace of our pre-
natal unconsciousness, of that milky sweetness that
soothed our dreams of innocence; the Mother who knows
no justice but that of forgiveness, no law but that of love.
Our weak and imperfect conception of God as a God
with a long beard and a voice of thunder, of a God who
promulgates laws and pronounces dooms, of a God who
is the Master of a household, a Roman Paterfamilias,
required counterpoise and complement, and since fundamentally we are unable to conceive of the personal and
living God as exalted above human and even masculine
characteristics, and still less as a neutral or hermaphro-
dite God, we have recourse to providing Him with a
feminine God, and by the side of the God-Father we
have placed the Goddess-Mother, she who always forgives, because, since she sees with love-blind eyes, she
sees always the hidden cause of the fault and in that
hidden cause the only justice of forgiveness. . . ."

And to this I must now add that not only are we unable
to conceive of the full and living God as masculine

simply, but we are unable to conceive of Him as individual simply, as the projection of a solitary I, an unsocial I, an I that is in reality an abstract I. My living I is an I that is really a We; my living personal I lives only in other, of other, and by other I's; I am sprung from a multitude of ancestors, I carry them within me in extract, and at the same time I carry within me, potentially, a multitude of descendants, and God, the projection of my I to the infinite—or rather I, the projection of God to the finite—must also be multitude. Hence, in order to save the personality of God—that is to say, in order to save the living God—faith's need—the need of the feeling and the imagination—of conceiving Him and feeling Him as possessed of a certain internal multiplicity.

This need the pagan feeling of a living divinity obviated by polytheism. It is the agglomeration of its gods, the republic of them, that really constitutes its Divinity. The real God of Hellenic paganism is not so much Father Zeus (*Jupiter*) as the whole society of gods and demi-gods. Hence the solemnity of the invocation of Demosthenes when he invoked all the gods and all the goddesses : τοῖς θεοῖς εὔχομαι πᾶσι καὶ πάσαις. And when the rationalizers converted the term god, θεός, which is properly an adjective, a quality predicated of each one of the gods, into a substantive, and added the definite article to it, they produced *the* god, ὁ θεός, the dead and abstract god of philosophical rationalism, a substantivized quality and therefore void of personality. For the masculine concrete god (*el* dios) is nothing but the neuter abstract divine quality (*lo* divino). Now the transition from feeling the divinity in all things to substantivating it and converting the Divinity into God, cannot be achieved without feeling undergoing a certain risk. And the Aristotelian God, the God of the logical proofs, is nothing more than the Divinity, a concept and not a living person who can be felt and with whom through love man can communicate. This God is merely a substantivized adjective; He is a constitutional God who reigns but does not govern, and Knowledge is His constitutional charter.

And even in Greco-Latin paganism itself the tendency towards a living monotheism is apparent in the fact that Zeus was conceived of and felt a father, Ζεὺς πατήρ, as Homer calls him, the *Ju-piter* or *Ju-pater* of the Latins, and as a father of a whole widely extended family of gods and goddesses who together with him constituted the Divinity.

The conjunction of pagan polytheism with Judaic monotheism, which had endeavoured by other means to save the personality of God, gave birth to the feeling of the Catholic God, a God who is a society, as the pagan God of whom I have spoken was a society, and who at the same time is one, as the God of Israel finally became one. Such is the Christian Trinity, whose deepest sense rationalistic deism has scarcely ever succeeded in understanding, that deism, which though more or less impregnated with Christianity, always remains Unitarian or Socinian.

And the truth is that we feel God less as a superhuman consciousness than as the actual consciousness of the whole human race, past, present, and future, as the collective consciousness of the whole race, and still more, as the total and infinite consciousness which embraces and sustains all consciousnesses, infra-human, human, and perhaps, super-human. The divinity that there is in everything, from the lowest—that is to say, from the least conscious—of living forms, to the highest, including our own human consciousness, this divinity we feel to be personalized, conscious of itself, in God. And this gradation of consciousnesses, this sense of the gulf between the human and the fully divine, the universal, consciousness, finds its counterpart in the belief in angels with their different hierarchies, as intermediaries between our human consciousness and that of God. And these

gradations a faith consistent with itself must believe to be
infinite, for only by an infinite number of degrees is it
possible to pass from the finite to the infinite.

Deistic rationalism conceives God as the Reason of
the Universe, but its logic compels it to conceive Him as
an impersonal reason—that is to say, as an idea—while
deistic vitalism feels and imagines God as Consciousness,
and therefore as a person or rather as a society of persons.
The consciousness of each one of us, in effect, is a society
of persons; in me there are various I's and even the I's
of those among whom I live, live in me.

The God of deistic rationalism, in effect, the God of the
logical proofs of His existence, the *ens realissimum* and
the immobile prime mover, is nothing more than a
Supreme Reason, but in the same sense in which we can
call the law of universal gravitation the reason of the
falling of bodies, this law being merely the explanation
of the phenomenon.   But will anyone say that that which
we call the law of universal gravitation, or any other
law or mathematical principle, is a true and independent
reality, that it is an angel, that it is something which
possesses consciousness of itself and others, that it is a
person?   No, it is nothing but an idea without any reality
outside of the mind of him who conceives it.   And similarly this God-Reason either possesses consciousness of
himself or he possesses no reality outside the mind that
conceives him.   And if he possesses consciousness of
himself, he becomes a personal reason, and then all the
value of the traditional proofs disappears, for these proofs
only proved a reason, but not a supreme consciousness.
Mathematics prove an order, a constancy, a reason in the
series of mechanical phenomena, but they do not prove
that this reason is conscious of itself.   This reason is a
logical necessity, but the logical necessity does not prove
the teleological or finalist necessity.   And where there
is no finality there is no personality, there is no consciousness.

The rational God, therefore—that is to say, the God who is simply the Reason of the Universe and nothing more—consummates his own destruction, is destroyed in our mind in so far as he is such a God, and is only born again in us when we feel him in our heart as a living person, as Consciousness, and no longer merely as the impersonal and objective Reason of the Universe. If we wish for a rational explanation of the construction of a machine, all that we require to know is the mechanical science of its constructor; but if we would have a reason for the existence of such a machine, then, since it is the work not of Nature but of man, we must suppose a conscious, constructive being. But the second part of this reasoning is not applicable to God, even though it be said that in Him the mechanical science and the mechanician, by means of which the machine was constructed, are one and the same thing. From the rational point of view this identification is merely a begging of the question. And thus it is that reason destroys this Supreme Reason, in so far as the latter is a person.

The human reason, in effect, is a reason that is based upon the irrational, upon the total vital consciousness, upon will and feeling; our human reason is not a reason that can prove to us the existence of a Supreme Reason, which in its turn would have to be based upon the Supreme Irrational, upon the Universal Consciousness. And the revelation of this Supreme Consciousness in our feeling and imagination, by love, by faith, by the process of personalization, is that which leads us to believe in the living God.

And this God, the living God, your God, our God, is in me, is in you, lives in us, and we live and move and have our being in Him. And He is in us by virtue of the hunger, the longing, which we have for Him, He is Himself creating the longing for Himself. And He is the God of the humble, for in the words of the Apostle, God chose the foolish things of the world to confound the

12

wise, and the weak things of the world to confound the things which are mighty (1 Cor. i. 27). And God is in each one of us in the measure in which each one feels Him and loves Him. "If of two men," says Kierkegaard, "one prays to the true God without sincerity of heart, and the other prays to an idol with all the passion of an infinite yearning, it is the first who really prays to an idol, while the second really prays to God." It would be better to say that the true God is He to whom man truly prays and whom man truly desires. And there may even be a truer revelation in superstition itself than in theology. The venerable Father of the long beard and white locks who appears among the clouds carrying the globe of the world in his hand is more living and more real than the *ens realissimum* of theodicy.

Reason is an analytical, that is, a dissolving force, whenever it transfers its activity from the form of intuitions, whether those of the individual instinct of preservation or those of the social instinct of perpetuation, and applies it to the essence and matter of them. Reason orders the sensible perceptions which give us the material world; but when its analysis is exercised upon the reality of the perceptions themselves, it dissolves them and plunges us into a world of appearances, a world of shadows without consistency, for outside the domain of the formal, reason is nihilist and annihilating. And it performs the same terrible office when we withdraw it from its proper domain and apply it to the scrutiny of the imaginative intuitions which give us the spiritual world. For reason annihilates and imagination completes, integrates or totalizes; reason by itself alone kills, and it is imagination that gives life. If it is true that imagination by itself alone, in giving us life without limit, leads us to lose our identity in the All and also kills us as individuals, it kills us by excess of life. Reason, the head, speaks to us the word Nothing! imagination, the heart, the word All! and between all and nothing, by

the fusion of the all and the nothing within us, we live
in God, who is All, and God lives in us who, without
Him, are nothing. Reason reiterates, Vanity of vanities!
all is vanity! And imagination answers, Plenitude of
plenitudes! all is plenitude! And thus we live the
vanity of plenitude or the plenitude of vanity.

And so deeply rooted in the depths of man's being is
this vital need of living a world[1] illogical, irrational,
personal or divine, that those who do not believe in
God, or believe that they do not believe in Him, believe nevertheless in some little pocket god or even
devil of their own, or in an omen, or in a horseshoe
picked up by chance on the roadside and carried about
with them to bring them good luck and defend them
from that very reason whose loyal and devoted henchmen
they imagine themselves to be.

The God whom we hunger after is the God to whom
we pray, the God of the *Pater Noster,* of the Lord's
Prayer; the God whom we beseech, before all and above
all, and whether we are aware of it or not, to instil faith
into us, to make us believe in Him, to make Himself in
us, the God to whom we pray that His name may be
hallowed and that His will may be done—His will, not
His reason—on earth as it is in heaven; but feeling that
His will cannot be other than the essence of our will, the
desire to persist eternally.

And such a God is the God of love—*how* He is it profits
us not to ask, but rather let each consult his own heart
and give his imagination leave to picture Him in the
remoteness of the Universe, gazing down upon him with
those myriad eyes of His that shine in the night-darkened
heavens. He in whom you believe, reader, He is your
God, He who has lived with you and within you, who
was born with you, who was a child when you were a
child, who became a man according as you became a
man, who will vanish when you yourself vanish, and who

is your principle of continuity in the spiritual life, for
He is the principle of solidarity among all men and in
each man and between men and the Universe, and He
is, as you are, a person. And if you believe in God,
God believes in you, and believing in you He creates
you continually. For in your essence you are nothing
but the idea that God possesses of you—but a living idea,
because the idea of a God who is living and conscious of
Himself, of a God-Consciousness, and apart from what
you are in the society of God you are nothing.

How to define God? Yes, that is our longing. That
was the longing of the man Jacob, when, after wrestling
all the night until the breaking of the day with that divine
visitant, he cried, " Tell me, I pray thee, thy name!"
(Gen. xxxii. 29). Listen to the words of that great
Christian preacher, Frederick William Robertson, in a
sermon preached in Trinity Chapel, Brighton, on the
10th of June, 1849: "And this is our struggle—*the*
struggle. Let any true man go down into the deeps of
his own being, and answer us—what is the cry that comes
from the most real part of his nature? Is it the cry for
daily bread? Jacob asked for that in his *first* communing
with God—preservation, safety. Is it even this—to be
forgiven our sins? Jacob had a sin to be forgiven, and
in that most solemn moment of his existence he did not
say a syllable about it. Or is it this—'Hallowed be
Thy name'? No, my brethren. Out of our frail and
yet sublime humanity, the demand that rises in the
earthlier hours of our religion may be this—'Save my
soul '; but in the most unearthly moments it is this—' Tell
me thy name.' We move through a world of mystery;
and the deepest question is, What is the being that is
ever near, sometimes felt, never seen; that which has
haunted us from childhood with a dream of something
surpassingly fair, which has never yet been realized;
that which sweeps through the soul at times as a desolation, like the blast from the wings of the Angel of Death,

leaving us stricken and silent in our loneliness; that which has touched us in our tenderest point, and the flesh has quivered with agony, and our mortal affections have shrivelled up with pain; that which comes to us in aspirations of nobleness and conceptions of superhuman excellence? Shall we say It or He? What is It? Who is He? Those anticipations of Immortality and God—what are they? Are they the mere throbbings of my own heart, heard and mistaken for a living something beside me? Are they the sound of my own wishes, echoing through the vast void of Nothingness? or shall I call them God, Father, Spirit, Love? A living Being within me or outside me? Tell me Thy name, thou awful mystery of Loveliness! This is the struggle of all earnest life."[1]

Thus Robertson. To which I must add this comment, that Tell me thy name! is essentially the same as Save my soul! We ask Him His name in order that He may save our soul, that He may save the human soul, that He may save the human finality of the Universe. And if they tell us that He is called He, that He is the *ens realissimum* or the Supreme Being or any other metaphysical name, we are not contented, for we know that every metaphysical name is an X, and we go on asking Him His name. And there is only one name that satisfies our longing, and that is the name Saviour, Jesus. God is the love that saves. As Browning said in his *Christmas Eve and Easter Day,*

> For the loving worm within its clod,
> Were diviner than a loveless God
> Amid his worlds, I will dare to say.

The essence of the divine is Love, Will that personalizes and eternalizes, that feels the hunger for eternity and infinity.

It is ourselves, it is our eternity that we seek in God,

---

[1] *Sermons*, by the Rev. Frederick W Robertson First series, sermon iii., "Jacob's Wrestling." Kegan Paul, Trench, Trübner and Co., London, 1898

it is our divinization.   It was Browning again who said, in *Saul,*

'Tis the weakness in strength that I cry for ! my flesh that I seek
In the Godhead !

But this God who saves us, this personal God, the Consciousness of the Universe who envelops and sustains our consciousnesses, this God who gives human finality to the whole creation—does He exist?   Have we proofs of His existence?

This question leads in the first place to an enquiry into the meaning of this notion of existence.   What is it to exist and in what sense do we speak of things as not existing?

In its etymological signification to exist is to be outside of ourselves, outside of our mind: *ex-sistere.*   But is there anything outside of our mind, outside of our consciousness which embraces the sum of the known? Undoubtedly there is.   The matter of knowledge comes to us from without.   And what is the mode of this matter?   It is impossible for us to know, for to know is to clothe matter with form, and hence we cannot know the formless as formless.   To do so would be tantamount to investing chaos with order.

This problem of the existence of God, a problem that is rationally insoluble, is really identical with the problem of consciousness, of the *ex-sistentia* and not of the *in-sistentia* of consciousness, it is none other than the problem of the substantial existence of the soul, the problem of the perpetuity of the human soul, the problem of the human finality of the Universe itself.   To believe in a living and personal God, in an eternal and universal consciousness that knows and loves us, is to believe that the Universe exists *for* man.   For man, or for a consciousness of the same order as the human consciousness, of the same nature, although sublimated, a consciousness that is capable of knowing us, in the depth of whose being our memory may live for ever.

Perhaps, as I have said before, by a supreme and
desperate effort of resignation we might succeed in
making the sacrifice of our personality provided that we
knew that at our death it would go to enrich a Supreme
Personality; provided that we knew that the Universal
Soul was nourished by our souls and had need of them.
We might perhaps meet death with a desperate resignation or with a resigned despair, delivering up our soul to
the soul of humanity, bequeathing to it our work, the
work that bears the impress of our person, if it were certain that this humanity were destined to bequeath its soul
in its turn to another soul, when at long last consciousness shall have become extinct upon this desire-tormented
Earth.    But is it certain?

And if the soul of humanity is eternal, if the human
collective consciousness is eternal, if there is a Consciousness of the Universe, and if this Consciousness is eternal,
why must our own individual consciousness—yours,
reader, mine—be not eternal?

In the vast all of the Universe, must there be this unique
anomaly—a consciousness that knows itself, loves itself
and feels itself, joined to an organism which can only
live within such and such degrees of heat, a merely
transitory phenomenon?    No, it is not mere curiosity
that inspires the wish to know whether or not the stars
are inhabited by living organisms, by consciousnesses
akin to our own, and a profound longing enters into that
dream that our souls shall pass from star to star through
the vast spaces of the heavens, in an infinite series of
transmigrations.    The feeling of the divine makes us
wish and believe that everything is animated, that consciousness, in a greater or less degree, extends through
everything.    We wish not only to save ourselves, but
to save the world from nothingness.    And therefore God.
Such is His finality as we feel it.

What would a universe be without any consciousness
capable of reflecting it and knowing it?    What would

objectified reason be without will and feeling? For us it would be equivalent to nothing—a thousand times more dreadful than nothing.

If such a supposition is reality, our life is deprived of sense and value.

It is not, therefore, rational necessity, but vital anguish that impels us to believe in God. And to believe in God—I must reiterate it yet again—is, before all and above all, to feel a hunger for God, a hunger for divinity, to be sensible of His lack and absence, to wish that God may exist. And it is to wish to save the human finality of the Universe. For one might even come to resign oneself to being absorbed by God, if it be that our consciousness is based upon a Consciousness, if consciousness is the end of the Universe.

"The wicked man hath said in his heart, There is no God." And this is truth. For in his head the righteous man may say to himself, God does not exist! But only the wicked can say it in his heart. Not to believe that there is a God or to believe that there is not a God, is one thing; to resign oneself to there not being a God is another thing, and it is a terrible and inhuman thing; but not to wish that there be a God exceeds every other moral monstrosity; although, as a matter of fact, those who deny God deny Him because of their despair at not finding Him.

And now reason once again confronts us with the Sphinx-like question—the Sphinx, in effect, is reason—Does God exist? This eternal and eternalizing person who gives meaning—and I will add, a human meaning, for there is none other—to the Universe, is it a substantial something, existing independently of our consciousness, independently of our desire? Here we arrive at the insoluble, and it is best that it should be so. Let it suffice for reason that it cannot prove the impossibility of His existence.

To believe in God is to long for His existence and,

further, it is to act as if He existed; it is to live by this longing and to make it the inner spring of our action. This longing or hunger for divinity begets hope, hope begets faith, and faith and hope beget charity. Of this divine longing is born our sense of beauty, of finality, of goodness.

Let us see how this may be.

# FAITH, HOPE, AND CHARITY

Sanctius ac reverentius visum de actis deorum credere quam scire.—
TACITUS : *Germania*, 34.

THE road that leads us to the living God, the God of the
heart, and that leads us back to Him when we have left
Him for the lifeless God of logic, is the road of faith, not
of rational or mathematical conviction.

And what is faith ?

This is the question propounded in the Catechism of
Christian Doctrine that was taught us at school, and the
answer runs : Faith is believing what we have not seen.

This, in an essay written some twelve years ago, I
amended as follows : " Believing what we have not seen,
no ! but creating what we do not see." And I have
already told you that believing in God is, in the first
instance at least, wishing that God may be, longing for
the existence of God.

The theological virtue of faith, according to the
Apostle Paul, whose definition serves as the basis of the
traditional Christian disquisitions upon it, is " the substance of things hoped for, the evidence of things not
seen," ἐλπιζομένων ὑπόστασις, πραγμάτων ἔλεγχος οὐ
βλεπομένων (Heb. xi. 1).

The substance, or rather the support and basis, of
hope, the guarantee of it. That which connects, or,
rather than connects, subordinates, faith to hope. And
in fact we do not hope because we believe, but rather we
believe because we hope. It is hope in God, it is the
ardent longing that there may be a God who guarantees
the eternity of consciousness, that leads us to believe in
Him.

But faith, which after all is something compound, comprising a cognitive, logical, or rational element together with an affective, biotic, sentimental, and strictly irrational element, is presented to us under the form of knowledge. And hence the insuperable difficulty of separating it from some dogma or other. Pure faith, free from dogmas, about which I wrote a great deal years ago, is a phantasm. Neither is the difficulty overcome by inventing the theory of faith in faith itself. Faith needs a matter to work upon.

Believing is a form of knowing, even if it be no more than a knowing and even a formulating of our vital longing. In ordinary language the term "believing," however, is used in a double and even a contradictory sense. It may express, on the one hand, the highest degree of the mind's conviction of the truth of a thing, and, on the other hand, it may imply merely a weak and hesitating persuasion of its truth. For if in one sense believing expresses the firmest kind of assent we are capable of giving, the expression " I believe that it is so, although I am not sure of it," is nevertheless common in ordinary speech.

And this agrees with what we have said above with respect to uncertainty as the basis of faith. The most robust faith, in so far as it is distinguished from all other knowledge that is not *pistic* or of faith—faithful, as we might say—is based on uncertainty. And this is because faith, the guarantee of things hoped for, is not so much rational adhesion to a theoretical principle as trust in a person who assures us of something. Faith supposes an objective, personal element. We do not so much believe something as believe someone who promises us or assures us of this or the other thing. We believe in a person and in God in so far as He is a person and a personalization of the Universe.

This personal or religious element in faith is evident. Faith, it is said, is in itself neither theoretical knowledge nor rational adhesion to a truth, nor yet is its essence sufficiently explained by defining it as trust in God. Seeberg says of faith that it is " the inward submission to the spiritual authority of God, immediate obedience. And in so far as this obedience is the means of attaining a rational principle, faith is a personal conviction."[1]

The faith which St. Paul defined, πίστις in Greek, is better translated as trust, confidence. The word *pistis* is derived from the verb πείθω, which in its active voice means to persuade and in its middle voice to trust in someone, to esteem him as worthy of trust, to place confidence in him, to obey. And *fidare se*, to trust, is derived from the root *fid*—whence *fides*, faith, and also confidence. The Greek root πιθ and the Latin *fid* are twin brothers. In the root of the word "faith" itself, therefore, there is implicit the idea of confidence, of surrender to the will of another, to a person. Confidence is placed only in persons. We trust in Providence, which we conceive as something personal and conscious, not in Fate, which is something impersonal. And thus it is in the person who tells us the truth, in the person who gives us hope, that we believe, not directly and immediately in truth itself or in hope itself.

And this personal or rather personifying element in faith extends even to the lowest forms of it, for it is this that produces faith in pseudo-revelation, in inspiration, in miracle. There is a story of a Parisian doctor, who, when he found that a quack-healer was drawing away his clientèle, removed to a quarter of the city as distant as possible from his former abode, where he was totally unknown, and here he gave himself out as a quack-healer and conducted himself as such. When he was denounced as an illegal practitioner he produced his doctor's certificate, and explained his action more or less as follows : " I am indeed a doctor, but if I had announced myself as

[1] Reinold Seeberg, *Christliche-protestantische Ethik* in *Systematische christliche Religion*, in *Die Kultur der Gegenwart* series.

such I should not have had as large a clientèle as I have
as a quack-healer.  Now that all my clients know that I
have studied medicine, however, and that I am a properly
qualified medical man, they will desert me in favour of
some quack who can assure them that he has never
studied, but cures simply by inspiration."  And true it
is that a doctor is discredited when it is proved that he has
never studied medicine and possesses no qualifying
certificate, and that a quack is discredited when it is proved
that he has studied and is a qualified practitioner.  For
some believe in science and in study, while others believe
in the person, in inspiration, and even in ignorance.

"There is one distinction in the world's geography
which comes immediately to our minds when we thus
state the different thoughts and desires of men concerning their religion.  We remember how the whole
world is in general divided into two hemispheres
upon this matter.  One half of the world—the great
dim East—is mystic.  It insists upon not seeing anything too clearly.  Make any one of the great ideas of
life distinct and clear, and immediately it seems to the
Oriental to be untrue.  He has an instinct which tells
him that the vastest thoughts are too vast for the human
mind, and that if they are made to present themselves in
forms of statement which the human mind can comprehend, their nature is violated and their strength is lost.

"On the other hand, the Occidental, the man of the
West, demands clearness and is impatient with mystery.
He loves a definite statement as much as his brother of
the East dislikes it.  He insists on knowing what the
eternal and infinite forces mean to his personal life, how
they will make him personally happier and better, almost
how they will build the house over his head, and cook the
dinner on his hearth.  This is the difference between the
East and the West, between man on the banks of the
Ganges and man on the banks of the Mississippi.  Plenty
of exceptions, of course, there are—mystics in Boston and

St. Louis, hard-headed men of facts in Bombay and Calcutta. The two great dispositions cannot be shut off from one another by an ocean or a range of mountains. In some nations and places—as, for instance, among the Jews and in our own New England—they notably commingle. But in general they thus divide the world between them. The East lives in the moonlight of mystery, the West in the sunlight of scientific fact. The East cries out to the Eternal for vague impulses. The West seizes the present with light hands, and will not let it go till it has furnished it with reasonable, intelligible motives. Each misunderstands, distrusts, and in large degree despises the other. But the two hemispheres together, and not either one by itself, make up the total world." Thus, in one of his sermons, spoke the great Unitarian preacher Phillips Brooks, late Bishop of Massachusetts (*The Mystery of Iniquity and Other Sermons*, sermon xvi.).

We might rather say that throughout the whole world, in the East as well as in the West, rationalists seek definition and believe in the concept, while vitalists seek inspiration and believe in the person. The former scrutinize the Universe in order that they may wrest its secrets from it; the latter pray to the Consciousness of the Universe, strive to place themselves in immediate relationship with the Soul of the World, with God, in order that they may find the guarantee or substance of what they hope for, which is not to die, and the evidence of what they do not see.

And since a person is a will, and will always has reference to the future, he who believes, believes in what is to come—that is, in what he hopes for. We do not believe, strictly speaking, in what is or in what was, except as the guarantee, as the substance, of what will be. For the Christian, to believe in the resurrection of Christ—that is to say, in tradition and in the Gospel, which assure him that Christ has risen, both of them personal forces—is to believe that he himself will one day rise again by the grace of Christ. And even scientific faith—for such there is—refers to the future and is an act of trust. The man of science believes that at a certain future date an eclipse of the sun will take place; he believes that the laws which have governed the world hitherto will continue to govern it.

To believe, I repeat, is to place confidence in someone, and it has reference to a person. I say that I know that there is an animal called the horse, and that it has such and such characteristics, because I have seen it; and I say that I believe in the existence of the giraffe or the ornithorhyncus, and that it possesses such and such qualities, because I believe those who assure me that they have seen it. And hence the element of uncertainty attached to faith, for it is possible that a person may be deceived or that he may deceive us.

But, on the other hand, this personal element in belief gives it an effective and loving character, and above all, in religious faith, a reference to what is hoped for. Perhaps there is nobody who would sacrifice his life for the sake of maintaining that the three angles of a triangle are together equal to two right angles, for such a truth does not demand the sacrifice of our life; but, on the other hand, there are many who have lost their lives for the sake of maintaining their religious faith. Indeed it is truer to say that martyrs make faith than that faith makes martyrs. For faith is not the mere adherence of the intellect to an abstract principle; it is not the recognition of a theoretical truth, a process in which the will merely sets in motion our faculty of comprehension; faith is an act of the will—it is a movement of the soul towards a practical truth, towards a person, towards something that makes us not merely comprehend life, but that makes us live.[1]

Faith makes us live by showing us that life, although

---

[1] Cf St Thomas Aquinas, *Summa*, secunda secundæ, quæstio iv , art 2

it is dependent upon reason, has its well-spring and
source of power elsewhere, in something supernatural
and miraculous. Cournot the mathematician, a man of
singularly well-balanced and scientifically equipped
mind, has said that it is this tendency towards the supernatural and miraculous that gives life, and that when it
is lacking, all the speculations of the reason lead to
nothing but affliction of spirit (*Traité de l'enchaînement
des idées fondamentales dans les sciences et dans
l'histoire*, § 329). And in truth we wish to live.

But, although we have said that faith is a thing of the
will, it would perhaps be better to say that it is will
itself—the will not to die, or, rather, that it is some other
psychic force distinct from intelligence, will, and feeling. We should thus have feeling, knowing, willing,
and believing or creating. For neither feeling, nor
intelligence, nor will creates; they operate upon a
material already given, upon the material given them
by faith. Faith is the creative power in man. But
since it has a more intimate relation with the will than
with any other of his faculties, we conceive it under the
form of volition. It should be borne in mind, however,
that wishing to believe—that is to say, wishing to create
—is not precisely the same as believing or creating,
although it is its starting-point.

Faith, therefore, if not a creative force, is the fruit of
the will, and its function is to create. Faith, in a certain
sense, creates its object. And faith in God consists in
creating God; and since it is God who gives us faith in
Himself, it is God who is continually creating Himself
in us. Therefore St. Augustine said: "I will seek
Thee, Lord, by calling upon Thee, and I will call upon
Thee by believing in Thee. My faith calls upon Thee,
Lord, the faith which Thou hast given me, with which
Thou hast inspired me through the Humanity of Thy
Son, through the ministry of Thy preacher" (*Confes-
sions*, book i., chap. i.). The power of creating God in

our own image and likeness, of personalizing the Universe, simply means that we carry God within us, as the substance of what we hope for, and that God is continually creating us in His own image and likeness.

And we create God—that is to say, God creates Himself in us—by compassion, by love. To believe in God is to love Him, and in our love to fear Him; and we begin by loving Him even before knowing Him, and by loving Him we come at last to see and discover Him in all things.

Those who say that they believe in God and yet neither love nor fear Him, do not in fact believe in Him but in those who have taught them that God exists, and these in their turn often enough do not believe in Him either. Those who believe that they believe in God, but without any passion in their heart, without anguish of mind, without uncertainty, without doubt, without an element of despair even in their consolation, believe only in the God-Idea, not in God Himself. And just as belief in God is born of love, so also it may be born of fear, and even of hate, and of such kind was the belief of Vanni Fucci, the thief, whom Dante depicts insulting God with obscene gestures in Hell (*Inf.*, xxv., 1-3). For the devils also believe in God, and not a few atheists.

Is it not perhaps a mode of believing in God, this fury with which those deny and even insult Him, who, because they cannot bring themselves to believe in Him, wish that He may not exist? Like those who believe, they, too, wish that God may exist; but being men of a weak and passive or of an evil disposition, in whom reason is stronger than will, they feel themselves caught in the grip of reason and haled along in their own despite, and they fall into despair, and because of their despair they deny, and in their denial they affirm and create the thing that they deny, and God reveals Himself in them, affirming Himself by their very denial of Him.

But it will be objected to all this that to demonstrate

13

that faith creates its own object is to demonstrate that this object is an object for faith alone, that outside faith it has no objective reality; just as, on the other hand, to maintain that faith is necessary because it affords consolation to the masses of the people, or imposes a wholesome restraint upon them, is to declare that the object of faith is illusory. What is certain is that for thinking believers to-day, faith is, before all and above all, wishing that God may exist.

Wishing that God may exist, and acting and feeling as if He did exist. And desiring God's existence and acting conformably with this desire, is the means whereby we create God—that is, whereby God creates Himself in us, manifests Himself to us, opens and reveals Himself to us. For God goes out to meet him who seeks Him with love and by love, and hides Himself from him who searches for Him with the cold and loveless reason. God wills that the heart should have rest, but not the head, reversing the order of the physical life in which the head sleeps and rests at times while the heart wakes and works unceasingly. And thus knowledge without love leads us away from God; and love, even without knowledge, and perhaps better without it, leads us to God, and through God to wisdom. Blessed are the pure in heart, for they shall see God!

And if you should ask me how I believe in God—that is to say, how God creates Himself in me and reveals Himself to me—my answer may, perhaps, provoke your smiles or your laughter, or it may even scandalize you.

I believe in God as I believe in my friends, because I feel the breath of His affection, feel His invisible and intangible hand, drawing me, leading me, grasping me; because I possess an inner consciousness of a particular providence and of a universal mind that marks out for me the course of my own destiny. And the concept of law—it is nothing but a concept after all!—tells me nothing and teaches me nothing.

Once and again in my life I have seen myself suspended in a trance over the abyss; once and again I
have found myself at the cross-roads, confronted by a
choice of ways and aware that in choosing one I should
be renouncing all the others—for there is no turning
back upon these roads of life; and once and again in
such unique moments as these I have felt the impulse of
a mighty power, conscious, sovereign, and loving.
And then, before the feet of the wayfarer, opens out the
way of the Lord.

It is possible for a man to feel the Universe calling to
him and guiding him as one person guides and calls to
another, to hear within him its voice speaking without
words and saying: " Go and preach to all peoples !"
How do you know that the man you see before you
possesses a consciousness like you, and that an animal
also possesses such a consciousness, more or less dimly,
but not a stone? Because the man acts towards you like a
man, like a being made in your likeness, and because the
stone does not act towards you at all, but suffers you to
act upon it. And in the same way I believe that the
Universe possesses a certain consciousness like myself,
because its action towards me is a human action, and I
feel that it is a personality that environs me.

Here is a formless mass; it appears to be a kind of
animal; it is impossible to distinguish its members; I
only see two eyes, eyes which gaze at me with a human
gaze, the gaze of a fellow-being, a gaze which asks for
pity; and I hear it breathing. I conclude that in this
formless mass there is a consciousness. In just such a
way and none other, the starry-eyed heavens gaze down
upon the believer, with a superhuman, a divine, gaze, a
gaze that asks for supreme pity and supreme love, and in
the serenity of the night he hears the breathing of God,
and God touches him in his heart of hearts and reveals
Himself to him. It is the Universe, living, suffering,
loving, and asking for love.

From loving little trifling material things, which lightly come and lightly go, having no deep root in our affections, we come to love the more lasting things, the things which our hands cannot grasp; from loving goods we come to love the Good; from loving beautiful things we come to love Beauty; from loving the true we come to love the Truth; from loving pleasures we come to love Happiness; and, last of all, we come to love Love. We emerge from ourselves in order to penetrate further into our supreme I; individual consciousness emerges from us in order to submerge itself in the total Consciousness of which we form a part, but without being dissolved in it. And God is simply the Love that springs from universal suffering and becomes consciousness.

But this, it will be said, is merely to revolve in an iron ring, for such a God is not objective. And at this point it may not be out of place to give reason its due and to examine exactly what is meant by a thing existing, being objective.

What is it, in effect, to exist? and when do we say that a thing exists? A thing exists when it is placed outside us, and in such a way that it shall have preceded our perception of it and be capable of continuing to subsist outside us after we have disappeared. But have I any certainty that anything has preceded me or that anything must survive me? Can my consciousness know that there is anything outside it? Everything that I know or can know is within my consciousness. We will not entangle ourselves, therefore, in the insoluble problem of an objectivity outside our perceptions. Things exist in so far as they act. To exist is to act.

But now it will be said that it is not God, but the idea of God, that acts in us. To which we shall reply that it is sometimes God acting by His idea, but still very often it is rather God acting in us by Himself. And the retort will be a demand for proofs of the objective truth of the existence of God, since we ask for signs. And we shall have to answer with Pilate : What is truth ?

And having asked this question, Pilate turned away without waiting for an answer and proceeded to wash his hands in order that he might exculpate himself for having allowed Christ to be condemned to death. And there are many who ask this question, What is truth ? but without any intention of waiting for the answer, and solely in order that they may turn away and wash their hands of the crime of having helped to kill and eject God from their own consciousness or from the consciousness of others.

What is truth ? There are two kinds of truth—the logical or objective, the opposite of which is error, and the moral or subjective, the opposite of which is falsehood. And in a previous essay I have endeavoured to show that error is the fruit of falsehood.[1]

Moral truth, the road that leads to intellectual truth, which also is moral, inculcates the study of science, which is over and above all a school of sincerity and humility. Science teaches us, in effect, to submit our reason to the truth and to know and judge of things as they are—that is to say, as they themselves choose to be and not as we would have them be. In a religiously scientific investigation, it is the data of reality themselves, it is the perceptions which we receive from the outside world, that formulate themselves in our mind as laws—it is not we ourselves who thus formulate them. It is the numbers themselves which in our mind create mathematics. Science is the most intimate school of resignation and humility, for it teaches us to bow before the seemingly most insignificant of facts. And it is the gateway of religion ; but within the temple itself its function ceases.

---

[1] "*Qué es Verdad?*" ("What is truth?"), published in *La España Moderna*, March, 1906, vol 207 (reprinted in the edition of collected *Ensayos*, vol. vi., Madrid, 1918)

And just as there is logical truth, opposed to error, and moral truth, opposed to falsehood, so there is also esthetic truth or verisimilitude, which is opposed to extravagance, and religious truth or hope, which is opposed to the inquietude of absolute despair. For esthetic verisimilitude, the expression of which is sensible, differs from logical truth, the demonstration of which is rational; and religious truth, the truth of faith, the substance of things hoped for, is not equivalent to moral truth, but superimposes itself upon it. He who affirms a faith built upon a basis of uncertainty does not and cannot lie.

And not only do we not believe with reason, nor yet above reason nor below reason, but we believe against reason. Religious faith, it must be repeated yet again, is not only irrational, it is contra-rational. Kierkegaard says : " Poetry is illusion before knowledge; religion illusion after knowledge. Between poetry and religion the worldly wisdom of living plays its comedy. Every individual who does not live either poetically or religiously is a fool" (*Afsluttende uvidenskabelig Efterskrift,* chap. iv., sect. 2a, § 2). The same writer tells us that Christianity is a desperate sortie (*salida*). Even so, but it is only by the very desperateness of this sortie that we can win through to hope, to that hope whose vitalizing illusion is of more force than all rational knowledge, and which assures us that there is always something that cannot be reduced to reason. And of reason the same may be said as was said of Christ: that he who is not with it is against it. That which is not rational is contra-rational; and such is hope.

By this circuitous route we always arrive at hope in the end.

To the mystery of love, which is the mystery of suffering, belongs a mysterious form, and this form is time. We join yesterday to to-morrow with links of longing, and the now is, strictly, nothing but the endeavour of

the before to make itself the after; the present is simply
the determination of the past to become the future.  The
now is a point which, if not sharply articulated, vanishes;
and, nevertheless, in this point is all eternity, the substance of time.

Everything that has been can be only as it was, and
everything that is can be only as it is; the possible is
always relegated to the future, the sole domain of liberty,
wherein imagination, the creative and liberating energy,
the incarnation of faith, has space to roam at large.

Love ever looks and tends to the future, for its work
is the work of our perpetuation; the property of love is
to hope, and only upon hopes does it nourish itself.  And
thus when love sees the fruition of its desire it becomes
sad, for it then discovers that what it desired was not its
true end, and that God gave it this desire merely as a
lure to spur it to action; it discovers that its end is further
on, and it sets out again upon its toilsome pilgrimage
through life, revolving through a constant cycle of illusions and disillusions.  And continually it transforms
its frustrated hopes into memories, and from these
memories it draws fresh hopes.  From the subterranean
ore of memory we extract the jewelled visions of our
future; imagination shapes our remembrances into
hopes.  And humanity is like a young girl full of longings, hungering for life and thirsting for love, who
weaves her days with dreams, and hopes, hopes ever,
hopes without ceasing, for the eternal and predestined
lover, for him who, because he was destined for her from
the beginning, from before the dawn of her remotest
memory, from before her cradle-days, shall live with her
and for her into the illimitable future, beyond the
stretch of her furthest hopes, beyond the grave itself.
And for this poor lovelorn humanity, as for the girl ever
awaiting her lover, there is no kinder wish than that
when the winter of life shall come it may find the sweet
dreams of its spring changed into memories sweeter still,

and memories that shall burgeon into new hopes.  In
the days when our summer is over, what a flow of calm
felicity, of resignation to destiny, must come from remembering hopes which have never been realized and
which, because they have never been realized, preserve
their pristine purity.

Love hopes, hopes ever and never wearies of hoping;
and love of God, our faith in God, is, above all, hope in
Him.  For God dies not, and he who hopes in God shall
live for ever.  And our fundamental hope, the root and
stem of all our hopes, is the hope of eternal life.

And if faith is the substance of hope, hope in its turn
is the form of faith.  Until it gives us hope, our faith is
a formless faith, vague, chaotic, potential; it is but the
possibility of believing, the longing to believe.  But we
must needs believe in something, and we believe in what
we hope for, we believe in hope.  We remember the
past, we know the present, we only believe in the future.
To believe what we have not seen is to believe what we
shall see.  Faith, then, I repeat once again, is faith in
hope; we believe what we hope for.

Love makes us believe in God, in whom we hope and
from whom we hope to receive life to come; love makes
us believe in that which the dream of hope creates for us.

Faith is our longing for the eternal, for God; and
hope is God's longing, the longing of the eternal, of the
divine in us, which advances to meet our faith and uplifts
us.  Man aspires to God by faith and cries to Him: " I
believe—give me, Lord, wherein to believe!"  And
God, the divinity in man, sends him hope in another life
in order that he may believe in it.  Hope is the reward
of faith.  Only he who believes truly hopes; and only
he who truly hopes believes.  We only believe what we
hope, and we only hope what we believe.

It was hope that called God by the name of Father;
and this name, so comforting yet so mysterious, is still
bestowed upon Him by hope.  The father gave us life

and gives bread wherewith to sustain it, and we ask the father to preserve our life for us.  And if Christ was he who, with the fullest heart and purest mouth, named with the name of Father his Father and ours, if the noblest feeling of Christianity is the feeling of the Fatherhood of God, it is because in Christ the human race sublimated its hunger for eternity.

It may perhaps be said that this longing of faith, that this hope, is more than anything else an esthetic feeling. Possibly the esthetic feeling enters into it, but without completely satisfying it.

We seek in art an image of eternalization.  If for a brief moment our spirit finds peace and rest and assuagement in the contemplation of the beautiful, even though it finds therein no real cure for its distress, it is because the beautiful is the revelation of the eternal, of the divine in things, and beauty but the perpetuation of momentaneity.  Just as truth is the goal of rational knowledge, so beauty is the goal of hope, which is perhaps in its essence irrational.

Nothing is lost, nothing wholly passes away, for in some way or another everything is perpetuated; and everything, after passing through time, returns to eternity.  The temporal world has its roots in eternity, and in eternity yesterday is united with to-day and to-morrow.  The scenes of life pass before us as in a cinematograph show, but on the further side of time the film is one and indivisible.

Physicists affirm that not a single particle of matter nor a single tremor of energy is lost, but that each is transformed and transmitted and persists.  And can it be that any form, however fugitive it may be, is lost? We must needs believe—believe and hope!—that it is not, but that somewhere it remains archived and perpetuated, and that there is some mirror of eternity in which, without losing themselves in one another, all the images that pass through time are received.  Every

impression that reaches me remains stored up in my
brain even though it may be so deep or so weak that it is
buried in the depths of my subconsciousness; but from
these depths it animates my life; and if the whole of my
spirit, the total content of my soul, were to awake to
full consciousness, all these dimly perceived and forgotten fugitive impressions would come to life again,
including even those which I had never been aware of.
I carry within me everything that has passed before me,
and I perpetuate it with myself, and it may be that it all
goes into my germs, and that all my ancestors live un-
diminished in me and will continue so to live, united
with me, in my descendants.    And perhaps I, the whole
I, with all this universe of mine, enter into each one of
my actions, or, at all events, that which is essential in
me enters into them—that which makes me myself, my
individual essence.

And how is this individual essence in each several
thing—that which makes it itself and not another—
revealed to us save as beauty?    What is the beauty of
anything but its eternal essence, that which unites its
past with its future, that element of it that rests and
abides in the womb of eternity? or, rather, what is it but
the revelation of its divinity?

And this beauty, which is the root of eternity, is revealed to us by love; it is the supreme revelation of the
love of God and the token of our ultimate victory over
time.    It is love that reveals to us the eternal in us and
in our neighbours.

Is it the beautiful, the eternal, in things, that awakens
and kindles our love for them, or is it our love for things
that reveals to us the beautiful, the eternal, in them?
Is not beauty perhaps a creation of love, in the same way
and in the same sense that the sensible world is a creation
of the instinct of preservation and the supersensible world
of that of perpetuation?    Is not beauty, and together with
beauty eternity, a creation of love?    ".Though our outward

man perish," says the Apostle, "yet the inward man is renewed day by day" (2 Cor. iv. 16). The man of passing appearances perishes and passes away with them; the man of reality remains and grows. "For our light affliction, which is but for a moment, worketh for us a far more exceeding and eternal weight of glory" (ver. 17). Our suffering causes us anguish, and this anguish, bursting because of its own fullness, seems to us consolation. "While we look not at the things which are seen, but at the things which are not seen: for the things which are seen are temporal; but the things which are not seen are eternal" (ver. 18).

This suffering gives hope, which is the beautiful in life, the supreme beauty, or the supreme consolation. And since love is full of suffering, since love is compassion and pity, beauty springs from compassion and is simply the temporal consolation that compassion seeks. A tragic consolation! And the supreme beauty is that of tragedy. The consciousness that everything passes away, that we ourselves pass away, and that everything that is ours and everything that environs us passes away, fills us with anguish, and this anguish itself reveals to us the consolation of that which does not pass away, of the eternal, of the beautiful.

And this beauty thus revealed, this perpetuation of momentaneity, only realizes itself practically, only lives through the work of charity. Hope in action is charity, and beauty in action is goodness.

Charity, which eternalizes everything it loves, and in giving us the goodness of it brings to light its hidden beauty, has its root in the love of God, or, if you like, in charity towards God, in pity for God. Love, pity, personalizes everything, we have said; in discovering the suffering in everything and in personalizing everything, it personalizes the Universe itself as well—for the Universe also suffers—and it discovers God to us. For

God is revealed to us because He suffers and because we suffer; because He suffers He demands our love, and because we suffer He gives us His love, and He covers our anguish with the eternal and infinite anguish.

This was the scandal of Christianity among Jews and Greeks, among Pharisees and Stoics, and this, which was its scandal of old, the scandal of the Cross, is still its scandal to-day, and will continue to be so, even among Christians themselves—the scandal of a God who becomes man in order that He may suffer and die and rise again, because He has suffered and died, the scandal of a God subject to suffering and death. And this truth that God suffers—a truth that appals the mind of man—is the revelation of the very heart of the Universe and of its mystery, the revelation that God revealed to us when He sent His Son in order that he might redeem us by suffering and dying. It was the revelation of the divine in suffering, for only that which suffers is divine.

And men made a god of this Christ who suffered, and through him they discovered the eternal essence of a living, human God—that is, of a God who suffers—it is only the dead, the inhuman, that does not suffer—a God who loves and thirsts for love, for pity, a God who is a person. Whosoever knows not the Son will never know the Father, and the Father is only known through the Son; whosoever knows not the Son of Man—he who suffers bloody anguish and the pangs of a breaking heart, whose soul is heavy within him even unto death, who suffers the pain that kills and brings to life again—will never know the Father, and can know nothing of the suffering God.

He who does not suffer, and who does not suffer because he does not live, is that logical and frozen *ens realissimum*, the *primum movens*, that impassive entity, which because of its impassivity is nothing but a pure idea. The category does not suffer, but neither does it live or exist as a person. And how is the world to derive

its origin and life from an impassive idea? Such a
world would be but the idea of the world. But the world
suffers, and suffering is the sense of the flesh of reality;
it is the spirit's sense of its mass and substance; it is the
self's sense of its own tangibility; it is immediate reality.

Suffering is the substance of life and the root of personality, for it is only suffering that makes us persons.
And suffering is universal, suffering is that which unites
all us living beings together; it is the universal or divine
blood that flows through us all. That which we call
will, what is it but suffering?

And suffering has its degrees, according to the depth
of its penetration, from the suffering that floats upon the
sea of appearances to the eternal anguish, the source of
the tragic sense of life, which seeks a habitation in the
depths of the eternal and there awakens consolation;
from the physical suffering that contorts our bodies to
the religious anguish that flings us upon the bosom of
God, there to be watered by the divine tears.

Anguish is something far deeper, more intimate, and
more spiritual than suffering. We are wont to feel the
touch of anguish even in the midst of that which we call
happiness, and even because of this happiness itself, to
which we cannot resign ourselves and before which we
tremble. The happy who resign themselves to their
apparent happiness, to a transitory happiness, seem to
be as men without substance, or, at any rate, men who
have not discovered this substance in themselves, who
have not touched it. Such men are usually incapable of
loving or of being loved, and they go through life without really knowing either pain or bliss.

There is no true love save in suffering, and in this
world we have to choose either love, which is suffering,
or happiness. And love leads us to no other happiness
than that of love itself and its tragic consolation of
uncertain hope. The moment love becomes happy and
satisfied, it no longer desires and it is no longer love.

The satisfied, the happy, do not love; they fall asleep in habit, near neighbour to annihilation. To fall into a habit is to begin to cease to be. Man is the more man— that is, the more divine—the greater his capacity for suffering, or, rather, for anguish.

At our coming into the world it is given to us to choose between love and happiness, and we wish—poor fools !— for both : the happiness of loving and the love of happiness. But we ought to ask for the gift of love and not of happiness, and to be preserved from dozing away into habit, lest we should fall into a fast sleep, a sleep without waking, and so lose our consciousness beyond power of recovery. We ought to ask God to make us conscious of ourselves in ourselves, in our suffering.

What is Fate, what is Fatality, but the brotherhood of love and suffering ? What is it but that terrible mystery in virtue of which love dies as soon as it touches the happiness towards which it reaches out, and true happiness dies with it ? Love and suffering mutually engender one another, and love is charity and compassion, and the love that is not charitable and compassionate is not love. Love, in a word, is resigned despair.

That which the mathematicians call the problem of maxima and minima, which is also called the law of economy, is the formula for all existential—that is, passional—activity. In material mechanics and in social mechanics, in industry and in political economy, every problem resolves itself into an attempt to obtain the greatest possible resulting utility with the least possible effort, the greatest income with the least expenditure, the most pleasure with the least pain. And the terrible and tragic formula of the inner, spiritual life is either to obtain the most happiness with the least love, or the most love with the least happiness. And it is necessary to choose between the one and the other, and to know that he who approaches the infinite of love, the love that is infinite, approaches the zero of happiness,

the supreme anguish.  And in reaching this zero he is
beyond the reach of the misery that kills.  " Be not,
and thou shalt be mightier than aught that is," said
Brother Juan de los Angeles in one of his *Diálogos de la
conquista del reino de Dios* (Dial. iii. 8).

And there is something still more anguishing than
suffering.  A man about to receive a much-dreaded blow
expects to have to suffer so severely that he may even
succumb to the suffering, and when the blow falls he
feels scarcely any pain; but afterwards, when he has
come to himself and is conscious of his insensibility, he
is seized with terror, a tragic terror, the most terrible of
all, and choking with anguish he cries out : " Can it be
that I no longer exist?"  Which would you find most
appalling—to feel such a pain as would deprive you of
your senses on being pierced through with a white-hot
iron, or to see yourself thus pierced through without
feeling any pain?  Have you never felt the horrible
terror of feeling yourself incapable of suffering and of
tears?  Suffering tells us that we exist; suffering tells
us that those whom we love exist; suffering tells us that
the world in which we live exists; and suffering tells us
that God exists and suffers; but it is the suffering of
anguish, the anguish of surviving and being eternal.
Anguish discovers God to us and makes us love
Him.

To believe in God is to love Him, and to love Him is
to feel Him suffering, to pity Him.

It may perhaps appear blasphemous to say that God
suffers, for suffering implies limitation.  Nevertheless,
God, the Consciousness of the Universe, is limited by the
brute matter in which He lives, by the unconscious, from
which He seeks to liberate Himself and to liberate us.
And we, in our turn, must seek to liberate Him.  God
suffers in each and all of us, in each and all of the consciousnesses imprisoned in transitory matter, and we all
suffer in Him.  Religious anguish is but the divine

suffering, the feeling that God suffers in me and that I suffer in Him.

The universal suffering is the anguish of all in seeking to be all else but without power to achieve it, the anguish of each in being he that he is, being at the same time all that he is not, and being so for ever. The essence of a being is not only its endeavour to persist for ever, as Spinoza taught us, but also its endeavour to universalize itself; it is the hunger and thirst for eternity and infinity. Every created being tends not only to preserve itself in itself, but to perpetuate itself, and, moreover, to invade all other beings, to be others without ceasing to be itself, to extend its limits to the infinite, but without breaking them. It does not wish to throw down its walls and leave everything laid flat, common and undefended, confounding and losing its own individuality, but it wishes to carry its walls to the extreme limits of creation and to embrace everything within them. It seeks the maximum of individuality with the maximum also of personality: it aspires to the identification of the Universe with itself; it aspires to God.

And this vast I, within which each individual I seeks to put the Universe—what is it but God? And because I aspire to God, I love Him; and this aspiration of mine towards God is my love for Him, and just as I suffer in being He, He also suffers in being I, and in being each one of us.

I am well aware that in spite of my warning that I am attempting here to give a logical form to a system of a-logical feelings, I shall be scandalizing not a few of my readers in speaking of a God who suffers, and in applying to God Himself, as God, the passion of Christ. The God of so-called rational theology excludes in effect all suffering. And the reader will no doubt think that this idea of suffering can have only a metaphorical value when applied to God, similar to that which is supposed to attach to those passages in the Old Testament which describe the human passions of the God of Israel. For anger, wrath, and vengeance are impossible without suffering. And as for saying that God suffers through being bound by matter, I shall be told that, in the words of Plotinus (*Second Ennead,* ix., 7), the Universal Soul cannot be bound by the very thing—namely, bodies or matter—which is bound by It.

Herein is involved the whole problem of the origin of evil, the evil of sin no less than the evil of pain, for if God does not suffer, He causes suffering; and if His life, since God lives, is not a process of realizing in Himself a total consciousness which is continually becoming fuller —that is to say, which is continually becoming more and more God—it is a process of drawing all things towards Himself, of imparting Himself to all, of constraining the consciousness of each part to enter into the consciousness of the All, which is He Himself, until at last He comes to be all in all—πάντα ἐν πᾶσι, according to the expression of St. Paul, the first Christian mystic. We will discuss this more fully, however, in the next chapter on the apocatastasis or beatific union.

For the present let it suffice to say that there is a vast current of suffering urging living beings towards one another, constraining them to love one another and to seek one another, and to endeavour to complete one another, and to be each himself and others at the same time. In God everything lives, and in His suffering everything suffers, and in loving God we love His creatures in Him, just as in loving and pitying His creatures we love and pity God in them. No single soul can be free so long as there is anything enslaved in God's world, neither can God Himself, who lives in the soul of each one of us, be free so long as our soul is not free.

My most immediate sensation is the sense and love of my own misery, my anguish, the compassion I feel for myself, the love I bear for myself. And when this compassion is vital and superabundant, it overflows from me

14

upon others, and from the excess of my own compassion
I come to have compassion for my neighbours. My
own misery is so great that the compassion for myself
which it awakens within me soon overflows and reveals
to me the universal misery.

And what is charity but the overflow of pity? What
is it but reflected pity that overflows and pours itself out
in a flood of pity for the woes of others and in the
exercise of charity?

When the overplus of our pity leads us to the consciousness of God within us, it fills us with so great
anguish for the misery shed abroad in all things, that we
have to pour our pity abroad, and this we do in the
form of charity. And in this pouring abroad of our pity
we experience relief and the painful sweetness of goodness. This is what Teresa de Jesús, the mystical doctor,
called "sweet-tasting suffering" (*dolor sabroso*), and she
knew also the lore of suffering loves. It is as when one
looks upon some thing of beauty and feels the necessity
of making others sharers in it. For the creative impulse, in which charity consists, is the work of suffering
love.

We feel, in effect, a satisfaction in doing good when
good superabounds within us, when we are swollen with
pity; and we are swollen with pity when God, filling our
soul, gives us the suffering sensation of universal life,
of the universal longing for eternal divinization. For
we are not merely placed side by side with others in the
world, having no common root with them, neither is their
lot indifferent to us, but their pain hurts us, their
anguish fills us with anguish, and we feel our com-
munity of origin and of suffering even without knowing
it. Suffering, and pity which is born of suffering, are
what reveal to us the brotherhood of every existing thing
that possesses life and more or less of consciousness.
"Brother Wolf" St. Francis of Assisi called the poor
wolf that feels a painful hunger for the sheep, and feels,

too, perhaps, the pain of having to devour them; and
this brotherhood reveals to us the Fatherhood of God,
reveals to us that God is a Father and that He exists.
And as a Father He shelters our common misery.

Charity, then, is the impulse to liberate myself and all
my fellows from suffering, and to liberate God, who
embraces us all.

Suffering is a spiritual thing. It is the most immediate revelation of consciousness, and it may be that our
body was given us simply in order that suffering might
be enabled to manifest itself. A man who had never
known suffering, either in greater or less degree, would
scarcely possess consciousness of himself. The child
first cries at birth when the air, entering into his lungs
and limiting him, seems to say to him: You have to
breathe me in order that you may live!

We must needs believe with faith, whatever counsels
reason may give us, that the material or sensible world
which the senses create for us exists solely in order to
embody and sustain that other spiritual or imaginable
world which the imagination creates for us. Consciousness tends to be ever more and more consciousness, to
intensify its consciousness, to acquire full consciousness
of its complete self, of the whole of its content. We
must needs believe with faith, whatever counsels reason
may give us, that in the depths of our own bodies, in
animals, in plants, in rocks, in everything that lives, in
all the Universe, there is a spirit that strives to know
itself, to acquire consciousness of itself, to be itself—for
to be oneself is to know oneself—to be pure spirit; and
since it can only achieve this by means of the body, by
means of matter, it creates and makes use of matter at
the same time that it remains the prisoner of it. The
face can only see itself when portrayed in the mirror,
but in order to see itself it must remain the prisoner of
the mirror in which it sees itself, and the image which
it sees therein is as the mirror distorts it; and if the

mirror breaks, the image is broken; and if the mirror is blurred, the image is blurred.

Spirit finds itself limited by the matter in which it has to live and acquire consciousness of itself, just as thought is limited by the word in which as a social medium it is incarnated. Without matter there is no spirit, but matter makes spirit suffer by limiting it. And suffering is simply the obstacle which matter opposes to spirit; it is the clash of the conscious with the unconscious.

Suffering is, in effect, the barrier which unconsciousness, matter, sets up against consciousness, spirit; it is the resistance to will, the limit which the visible universe imposes upon God; it is the wall that consciousness runs up against when it seeks to extend itself at the expense of unconsciousness; it is the resistance which unconsciousness opposes to its penetration by consciousness.

Although in deference to authority we may believe, we do not in fact know, that we possess heart, stomach, or lungs so long as they do not cause us discomfort, suffering, or anguish. Physical suffering, or even discomfort, is what reveals to us our own internal core. And the same is true of spiritual suffering and anguish, for we do not take account of the fact that we possess a soul until it hurts us.

Anguish is that which makes consciousness return upon itself. He who knows no anguish knows what he does and what he thinks, but he does not truly know that he does it and that he thinks it. He thinks, but he does not think that he thinks, and his thoughts are as if they were not his. Neither does he properly belong to himself. For it is only anguish, it is only the passionate longing never to die, that makes a human spirit master of itself.

Pain, which is a kind of dissolution, makes us discover our internal core; and in the supreme dissolution, which is death, we shall, at last, through the pain of annihilation, arrive at the core of our temporal core—at God, whom in our spiritual anguish we breathe and learn to love.

Even so must we believe with faith, whatever counsels reason may give us.

The origin of evil, as many discovered of old, is nothing other than what is called by another name the inertia of matter, and, as applied to the things of the spirit, sloth. And not without truth has it been said that sloth is the mother of all vices, not forgetting that the supreme sloth is that of not longing madly for immortality.

Consciousness, the craving for more, more, always more, hunger of eternity and thirst of infinity, appetite for God—these are never satisfied. Each consciousness seeks to be itself and to be all other consciousnesses without ceasing to be itself: it seeks to be God. And matter, unconsciousness, tends to be less and less, tends to be nothing, its thirst being a thirst for repose. Spirit says: I wish to be! and matter answers: I wish not to be!

And in the order of human life, the individual would tend, under the sole instigation of the instinct of preservation, the creator of the material world, to destruction, to annihilation, if it were not for society, which, in implanting in him the instinct of perpetuation, the creator of the spiritual world, lifts and impels him towards the All, towards immortalization. And everything that man does as a mere individual, opposed to society, for the sake of his own preservation, and at the expense of society, if need be, is bad; and everything that he does as a social person, for the sake of the society in which he himself is included, for the sake of its perpetuation and of the perpetuation of himself in it, is good. And many of those who seem to be the greatest egoists, trampling everything under their feet in their zeal to bring their work to a successful issue, are in reality men whose souls are aflame and overflowing with charity, for they subject and subordinate their petty personal I to the social I that has a mission to accomplish.

He who would tie the working of love, of spiritualization, of liberation, to transitory and individual forms, crucifies God in matter; he crucifies God who makes the ideal subservient to his own temporal interests or worldly glory. And such a one is a deicide.

The work of charity, of the love of God, is to endeavour to liberate God from brute matter, to endeavour to give consciousness to everything, to spiritualize or universalize everything; it is to dream that the very rocks may find a voice and work in accordance with the spirit of this dream; it is to dream that everything that exists may become conscious, that the Word may become life.

We have but to look at the eucharistic symbol to see an instance of it. The Word has been imprisoned in a piece of material bread, and it has been imprisoned therein to the end that we may eat it, and in eating it make it our own, part and parcel of our body in which the spirit dwells, and that it may beat in our heart and think in our brain and be consciousness. It has been imprisoned in this bread in order that, after being buried in our body, it may come to life again in our spirit.

And we must spiritualize everything. And this we shall accomplish by giving our spirit, which grows the more the more it is distributed, to all men and to all things. And we give our spirit when we invade other spirits and make ourselves the master of them.

All this is to be believed with faith, whatever counsels reason may give us.

And now we are about to see what practical consequences all these more or less fantastical doctrines may have in regard to logic, to esthetics, and, above all, to ethics—their religious concretion, in a word. And perhaps then they will gain more justification in the eyes of the reader who, in spite of my warnings, has hitherto been looking for the scientific or even philosophic development of an irrational system.

I think it may not be superfluous to recall to the reader once again what I said at the conclusion of the sixth chapter, that entitled " In the Depths of the Abyss "; but·we now approach the practical or pragmatical part of this treatise. First, however, we must see how the religious sense may become concrete in the hopeful vision of another life.

# X

## RELIGION, THE MYTHOLOGY OF THE BEYOND AND THE APOCATASTASIS

Καὶ γὰρ ἴσως καὶ μάλιστα πρέπει μέλλοντα ἐχεῖσε ἀποδημεῖν διασκοπεῖν τε καὶ μυθολογεῖν περὶ τῆς ἀποδημίας τῆς ἔχει, ποιαν τινὰ αὐτὴν οἰόμεθα εἶναι.—PLATO. *Phædo.*

RELIGION is founded upon faith, hope, and charity, which in their turn are founded upon the feeling of divinity and of God. Of faith in God is born our faith in men, of hope in God hope in men, and of charity or piety towards God—for as Cicero said,[1] *est enim pietas iustitia adversum deos*—charity towards men. In God is resumed not only Humanity, but the whole Universe, and the Universe spiritualized and penetrated with consciousness, for as the Christian Faith teaches, God shall at last be all in all. St. Teresa said, and Miguel de Molinos repeated with a harsher and more despairing inflection, that the soul must realize that nothing exists but itself and God.

And this relation with God, this more or less intimate union with Him, is what we call religion.

What is religion? In what does it differ from the religious sense and how are the two related? Every man's definition of religion is based upon his own inward experience of it rather than upon his observation of it in others, nor indeed is it possible to define it without in some way or another experiencing it. Tacitus said (*Hist.* v. 4), speaking of the Jews, that they regarded as profane everything that the Romans held to be sacred,

[1] *De natura deorum*, lib. i., cap. 41.

216

and that what was sacred to them was to the Romans impure : *profana illic omnia quæ apud nos sacra, rursum conversa apud illos quæ nobis incesta.* Therefore he, the Roman, describes the Jews as a people dominated by superstition and hostile to religion, *gens superstitioni obnoxia, religionibus adversa,* while as regards Christianity, with which he was very imperfectly acquainted, scarcely distinguishing it from Judaism, he deemed it to be a pernicious superstition, *existialis superstitio,* inspired by a hatred of mankind, *odium generis humani (Ab excessu Aug.,* xv., 44). And there have been many others who have shared his opinion. But where does religion end and superstition begin, or perhaps rather we should say at what point does superstition merge into religion? What is the criterion by means of which we discriminate between them?

It would be of little profit to recapitulate here, even summarily, the principal definitions, each bearing the impress of the personal feeling of its definer, which have been given of religion. Religion is better described than defined and better felt than described. But if there is any one definition that latterly has obtained acceptance, it is that of Schleiermacher, to the effect that religion consists in the simple feeling of a relationship of dependence upon something above us and a desire to establish relations with this mysterious power. Nor is there much amiss with the statement of W. Hermann[1] that the religious longing of man is a desire for truth concerning his human existence. And to cut short these extraneous citations, I will end with one from the judicious and perspicacious Cournot : " Religious manifestations are the necessary consequence of man's predisposition to believe in the existence of an invisible, supernatural and miraculous world, a predisposition which it has been possible to consider sometimes as a reminiscence of an anterior state, sometimes as an intimation of a future

---

[1] *Op. cit.*

destiny " (*Traité de l'enchaînement des idées fondamentales dans les sciences et dans l'histoire,* § 396). And
it is this problem of human destiny, of eternal life, or of
the human finality of the Universe or of God, that we
have now reached.    All the highways of religion lead up
to this, for it is the very essence of all religion.

Beginning with the savage's personalization of the
whole Universe in his fetich, religion has its roots in the
vital necessity of giving human finality to the Universe,
to God, and this necessity obliges it, therefore, to attribute
to the Universe, to God, consciousness of self and of
purpose.    And it may be said that religion is simply
union with God, each one interpreting God according to
his own sense of Him.    God gives transcendent meaning
and finality to life; but He gives it relatively to each one
of us who believe in Him.    And thus God is for man as
much as man is for God, for God in becoming man, in
becoming human, has given Himself to man because of
His love of him.

And this religious longing for union with God is a
longing for a union that cannot be consummated in
science or in art, but only in life.    " He who possesses
science and art, has religion; he who possesses neither
science nor art, let him get religion," said Goethe in one
of his frequent accesses of paganism.    And yet in spite
of what he said, he himself, Goethe . . . ?

And to wish that we may be united with God is not to
wish that we may be lost and submerged in Him, for this
loss and submersion of self ends at last in the complete
dissolution of self in the dreamless sleep of Nirvana; it is
to wish to possess Him rather than to be possessed by
Him.    When his disciples, amazed at his saying that it
was impossible for a rich man to enter into the kingdom
of heaven, asked Jesus who then could be saved, the
Master replied that with men it was impossible but not
with God; and then said Peter, " Behold, we have forsaken all and followed thee; what shall we have there-

fore?'' And the reply of Jesus was, not that they should be absorbed in the Father, but that they should sit upon twelve thrones, judging the twelve tribes of Israel (Matt. xix. 23-26).

It was a Spaniard, and very emphatically a Spaniard, Miguel de Molinos, who said in his *Guia Espiritual*[1] that " he who would attain to the mystical science must abandon and be detached from five things : first, from creatures; second, from temporal things; third, from the very gifts of the Holy Spirit; fourth, from himself; and fifth, he must be detached even from God.'' And he adds that " this last is the completest of all, because that soul only that knows how to be so detached is that which attains to being lost in God, and only the soul that attains to being so lost succeeds in finding itself.'' Emphatically a true Spaniard, Molinos, and truly Spanish is this paradoxical expression of quietism or rather of nihilism— for he himself elsewhere speaks of annihilation—and not less Spanish, nay, perhaps even more Spanish, were the Jesuits who attacked him, upholding the prerogatives of the All against the claims of Nothingness. For religion is not the longing for self-annihilation, but for self-completion, it is the longing not for death but for life. " The eternal religion of the inward essence of man . . . the individual dream of the heart, is the worship of his own being, the adoration of life,'' as the tortured soul of Flaubert was intimately aware (*Par les champs et par les grèves,* vii.).

When at the beginning of the so-called modern age, at the Renaissance, the pagan sense of religion came to life again, it took concrete form in the knightly ideal with its codes of love and honour. But it was a paganism Christianized, baptized. " Woman—*la donna*—was the divinity enshrined within those savage breasts. Who-

---

[1] *Guía Espiritual que desembaraza al alma y la conduce por el interior camino para alcanzar la perfecta contemplación y el rico tesoro de la paz interior,* book iii., chap. xviii., § 185.

soever will investigate the memorials of primitive times
will find this ideal of woman in its full force and purity;
the Universe is woman. And so it was in Germany, in
France, in Provence, in Spain, in Italy, at the beginning
of the modern age. History was cast in this mould;
Trojans and Romans were conceived as knights-errant,
and so too were Arabs, Saracens, Turks, the Sultan and
Saladin. . . . In this universal fraternity mingle
angels, saints, miracles and paradise, strangely blended
with the fantasy and voluptuousness of the Oriental
world, and all baptized in the name of Chivalry." Thus,
in his *Storia della Letteratura italiana*, ii., writes
Francesco de Sanctis, and in an earlier passage he informs
us that for that breed of men " in paradise itself the
lover's delight was to look upon his lady—*Madonna*—
and that he had no desire to go thither if he might not
go in his lady's company." What, in fact, was Chivalry
—which Cervantes, intending to kill it, afterwards purified and Christianized in *Don Quixote*—but a real though
distorted religion, a hybrid between paganism and
Christianity, whose gospel perhaps was the legend of
Tristan and Iseult? And did not even the Christianity
of the mystics—those knights-errant of the spirit—possibly reach its culminating-point in the worship of the
divine woman, the Virgin Mary? What else was the
Mariolatry of a St. Bonaventura, the troubadour of
Mary? And this sentiment found its inspiration in love
of the fountain of life, of that which saves us from death.

But as the Renaissance advanced men turned from the
religion of woman to the religion of science; desire, the
foundation of which was curiosity, ended in curiosity, in
eagerness to taste of the fruit of the tree of good and evil.
Europe flocked to the University of Bologna in search of
learning. Chivalry was succeeded by Platonism. Men
sought to discover the mystery of the world and of life.
But it was really in order to save life, which they had also
sought to save in the worship of woman. Human con-

sciousness sought to penetrate the Universal Consciousness, but its real object, whether it was aware of it or not, was to save itself.

For the truth is that we feel and imagine the Universal Consciousness—and in this feeling and imagination religious experience consists—simply in order that thereby we may save our own individual consciousnesses. And how?

Once again I must repeat that the longing for the immortality of the soul, for the permanence, in some form or another, of our personal and individual consciousness, is as much of the essence of religion as is the longing that there may be a God. The one does not exist apart from the other, the reason being that fundamentally they are one and the same thing. But as soon as we attempt to give a concrete and rational form to this longing for immortality and permanence, to define it to ourselves, we encounter even more difficulties than we encountered in our attempt to rationalize God.

The universal consent of mankind has again been invoked as a means of justifying this immortal longing for immortality to our own feeble reason. *Permanere animos arbitratur consensu nationum omnium*, said Cicero, echoing the opinion of the ancients (*Tuscul. Quæst.*, xvi., 36). But this same recorder of his own feelings confessed that, although when he read the arguments in favour of the immortality of the soul in the *Phædo* of Plato he was compelled to assent to them, as soon as he put the book aside and began to revolve the problem in his own mind, all his previous assent melted away, *assentio omnis illa illabitur* (cap. xi., 25). And what happened to Cicero happens to us all, and it happened likewise to Swedenborg, the most daring visionary of the other world. Swedenborg admitted that he who discourses of life after death, putting aside all erudite notions concerning the soul and its mode of union with the body, believes that after death he shall live in a glorious joy and vision, as a man among angels; but when he begins to reflect upon the doctrine of the union of the soul with the body, or upon the hypothetical opinion concerning the soul, doubts arise in him as to whether the soul is thus or otherwise, and when these doubts arise, his former idea is dissipated (*De cœlo et inferno*, § 183). Nevertheless, as Cournot says, "it is the destiny that awaits me, *me* or my *person*, that moves, perturbs and consoles me, that makes me capable of abnegation and sacrifice, whatever be the origin, the nature or the essence of this inexplicable bond of union, in the absence of which the philosophers are pleased to determine that my person must disappear" (*Traité*, etc., § 297).

Must we then embrace the pure and naked faith in an eternal life without trying to represent it to ourselves? This is impossible; it is beyond our power to bring ourselves or accustom ourselves to do so. And nevertheless there are some who call themselves Christians and yet leave almost altogether on one side this question of representation. Take any work of theology informed by the most enlightened—that is, the most rationalistic and liberal — Protestantism; take, for instance, the *Dogmatik* of Dr. Julius Kaftan, and of the 668 pages of which the sixth edition, that of 1909, consists, you will find only one, the last, that is devoted to this problem. And in this page, after affirming that Christ is not only the beginning and middle but also the end and consummation of History, and that those who are in Christ will attain to fullness of life, the eternal life of those who are in Christ, not a single word as to what that life may be. Half a dozen words at most about eternal death, that is, hell, "for its existence is demanded by the moral character of faith and of Christian hope." Its moral character, eh? not its religious character, for I am not aware that the latter knows any such exigency. And all this inspired by a prudent agnostic parsimony.

Yes, the prudent, the rational, and, some will say, the pious, attitude, is not to seek to penetrate into mysteries that are hidden from our knowledge, not to insist upon shaping a plastic representation of eternal glory, such as that of the *Divina Commedia*.  True faith, true Christian piety, we shall be told, consists in resting upon the confidence that God, by the grace of Christ, will, in some way or another, make us live in Him, in His Son; that, as our destiny is in His almighty hands, we should surrender ourselves to Him, in the full assurance that He will do with us what is best for the ultimate end of life, of spirit and of the universe.  Such is the teaching that has traversed many centuries, and was notably prominent in the period between Luther and Kant.

And nevertheless men have not ceased endeavouring to imagine to themselves what this eternal life may be, nor will they cease their endeavours so long as they are men and not merely thinking machines.  There are books of theology—or of what passes for theology—full of disquisitions upon the conditions under which the blessed dead live in paradise, upon their mode of enjoyment, upon the properties of the glorious body, for without some form of body the soul cannot be conceived.

And to this same necessity, the real necessity of forming to ourselves a concrete representation of what this other life may be, must in great part be referred the indestructible vitality of doctrines such as those of spiritualism, metempsychosis, the transmigration of souls from star to star, and the like; doctrines which as often as they are pronounced to be defeated and dead, are found to have come to life again, clothed in some more or less new form.  And it is merely supine to be content to ignore them and not to seek to discover their permanent and living essence.  Man will never willingly abandon his attempt to form a concrete representation of the other life.

But is an eternal and endless life after death indeed

thinkable? How can we conceive the life of a disembodied spirit? How can we conceive such a spirit? How can we conceive a pure consciousness, without a corporal organism? Descartes divided the world into thought and extension, a dualism which was imposed upon him by the Christian dogma of the immortality of the soul. But is extension, is matter, that which thinks and is spiritualized, or is thought that which is extended and materialized? The weightiest questions of metaphysics arise practically out of our desire to arrive at an understanding of the possibility of our immortality—from this fact they derive their value and cease to be merely the idle discussions of fruitless curiosity. For the truth is that metaphysics has no value save in so far as it attempts to explain in what way our vital longing can or cannot be realized. And thus it is that there is and always will be a rational metaphysic and a vital metaphysic, in perennial conflict with one another, the one setting out from the notion of cause, the other from the notion of substance.

And even if we were to succeed in imagining personal immortality, might we not possibly feel it to be something no less terrible than its negation? "Calypso was inconsolable at the departure of Ulysses; in her sorrow she was dismayed at being immortal," said the gentle, the mystical Fénelon at the beginning of his *Télémaque*. Was it not a kind of doom that the ancient gods, no less than the demons, were subject to—the deprivation of the power to commit suicide?

When Jesus took Peter and James and John up into a high mountain and was transfigured before them, his raiment shining as white as snow, and Moses and Elias appeared and talked with him, Peter said to the Master: "Master, it is good for us to be here; and let us make three tabernacles; one for thee and one for Moses and one for Elias," for he wished to eternalize that moment. And as they came down from the mountain, Jesus charged

them that they should tell no man what they had seen
until the Son of Man should have risen from the dead.
And they, keeping this saying to themselves, questioned
one with another what this rising from the dead should
mean, as men not understanding the purport of it.   And
it was after this that Jesus met the father whose son was
possessed with a dumb spirit and who cried out to him,
" Lord, I believe; help thou mine unbelief " (Mark ix.).

Those three apostles did not understand what this
rising from the dead meant. Neither did those Sadducees
who asked the Master whose wife she should be in the
resurrection who in this life had had seven husbands
(Matt. xxii.); and it was then that Jesus said that God is
not the God of the dead, but of the living.   And the
other life is not, in fact, thinkable to us except under the
same forms as those of this earthly and transitory life.
Nor is the mystery at all clarified by that metaphor of the
grain and the wheat that it bears, with which Paul
answers the question, "How are the dead raised up,
and with what body do they come?" (1 Cor. xv. 35).

How can a human soul live and enjoy God eternally
without losing its individual personality—that is to say,
without losing itself?   What is it to enjoy God?   What
is eternity as opposed to time?   Does the soul change or
does it not change in the other life?   If it does not
change, how does it live?   And if it changes, how does
it preserve its individuality through so vast a period of
time?   For though the other life may exclude space, it
cannot exclude time, as Cournot observes in the work
quoted above.

If there is life in heaven there is change.   Swedenborg
remarked that the angels change, because the delight of
the celestial life would gradually lose its value if they
always enjoyed it in its fullness, and because angels, like
men, love themselves, and he who loves himself experi-
ences changes of state; and he adds further that at times
the angels are sad, and that he, Swedenborg, discoursed

15

with some when they were sad (*De Cœlo et Inferno*, §§ 158, 160). In any case, it is impossible for us to conceive life without change, change of growth or of diminution, of sadness or of joy, of love or of hate.

In effect, an eternal life is unthinkable and an eternal life of absolute felicity, of beatific vision, is more unthinkable still.

And what precisely is this beatific vision? We observe in the first place that it is called vision and not action, something passive being therefore presupposed. And does not this beatific vision suppose loss of personal consciousness? A saint in heaven, says Bossuet, is a being who is scarcely sensible of himself, so completely is he possessed by God and immerged in His glory. . . . Our attention cannot stay on the saint, because one finds him outside of himself, and subject by an unchangeable love to the source of his being and his happiness (*Du culte qui est dû à Dieu*). And these are the words of Bossuet, the antiquietist. This loving vision of God supposes an absorption in Him. He who in a state of blessedness enjoys God in His fullness must perforce neither think of himself, nor remember himself, nor have any consciousness of himself, but be in perpetual ecstasy (ἔκστασις) outside of himself, in a condition of alienation. And the ecstasy that the mystics describe is a prelude of this vision.

He who sees God shall die, say the Scriptures (Judg. xiii. 22); and may it not be that the eternal vision of God is an eternal death, a swooning away of the personality? But St. Teresa, in her description of the last state of prayer, the rapture, transport, flight, or ecstasy of the soul, tells us that the soul is borne as upon a cloud or a mighty eagle, "but you see yourself carried away and know not whither," and it is "with delight," and "if you do not resist, the senses are not lost, at least I was so much myself as to be able to perceive that I was being lifted up"—that is to say, without

losing consciousness.  And God " appears to be not content with thus attracting the soul to Himself in so real a
way, but wishes to have the body also, though it be
mortal and of earth so foul."  " Ofttimes the soul is
absorbed—or, to speak more correctly, the Lord absorbs
it in Himself; and when He has held it thus for a
moment, the will alone remains in union with Him "—
not the intelligence alone.  We see, therefore, that it is
not so much vision as a union of the will, and meanwhile,
" the understanding and memory are distraught . . .
like one who has slept long and dreamed and is hardly
yet awake."  It is " a soft flight, a delicious flight, a
noiseless flight."  And in this delicious flight the consciousness of self is preserved, the awareness of distinction from God with whom one is united.  And one is
raised to this rapture, according to the Spanish mystic,
by the contemplation of the Humanity of Christ—that is
to say, of something concrete and human ; it is the vision
of the living God, not of the idea of God.  And in the
28th chapter she tells us that " though there were nothing
else to delight the sight in heaven but the great beauty
of the glorified bodies, that would be an excessive bliss,
particularly the vision of the Humanity of Jesus Christ
our  Lord. . . ."  " This  vision,"  she  continues,
" though imaginary, I did never see with my bodily eyes,
nor, indeed, any other, but only with the eyes of the
soul."  And thus it is that in heaven the soul does not
see God only, but everything in God, or rather it sees
that everything is God, for God embraces all things.
And this idea is further emphasized by Jacob Böhme.
The saint tells us in the *Moradas Setimas* (vii. 2) that
" this secret union takes place in the innermost centre of
the soul, where God Himself must dwell."  And she
goes on to say that " the soul, I mean the spirit of the
soul, is made one with God . . ."; and this union may
be likened to " two wax candles, the tips of which touch
each other so closely that there is but one light ; or again,

the wick, the wax, and the light become one, but the one candle can again be separated from the other, and the two candles remain distinct; or the wick may be withdrawn from the wax." But there is another more intimate union, and this is "like rain falling from heaven into a river or stream, becoming one and the same liquid, so that the river and the rain-water cannot be divided; or it resembles a streamlet flowing into the sea, which cannot afterwards be disunited from it; or it may be likened to a room into which a bright light enters through two windows—though divided when it enters, the light becomes one and the same." And what difference is there between this and the internal and mystical silence of Miguel de Molinos, the third and most perfect degree of which is the silence of thought? (*Guía Espiritual,* book i., chap. xvii., § 128). Do we not here very closely approach the view that "nothingness is the way to attain to that high state of a mind reformed"? (book iii., chap. xx., § 196). And what marvel is it that Amiel in his *Journal Intime* should twice have made use of the Spanish word *nada*, nothing, doubtless because he found none more expressive in any other language? And nevertheless, if we read our mystical doctor, St. Teresa, with care, we shall see that the sensitive element is never excluded, the element of delight—that is to say, the element of personal consciousness. The soul allows itself to be absorbed in God in order that it may absorb Him, in order that it may acquire consciousness of its own divinity.

A beatific vision, a loving contemplation in which the soul is absorbed in God and, as it were, lost in Him, appears either as an annihilation of self or as a prolonged tedium to our natural way of feeling. And hence a certain feeling which we not infrequently observe and which has more than once expressed itself in satires, not altogether free from irreverence or perhaps impiety, with reference to the heaven of eternal glory as a place of eternal boredom. And it is useless to despise feelings such as these, so wholly natural and spontaneous.

It is clear that those who feel thus have failed to take note of the fact that man's highest pleasure consists in acquiring and intensifying consciousness. Not the pleasure of knowing, exactly, but rather that of learning. In knowing a thing we tend to forget it, to convert it, if the expression may be allowed, into unconscious knowledge. Man's pleasure, his purest delight, is allied with the act of learning, of getting at the truth of things, of acquiring knowledge with differentiation. And hence the famous saying of Lessing which I have already quoted. There is a story told of an ancient Spaniard who accompanied Vasco Núñez de Balboa when he climbed that peak in Darien from which both the Atlantic and the Pacific are visible. On beholding the two oceans the old man fell on his knees and exclaimed, " I thank Thee, God, that Thou didst not let me die without having seen so great a wonder." But if this man had stayed there, very soon the wonder would have ceased to be wonderful, and with the wonder the pleasure, too, would have vanished. His joy was the joy of discovery. And perhaps the joy of the beatific vision may be not exactly that of the contemplation of the supreme Truth, whole and entire (for this the soul could not endure), but rather that of a continual discovery of the Truth, of a ceaseless act of learning involving an effort which keeps the sense of personal consciousness continually active.

It is difficult for us to conceive a beatific vision of mental quiet, of full knowledge and not of gradual apprehension, as in any way different from a kind of Nirvana, a spiritual diffusion, a dissipation of energy in the essence of God, a return to unconsciousness induced by the absence of shock, of difference—in a word, of activity.

May it not be that the very condition which makes our eternal union with God thinkable destroys our longing? What difference is there between being absorbed by God and absorbing Him in ourself? Is it the stream that is lost in the sea or the sea that is lost in the stream? It is all the same.

Our fundamental feeling is our longing not to lose the sense of the continuity of our consciousness, not to break the concatenation of our memories, the feeling of our own personal concrete identity, even though we may be gradually being absorbed in God, enriching Him. Who at eighty years of age remembers the child that he was at eight, conscious though he may be of the unbroken chain connecting the two? And it may be said that the problem for feeling resolves itself into the question as to whether there is a God, whether there is a human finality to the Universe. But what is finality? For just as it is always possible to ask the why of every why, so it is also always possible to ask the wherefore of every wherefore. Supposing that there is a God, then wherefore God? For Himself, it will be said. And someone is sure to reply : What is the difference between this consciousness and no-consciousness? But it will always be true, as Plotinus has said (*Enn.*, ii., ix., 8), that to ask why God made the world is the same as to ask why there is a soul. Or rather, not why, but wherefore (διά τι).

For him who places himself outside himself, in an objective hypothetical position—which is as much as to say in an inhuman position—the ultimate wherefore is as inaccessible—and strictly, as absurd—as the ultimate why. What difference in effect does it make if there is not any finality? What logical contradiction is involved in the Universe not being destined to any finality, either human or superhuman? What objection is there in reason to there being no other purpose in the sum of things save only to exist and happen as it does exist and happen? For him who places himself outside himself, none; but for him who lives and suffers and desires within himself—for him it is a question of life or death.

Seek, therefore, thyself! But in finding oneself, does not one find one's own nothingness? "Having become a sinner in seeking himself, man has become wretched in finding himself," said Bossuet (*Traité de la Concupiscence*, chap. xi.). "Seek thyself" begins with "Know thyself." To which Carlyle answers (*Past and Present*, book iii., chap xi.): "The latest Gospel in this world is, Know thy work and do it. 'Know thyself': long enough has that poor 'self' of thine tormented thee; thou wilt never get to 'know' it, I believe! Think it not thy business, this of knowing thyself; thou art an unknowable individual: know what thou canst work at; and work at it, like a Hercules. That will be thy better plan."

Yes, but what I work at, will not that too be lost in the end? And if it be lost, wherefore should I work at it? Yes, yes, it may be that to accomplish my work—and what is my work?—without thinking about myself, is to love God. And what is it to love God?

And on the other hand, in loving God in myself, am I not loving myself more than God, am I not loving myself in God?

What we really long for after death is to go on living this life, this same mortal life, but without its ills, without its tedium, and without death. Seneca, the Spaniard, gave expression to this in his *Consolatio ad Marciam* (xxvi.); what he desired was to live this life again: *ista moliri*. And what Job asked for (xix. 25-7) was to see God in the flesh, not in the spirit. And what but that is the meaning of that comic conception of *eternal recurrence* which issued from the tragic soul of poor Nietzsche, hungering for concrete and temporal immortality?

And this beatific vision which is the primary Catholic solution of the problem, how can it be realized, I ask again, without obliteration of the consciousness of self?

Will it not be like a sleep in which we dream without knowing what we dream? Who would wish for an eternal life like that? To think without knowing that we think is not to be sensible of ourselves, it is not to be ourselves. And is not eternal life perhaps eternal consciousness, not only seeing God, but seeing that we see Him, seeing ourselves at the same time and ourselves as distinct from Him? He who sleeps lives, but he has no consciousness of himself; and would anyone wish for an eternal sleep? When Circe advised Ulysses to descend to the abode of the dead in order to consult the soothsayer Teiresias, she told him that Teiresias alone among the shades of the dead was possessed of understanding, for all the others flitted about like shadows (*Odyssey*, x., 487-495). And can it be said that the others, apart from Teiresias, had really overcome death? Is it to overcome death to flit about like shadows without understanding?

And on the other hand, may we not imagine that possibly this earthly life of ours is to the other life what sleep is to waking? May not all our life be a dream and death an awakening? But an awakening to what? And supposing that everything is but the dream of God and that God one day will awaken? Will He remember His dream?

Aristotle, the rationalist, tells in his *Ethics* of the superior happiness of the contemplative life, βίος θεωρητικός; and all rationalists are wont to place happiness in knowledge. And the conception of eternal happiness, of the enjoyment of God, as a beatific vision, as knowledge and comprehension of God, is a thing of rationalist origin, it is the kind of happiness that corresponds with the God-Idea of Aristotelianism. But the truth is that, in addition to vision, happiness demands delight, and this is a thing which has very little to do with rationalism and is only attainable when we feel ourselves distinct from God.

Our Aristotelian Catholic theologian, the author of the endeavour to rationalize Catholic feeling, St. Thomas Aquinas, tells us in his *Summa* (*prima secundæ partis, quæstio* iv., *art.* 1) that "delight is requisite for happiness. For delight is caused by the fact of desire resting in attained good. Hence, since happiness is nothing but the attainment of the Sovereign Good, there cannot be happiness without concomitant delight." But where is the delight of him who rests? To rest, *requiescere*— is not that to sleep and not to possess even the consciousness that one is resting? "Delight is caused by the vision of God itself," the theologian continues. But does the soul feel itself distinct from God? "The delight that accompanies the activity of the understanding does not impede, but rather strengthens that activity," he says later on. Obviously! for what happiness were it else? And in order to save delectation, delight, pleasure, which, like pain, has always something material in it, and which we conceive of only as existing in a soul incarnate in a body, it was necessary to suppose that the soul in a state of blessedness is united with its body. Apart from some kind of body, how is delight possible? The immortality of the pure soul, without some sort of body or spirit-covering, is not true immortality. And at bottom, what we long for is a prolongation of this life, this life and no other, this life of flesh and suffering, this life which we imprecate at times simply because it comes to an end. The majority of suicides would not take their lives if they had the assurance that they would never die on this earth. The self-slayer kills himself because he will not wait for death.

When in the thirty-third canto of the *Paradiso*, Dante relates how he attained to the vision of God, he tells us that just as a man who beholds somewhat in his sleep retains on awakening nothing but the impression of the feeling in his mind, so it was with him, for when the

vision had all but passed away the sweetness that sprang
from it still distilled itself in his heart.

> *Cotal son io, che quasi tutta cessa*
> *mia visione ed ancor mi distilla*
> *nel cuor lo dulce che nacque da essa*

like snow that melts in the sun—

> *cosi la neve al sol si disigilla.*

That is to say, that the vision, the intellectual content,
passes, and that which remains is the delight, the *pas-
sione impressa,* the emotional, the irrational—in a word,
the corporeal.

What we desire is not merely spiritual felicity, not
merely vision, but delight, bodily happiness. The
other happiness, the rationalist *beatitude,* the happiness
of being submerged in understanding, can only—
I will not say satisfy or deceive, for I do not believe that
it ever satisfied or deceived even a Spinoza. At the conclusion of his *Ethic,* in propositions xxxv. and xxxvi. of
the fifth part, Spinoza affirms that God loves Himself
with an infinite intellectual love; that the intellectual
love of the mind towards God is the selfsame love with
which God loves Himself, not in so far as He is infinite,
but in so far as He can be manifested through the
essence of the human mind, considered under the form
of eternity—that is to say, that the intellectual love of
the mind towards God is part of the infinite love with
which God loves Himself. And after these tragic, these
desolating propositions, we are told in the last proposition of the whole book, that which closes and crowns
this tremendous tragedy of the *Ethic,* that happiness is
not the reward of virtue, but virtue itself, and that our
repression of our desires is not the cause of our enjoyment of virtue, but rather because we find enjoyment in
virtue we are able to repress our desires. Intellectual
love! intellectual love! what is this intellectual love?
Something of the nature of a red flavour, or a bitter

sound, or an aromatic colour, or rather something of
the same sort as a love-stricken triangle or an enraged
ellipse—a pure metaphor, but a tragic metaphor.   And
a metaphor corresponding tragically with that saying
that the heart also has its reasons.   Reasons of the
heart! loves of the head! intellectual delight! delicious
intellection!—tragedy, tragedy, tragedy!

And nevertheless there is something which may be
called intellectual love, and that is the love of understanding, that which Aristotle meant by the contemplative life, for there is something of action and of love
in the act of understanding, and the beatific vision is the
vision of the total truth.   Is there not perhaps at the
root of every passion something of curiosity?   Did not
our first parents, according to the Biblical story, fall
because of their eagerness to taste of the fruit of the tree
of the knowledge of good and evil, and to be as gods,
knowers of this knowledge?   The vision of God—that
is to say, the vision of the Universe itself, in its soul, in
its inmost essence—would not that appease all our longing?   And this vision can fail to satisfy only men of a
gross mind who do not perceive that the greatest joy of
man is to be more man—that is, more God—and that
man is more God the more consciousness he has.

And this intellectual love, which is nothing but the
so-called platonic love, is a means to dominion and
possession.   There is, in fact, no more perfect dominion
than knowledge; he who knows something, possesses
it.   Knowledge unites the knower with the known.   " I
contemplate thee and in contemplating thee I make thee
mine "—such is the formula.   And to know God, what
can that be but to possess Him?   He who knows God
is thereby himself God.

In *La Dégradation de l'énergie* (ive partie,
chap. xviii., 2) B. Brunhes relates a story concerning
the great Catholic mathematician Cauchy, communicated
to him by M. Sarrau, who had it from Père Gratry.

While Cauchy and Père Gratry were walking in the
gardens of the Luxembourg, their conversation turned
upon the happiness which those in heaven would have
in knowing at last, without any obscurity or limitation,
the truths which they had so long and so laboriously
sought to investigate on earth.  In allusion to the study
which Cauchy had made of the mechanistic theory of
the reflection of light, Père Gratry threw out the suggestion that one of the greatest intellectual joys of the
great geometrician in the future life would be to penetrate into the secret of light.  To which Cauchy replied
that it did not appear to him to be possible to know more
about this than he himself already knew, neither could
he conceive how the most perfect intelligence could
arrive at a clearer comprehension of the mystery of
reflection than that manifested in his own explanation
of it, seeing that he had furnished a mechanistic theory
of the phenomenon.  " His piety," Brunhes adds, " did
not extend to a belief that God Himself could have
created anything different or anything better."

From this narrative two points of interest emerge.
The first is the idea expressed in it as to what contemplation, intellectual love, or beatific vision, may mean
for men of a superior order of intelligence, men whose
ruling passion is knowledge; and the second is the
implicit faith shown in the mechanistic explanation of
the world.

This mechanistic tendency of the intellect coheres with
the well-known formula, " Nothing is created, nothing
is lost, everything is transformed "—a formula by
means of which it has been sought to interpret the
ambiguous principle of the conservation of energy, forgetting that practically, for us, for men, energy is
utilizable energy, and that this is continually being lost,
dissipated by the diffusion of heat, and degraded, its
tendency being to arrive at a dead-level and homogeneity.  That which has value, and more than value,

reality, for us, is the differential, which is the qualitative; pure, undifferentiated quantity is for us as if it did not exist, for it does not act. And the material Universe, the body of the Universe, would appear to be gradually proceeding—unaffected by the retarding action of living organisms or even by the conscious action of man—towards a state of perfect stability, of homogeneity (*vide* Brunhes, *op. cit.*). For, while spirit tends towards concentration, material energy tends towards diffusion.

And may not this have an intimate relation with our problem? May there not be a connection between this conclusion of scientific philosophy with respect to a final state of stability and homogeneity and the mystical dream of the apocatastasis? May not this death of the body of the Universe be the final triumph of its spirit, of God?

It is manifest that there is an intimate relation between the religious need of an eternal life after death and the conclusions—always provisional—at which scientific philosophy arrives with respect to the probable future of the material or sensible Universe. And the fact is that just as there are theologians of God and the immortality of the soul, so there are also those whom Brunhes calls (*op. cit.*, chap. xxvi., § 2) theologians of monism, and whom it would perhaps be better to call atheologians, people who pertinaciously adhere to the spirit of *a priori* affirmation; and this becomes intolerable, Brunhes adds, when they harbour the pretension of despising theology. A notable type of these gentlemen may be found in Haeckel, who has succeeded in solving the riddles of Nature!

These atheologians have seized upon the principle of the conservation of energy, the "Nothing is created, nothing is lost, everything is transformed" formula, the theological origin of which is seen in Descartes, and have made use of it as a means whereby we are able to

dispense with God. " The world built to last," Brunhes
comments, " resisting all wear and tear, or rather auto-
matically repairing the rents that appear in it—what a
splendid theme for oratorical amplification ! But these
same amplifications which served in the seventeenth
century to prove the wisdom of the Creator have been
used in our days as arguments for those who presume to
do without Him." It is the old story : so-called
scientific philosophy, the origin and inspiration of which
is fundamentally theological or religious, ending in an
atheology or irreligion, which is itself nothing else but
theology and religion. Let us call to mind the comments
of Ritschl upon this head, already quoted in this work.

To-day the last word of science, or rather of scientific
philosophy, appears to be that, by virtue of the degradation of energy, of the predominance of irreversible
phenomena, the material, sensible world is travelling
towards a condition of ultimate levelness, a kind of final
homogeneity. And this brings to our mind the
hypothesis, not only so much used but abused by
Spencer, of a primordial homogeneity, and his fantastic theory of the instability of the homogeneous. An
instability that required the atheological agnosticism of
Spencer in order to explain the inexplicable transition
from the homogeneous to the heterogeneous. For how,
without any action from without, can any heterogeneity
emerge from perfect and absolute homogeneity ? But
as it was necessary to get rid of every kind of creation,
" the unemployed engineer turned metaphysician," as
Papini called him, invented the theory of the instability
of the homogeneous, which is more . . . what shall I
say ? more mystical, and even more mythological if you
like, than the creative action of God.

The Italian positivist, Roberto Ardigo, was nearer
the mark when, objecting to Spencer's theory, he said
that the most natural supposition was that things always
were as they are now, that always there have been

worlds in process of formation, in the nebulous stage, worlds completely formed and worlds in process of dissolution; that heterogeneity, in short, is eternal. Another way, it will be seen, of not solving the riddle.

Is this perhaps the solution? But in that case the Universe would be infinite, and in reality we are unable to conceive a Universe that is both eternal and limited such as that which served as the basis of Nietzsche's theory of eternal recurrence. If the Universe must be eternal, if within it and as regards each of its component worlds, periods in which the movement is towards homogeneity, towards the degradation of energy, must alternate with other periods in which the movement is towards heterogeneity, then it is necessary that the Universe should be infinite, that there should be scope, always and in each world, for some action coming from without. And, in fact, the body of God cannot be other than eternal and infinite.

But as far as our own world is concerned, its gradual levelling-down—or, we might say, its death—appears to be proved. And how will this process affect the fate of our spirit? Will it wane with the degradation of the energy of our world and return to unconsciousness, or will it rather grow according as the utilizable energy diminishes and by virtue of the very efforts that it makes to retard this degradation and to dominate Nature?—for this it is that constitutes the life of the spirit. May it be that consciousness and its extended support are two powers in contraposition, the one growing at the expense of the other?

The fact is that the best of our scientific work, the best of our industry (that part of it I mean—and it is a large part—that does not tend to destruction), is directed towards retarding this fatal process of the degradation of energy. And organic life, the support of our consciousness, is itself an effort to avoid, so far as it is possible, this fatal period, to postpone it.

It is useless to seek to deceive ourselves with pagan pæans in praise of Nature, for as Leopardi, that Christian atheist, said with profound truth in his stupendous poem *La Ginestra,* Nature " gives us life like a mother, but loves us like a step-mother." The origin of human companionship was opposition to Nature; it was horror of impious Nature that first linked men together in the bonds of society. It is human society, in effect, the source of reflective consciousness and of the craving for immortality, that inaugurates the state of grace upon the state of Nature; and it is man who, by humanizing and spiritualizing Nature by his industry, supernaturalizes her.

In two amazing sonnets which he called *Redemption,* the tragic Portuguese poet, Antero de Quental, embodied his dream of a spirit imprisoned, not in atoms or ions or crystals, but—as is natural in a poet—in the sea, in trees, in the forest, in the mountains, in the wind, in all material individualities and forms; and he imagines that a day may come when all these captive souls, as yet in the limbo of existence, will awaken to consciousness, and, emerging as pure thought from the forms that imprisoned them, they will see these forms, the creatures of illusion, fall away and dissolve like a baseless vision. It is a magnificent dream of the penetration of everything by consciousness.

May it not be that the Universe, our Universe—who knows if there are others?—began with a zero of spirit —and zero is not the same as nothing—and an infinite of matter, and that its goal is to end with an infinite of spirit and a zero of matter? Dreams!

May it be that everything has a soul and that this soul begs to be freed?

> *Oh tierras de Alvargonzález,*
> *en el corazón de España,*
> *tierras pobres, tierras tristes,*
> *tan tristes que tienen alma!*

sings our poet Antonio Machado in his *Campos de Castilla.*[1] Is the sadness of the field in the fields themselves or in us who look upon them? Do they not suffer? But what can an individual soul in a world of matter actually be? Is it the rock or the mountain that is the individual? Is it the tree?

And nevertheless the fact always remains that spirit and matter are at strife. This is the thought that Espronceda expressed when he wrote:

> *Aquí, para vivir en santa calma,*
> *o sobra la materia, o sobra el alma.*[2]

And is there not in the history of thought, or of human imagination if you prefer it, something that corresponds to this process of the reduction of matter, in the sense of a reduction of everything to consciousness?

Yes, there is, and its author is the first Christian mystic, St. Paul of Tarsus, the Apostle of the Gentiles, he who because he had never with his bodily eyes looked upon the face of the fleshly and mortal Christ, the ethical Christ, created within himself an immortal and religious Christ—he who was caught up into the third heaven and there beheld secret and unspeakable things (2 Cor. xii.). And this first Christian mystic dreamed also of a final triumph of spirit, of consciousness, and this is what in theology is technically called the apocatastasis or restitution.

In 1 Cor. xv. 26-28 he tells us that " the last enemy that shall be destroyed is death, for he hath put all things under his feet. But when he saith all things are put under him, it is manifest that he is excepted, which did put all things under him. And when all things shall be subdued unto him, then shall the Son also himself be

---

[1] O land of Alvargonzález,
In the heart of Spain,
Sad land, poor land,
So sad that it has a soul !

[2] To living a life of blessed quiet here on earth,
Either matter or soul is a hindrance

subject unto him that put all things under him, that God
may be all in all '' : ἵνα ᾖ ὁ θεὸς πάντα ἐν πᾶσιν—that is to
say, that the end is that God, Consciousness, will end by
being all in all.

This doctrine is completed by Paul's teaching, in his
Epistle to the Ephesians, with regard to the end of the
whole history of the world.  In this Epistle, as you
know, he represents Christ—by whom " were all things
created, that are in heaven and that are in earth, visible
and invisible " (Col. i. 16)—as the head over all things
(Eph. i. 22), and in him, in this head, we all shall be
raised up that we may live in the communion of saints
and that we " may be able to comprehend with all saints
what is the breadth, and length, and depth, and height,
and to know the love of Christ, which passeth knowledge " (Eph. iii. 18, 19).  And this gathering of us
together in Christ, who is the head and, as it were, the
compendium, of Humanity, is what the Apostle calls the
gathering or collecting together or recapitulating of all
things in Christ, ἀνακεφαλαιώσασθαι τὰ πάντα ἐν Χριστῷ.
And this recapitulation—ἀνακεφαλαίωσις, anacefaleosis—
the end of the world's history and of the human race, is
merely another aspect of the apocatastasis.  The apocatastasis, God's coming to be all in all, thus resolves itself
into the anacefaleosis, the gathering together of all things
in Christ, in Humanity—Humanity therefore being the
end of creation.  And does not this apocatastasis, this
humanization or divinization of all things, do away with
matter?  But if matter, which is the principle of indi-
viduation, the scholastic *principium individuationis*, is
once done away with, does not everything return to pure
consciousness, which, in its pure purity, neither knows
itself nor is it anything that can be conceived or felt?
And if matter be abolished, what support is there left for
spirit?

Thus a different train of thought leads us to the same
difficulties, the same unthinkabilities.

It may be said, on the other hand, that the apocatastasis, God's coming to be all in all, presupposes that there was a time when He was not all in all. The supposition that all beings shall attain to the enjoyment of God implies the supposition that God shall attain to the enjoyment of all beings, for the beatific vision is mutual, and God is perfected in being better known, and His being is nourished and enriched with souls.

Following up the track of these wild dreams, we might imagine an unconscious God, slumbering in matter, and gradually wakening into consciousness of everything, consciousness of His own divinity; we might imagine the whole Universe becoming conscious of itself as a whole and becoming conscious of each of its constituent consciousnesses, becoming God. But in that case, how did this unconscious God begin? Is He not matter itself? God would thus be not the beginning but the end of the Universe; but can that be the end which was not the beginning? Or can it be that outside time, in eternity, there is a difference between beginning and end? "The soul of all things cannot be bound by that very thing— that is, matter—which it itself has bound," says Plotinus (*Enn*. ii., ix. 7). Or is it not rather the Consciousness of the Whole that strives to become the consciousness of each part and to make each partial consciousness conscious of itself—that is, of the total consciousness? Is not this universal soul a monotheist or solitary God who is in process of becoming a pantheist God? And if it is not so, if matter and pain are alien to God, wherefore, it will be asked, did God create the world? For what purpose did He make matter and introduce pain? Would it not have been better if He had not made anything? What added glory does He gain by the creation of angels or of men whose fall He must punish with eternal torment? Did He perhaps create evil for the sake of remedying it? Or was redemption His design, redemption complete and absolute, redemption of all things and of all men ? For this hypothesis is neither more rational nor more pious than the other.

In so far as we attempt to represent eternal happiness to ourselves, we are confronted by a series of questions to which there is no satisfactory—that is, rational—answer, and it matters not whether the supposition from which we start be monotheist, or pantheist, or even panentheist.

Let us return to the Pauline apocatastasis.

Is it not possible that in becoming all in all God completes Himself, becomes at last fully God, an infinite consciousness embracing all consciousnesses ? And what is an infinite consciousness ? Since consciousness supposes limitation, or rather since consciousness is consciousness of limitation, of distinction, does it not thereby exclude infinitude ? What value has the notion of infinitude applied to consciousness ? What is a consciousness that is all consciousness, without anything outside it that is not consciousness ? In such a case, of what is consciousness the consciousness ? Of its content ? Or may it not rather be that, starting from chaos, from absolute unconsciousness, in the eternity of the past, we continually approach the apocatastasis or final apotheosis without ever reaching it ?

May not this apocatastasis, this return of all things to God, be rather an ideal term to which we unceasingly approach—some of us with fleeter step than others—but which we are destined never to reach ? May not the absolute and perfect eternal happiness be an eternal hope, which would die if it were to be realized ? Is it possible to be happy without hope ? And there is no place for hope when once possession has been realized, for hope, desire, is killed by possession. May it not be, I say, that all souls grow without ceasing, some in a greater measure than others, but all having to pass some time through the same degree of growth, whatever that degree may be, and yet without ever arriving at the infinite, at God, to whom they continually approach ? Is not eternal

happiness an eternal hope, with its eternal nucleus of
sorrow in order that happiness shall not be swallowed up
in nothingness?

Follow more questions to which there is no answer.
" He shall be all in all," says the Apostle.   But will His
mode of being in each one be different or will it be the
same for all alike?   Will not God be wholly in one of the
damned?   Is He not in his soul?   Is He not in what is
called hell?   And in what sense is He in hell?

Whence arise new problems, those relating to the
opposition between heaven and hell, between eternal
happiness and eternal unhappiness.

May it not be that in the end all shall be saved, including Cain and Judas and Satan himself, as Origen's development of the Pauline apocatastasis led him to hope?

When our Catholic theologians seek to justify rationally—or in other words, ethically—the dogma of the
eternity of the pains of hell, they put forward reasons so
specious, ridiculous, and childish, that it would appear
impossible that they should ever have obtained currency.
For to assert that since God is infinite, an offence com-
mitted against Him is infinite also and therefore demands
an eternal punishment, is, apart from the inconceivability
of an infinite offence, to be unaware that, in human ethics,
if not in the human police system, the gravity of the
offence is measured not by the dignity of the injured
person but by the intention of the injurer, and that to
speak of an infinite culpable intention is sheer nonsense,
and nothing else.   In this connection those words which
Christ addressed to His Father are capable of application: " Father, forgive them, for they know not what
they do," and no man who commits an offence against
God or his neighbour knows what he does.   In human
ethics, or if you like in human police regulations—that
which is called penal law and is anything but law[1]
eternal punishment is a meaningless phrase.

[1] Eso que llaman derecho penal, y que es todo menos derecho.

" God is just and punishes us; that is all we need to
know; as far as we are concerned the rest is merely
curiosity." Such was the conclusion of Lamennais
(*Essai,* etc., iv^e partie, chap. vii.), an opinion shared by
many others. Calvin also held the same view. But is
there anyone who is content with this ? Pure curiosity !
—to call this load that wellnigh crushes our heart pure
curiosity !

May we not say, perhaps, that the evil man is
annihilated because he wished to be annihilated, or that
he did not wish strongly enough to eternalize himself
because he was evil ? May we not say that it is not
believing in the other life that makes a man good, but
rather that being good makes him believe in it ? And
what is being good and being evil ? These states pertain to the sphere of ethics, not of religion : or, rather,
does not the doing good though being evil pertain to
ethics, and the being good though doing evil to religion ?

Shall we not perhaps be told, on the other hand, that
if the sinner suffers an eternal punishment, it is because
he does not cease to sin ?—for the damned sin without
ceasing. This, however, is no solution of the problem,
which derives all its absurdity from the fact that punishment has been conceived as vindictiveness or vengeance,
not as correction, has been conceived after the fashion of
barbarous peoples. And in the same way hell has been
conceived as a sort of police institution, necessary in
order to put fear into the world. And the worst of it is
that it no longer intimidates, and therefore will have to
be shut up.

But, on the other hand, as a religious conception and
veiled in mystery, why not—although the idea revolts our
feelings—an eternity of suffering ? why not a God who is
nourished by our suffering ? Is our happiness the end of
the Universe ? or may we possibly sustain with our suffering some alien happiness ? Let us read again in the
*Eumenides* of that terrible tragedian, Æschylus, those

choruses of the Furies in which they curse the new gods
for overturning the ancient laws and snatching Orestes
from their hands—impassioned invectives against the
Apollinian redemption.    Does not redemption tear man,
their captive and plaything, from the hands of the gods,
who delight and amuse themselves in his sufferings, like
children, as the tragic poet says, torturing beetles?    And
let us remember the cry, "My God, my God, why hast
thou forsaken me?"

Yes, why not an eternity of suffering?    Hell is an
eternalization of the soul, even though it be an eternity
of pain.    Is not pain essential to life?

Men go on inventing theories to explain what they call
the origin of evil.    And why not the origin of good?    Why
suppose that it is good that is positive and original, and
evil that is negative and derivatory?    "Everything that
is, in so far as it is, is good," St. Augustine affirmed.
But why?    What does "being good" mean?    Good is
good for something, conducive to an end, and to say that
everything is good is equivalent to saying that everything
is making for its end.    But what is its end?    Our desire
is to eternalize ourselves, to persist, and we call good
everything that conspires to this end and bad everything
that tends to lessen or destroy our consciousness.    We
suppose that human consciousness is an end and not a
means to something else which may not be consciousness,
whether human or superhuman.

All metaphysical optimism, such as that of Leibnitz,
and all metaphysical pessimism, such as that of Schopenhauer, have no other foundation than this.    For Leibnitz
this world is the best because it conspires to perpetuate
consciousness, and, together with consciousness, will,
because intelligence increases will and perfects it, because
the end of man is the contemplation of God; while for
Schopenhauer this world is the worst of all possible
worlds, because it conspires to destroy will, because intelligence, representation, nullifies the will that begot it.

And similarly Franklin, who believed in another life, asserted that he was willing to live this life over again, the life that he had actually lived, " from its beginning to the end "; while Leopardi, who did not believe in another life, asserted that nobody would consent to live his life over again. These two views of life are not merely ethical, but religious; and the feeling of moral good, in so far as it is a teleological value, is of religious origin also.

And to return to our interrogations : Shall not all be saved, shall not all be made eternal, and eternal not in suffering but in happiness, those whom we call good and those whom we call bad alike?

And as regards this question of good and evil, does not the malice of him who judges enter in? Is the badness in the intention of him who does the deed or is it not rather in that of him who judges it to be bad? But the terrible thing is that man judges himself, creates himself his own judge.

Who then shall be saved? And now the imagination puts forth another possibility—neither more nor less rational than all those which have just been put forward interrogatively—and that is that only those are saved who have longed to be saved, that only those are eternalized who have lived in an agony of hunger for eternity and for eternalization. He who desires never to die and believes that he shall never die in the spirit, desires it because he deserves it, or rather, only he desires personal immortality who carries his immortality within him. The man who does not long passionately, and with a passion that triumphs over all the dictates of reason, for his own immortality, is the man who does not deserve it, and because he does not deserve it he does not long for it. And it is no injustice not to give a man that which he does not know how to desire, for " ask, and it shall be given you." It may be that to each will be given that which he desired. And perhaps the sin against the Holy Ghost—for which, according to the Evangelist, there is no remission—is none other than that of not desiring God, not longing to be made eternal.

> As is your sort of mind
> So is your sort of search ; you'll find
> What you desire, and that's to be
> A Christian,

said Robert Browning in *Christmas Eve and Easter Day.*

In his *Inferno* Dante condemned the Epicureans, those who did not believe in another life, to something more terrible than the not having it, and that is the consciousness of not having it, and this he expressed in plastic form by picturing them shut up in their tombs for all eternity, without light, without air, without fire, without movement, without life (*Inferno*, x., 10-15).

What cruelty is there in denying to a man that which he did not or could not desire?  In the sixth book of his *Æneid* (426-429) the gentle Virgil makes us hear the plaintive voices and sobbing of the babes who weep upon the threshold of Hades,

> *Continuo auditæ voces, vagitus et ingens,*
> *Infantumque animæ flentes in limine primo,*

unhappy in that they had but entered upon life and never known the sweetness of it, and whom, torn from their mothers' breasts, a dark day had cut off and drowned in bitter death—

> *Quos dulcis vitæ exsortes et ab ubere raptos*
> *Abstulit atra dies et funere mersit acerbo.*

But what life did they lose, if they neither knew life nor longed for it?  And yet is it true that they never longed for it?

It may be said that others craved life on their behalf, that their parents longed for them to be eternal to the end that they might be gladdened by them in paradise.  And so a fresh field is opened up for the imagination—namely, the consideration of the solidarity and representivity of eternal salvation.

There are many, indeed, who imagine the human race as one being, a collective and solidary individual, in whom each member may represent or may come to represent the total collectivity; and they imagine salvation as something collective. As something collective also, merit, and as something collective sin, and redemption. According to this mode of feeling and imagining, either all are saved or none is saved; redemption is total and it is mutual; each man is his neighbour's Christ.

And is there not perhaps a hint of this in the popular Catholic belief with regard to souls in purgatory, the belief that the living may devote suffrages and apply merits to the souls of their dead? This sense of the transmission of merits, both to the living and the dead, is general in popular Catholic piety.

Nor should it be forgotten that in the history of man's religious thought there has often presented itself the idea of an immortality restricted to a certain number of the elect, spirits representative of the rest and in a certain sense including them; an idea of pagan derivation—for such were the heroes and demi-gods—which sometimes shelters itself behind the pronouncement that there are many that are called and few that are chosen.

Recently, while I was engaged upon this essay, there came into my hands the third edition of the *Dialogue sur la vie et sur la mort*, by Charles Bonnefon, a book in which imaginative conceptions similar to those that I have been setting forth find succinct and suggestive expression. The soul cannot live without the body, Bonnefon says, nor the body without the soul, and thus neither birth nor death has any real existence—strictly speaking, there is no body, no soul, no birth, no death, all of which are abstractions and appearances, but only a thinking life, of which we form part and which can neither be born nor die. Hence he is led to deny human

individuality and to assert that no one can say " I am "
but only " we are," or, more correctly, " there is in us."
It is humanity, the species, that thinks and loves in us.
And souls are transmitted in the same way that bodies
are transmitted. " The living thought or the thinking
life which we are will find itself again immediately in a
form analogous to that which was our origin and corresponding with our being in the womb of a pregnant
woman." Each of us, therefore, has lived before and
will live again, although he does not know it. " If
humanity is gradually raised above itself, when the last
man dies, the man who will contain all the rest of mankind in himself, who shall say that he may not have
arrived at that higher order of humanity such as exists
elsewhere, in heaven? . . . As we are all bound
together in solidarity, we shall all, little by little, gather
the fruits of our travail." According to this mode of
imagining and thinking, since nobody is born, nobody
dies, no single soul has finished its struggle but many
times has been plunged into the midst of the human
struggle " ever since the type of embryo corresponding
with the same consciousness was represented in the succession of human phenomena." It is obvious that since
Bonnefon begins by denying personal individuality, he
leaves out of account our real longing, which is to save
our individuality; but on the other hand, since he,
Bonnefon, is a personal individual and feels this longing,
he has recourse to the distinction between the called and
the chosen, and to the idea of representative spirits, and
he concedes to a certain number of men this representative individual immortality. Of these elect he says that
" they will be somewhat more necessary to God than we
ourselves." And he closes this splendid dream by supposing that " it is not impossible that we shall arrive by
a series of ascensions at the supreme happiness, and that
our life shall be merged in the perfect Life as a drop of
water in the sea. Then we shall understand," he con-

tinues, "that everything was necessary, that every philosophy and every religion had its hour of truth, and that in all our wanderings and errors and in the darkest moments of our history we discerned the light of the distant beacon, and that we were all predestined to participate in the Eternal Light. And if the God whom we shall find again possesses a body—and we cannot conceive a living God without a body—we, together with each of the myriads of races that the myriads of suns have brought forth, shall be the conscious cells of his body. If this dream should be fulfilled, an ocean of love would beat upon our shores and the end of every life would be to add a drop of water to this ocean's infinity." And what is this cosmic dream of Bonnefon's but the plastic representation of the Pauline apocatastasis?

Yes, this dream, which has its origin far back in the dawn of Christianity, is fundamentally the same as the Pauline anacefaleosis, the fusion of all men in Man, in the whole of Humanity embodied in a Person, who is Christ, and the fusion not only of all men but of all things, and the subsequent subjection of all things to God, in order that God, Consciousness, may be all in all. And this supposes a collective redemption and a society beyond the grave.

In the middle of the eighteenth century, two pietists of Protestant origin, Johann Jakob Moser and Friedrich Christoph Oetinger, gave a new force and value to the Pauline anacefaleosis. Moser " declared that his religion consisted not in holding certain doctrines to be true and in living a virtuous life conformably therewith, but in being reunited to God through Christ. But this demands the thorough knowledge—a knowledge that goes on increasing until the end of life—of one's own sins and also of the mercy and patience of God, the transformation of all natural feelings, the appropriation of the atonement wrought by the death of Christ, the enjoyment of peace with God in the permanent witness

of the Holy Spirit to the remission of sins, the ordering
of life according to the pattern of Christ, which is the
fruit of faith alone, the drawing near to God and the
intercourse of the soul with Him, the disposition to die
in grace and the joyful expectation of the Judgement
which will bestow blessedness in the more intimate
enjoyment of God and in the *commerce with all the
saints* " (Ritschl, *Geschichte des Pietismus,* vol. iii.,
§ 43). The commerce with all the saints—that is to say,
the eternal human society. And for his part, Oetinger
considers eternal happiness not as the contemplation of
God in His infinitude, but, taking the Epistle to the
Ephesians as his authority, as the contemplation of God
in the harmony of the creature with Christ. The commerce with all the saints was, according to him, essential
to the content of eternal happiness. It was the realization of the kingdom of God, which thus comes to be the
kingdom of Man. And in his exposition of these doctrines of the two pietists, Ritschl confesses (*op. cit.,* iii.,
§ 46) that both witnesses have with these doctrines con-
tributed something to Protestantism that is of like value
with the theological method of Spener, another pietist.

We see, therefore, that the Christian, mystical, inward
longing ever since St. Paul, has been to give human
finality, or divine finality, to the Universe, to save
human consciousness, and to save it by converting all
humanity into a person. This longing is expressed in
the anacefaleosis, the gathering together of all things, all
things in earth and in heaven, the visible and the
invisible, in Christ, and also in the apocatastasis, the
return of all things to God, to consciousness, in order
that God may be all in all. And does not God's being
all in all mean that all things shall acquire consciousness
and that in this consciousness everything that has happened will come to life again, and that everything that
has existed in time will be eternalized? And within the
all, all individual consciousnesses, those which have

been, those that are, and those that will be, and as they have been, as they are, and as they will be, will exist in a condition of society and solidarity.

But does not this awakening to consciousness of everything that has been, necessarily involve a fusion of the identical, an amalgamation of like things? In this conversion of the human race into a true society in Christ, a communion of saints, a kingdom of heaven, will not individual differences, tainted as they are with deceit and even with sin, be obliterated, and in the perfect society will that alone remain of each man which was the essential part of him? Would it not perhaps result, according to Bonnefon's supposition, that this consciousness that lived in the twentieth century in this corner of this earth would feel itself to be the same with other such consciousnesses as have lived in other centuries and perhaps in other worlds?

And how can we conceive of an effective and real union, a substantial and intimate union, soul with soul, of all those who have been?

> If any two creatures grew into one
> They would do more than the world has done,

said Browning in *The Flight of the Duchess;* and Christ has told us that where two or three are gathered together in His name, there is He in the midst of them.

Heaven, then, so it is believed by many, is society, a more perfect society than that of this world; it is human society fused into a person. And there are not wanting some who believe that the tendency of all human progress is the conversion of our species into one collective being with real consciousness—is not perhaps an individual human organism a kind of confederation of cells?—and that when it shall have acquired full consciousness, all those who have existed will come to life again in it.

Heaven, so many think, is society. Just as no one can live in isolation, so no one can survive in isolation.

No one can enjoy God in heaven who sees his brother suffering in hell, for the sin and the merit were common to both. We think with the thoughts of others and we feel with the feelings of others. To see God when God shall be all in all is to see all things in God and to live in God with all things.

This splendid dream of the final solidarity of mankind is the Pauline anacefaleosis and apocatastasis. We Christians, said the Apostle (1 Cor. xii. 27) are the body of Christ, members of Him, flesh of His flesh and bone of His bone (Eph. v. 30), branches of the vine.

But in this final solidarization, in this true and supreme *Christination* of all creatures, what becomes of each individual consciousness? what becomes of Me, of this poor fragile I, this I that is the slave of time and space, this I which reason tells me is a mere passing accident, but for the saving of which I live and suffer and hope and believe? Granting that the human finality of the Universe is saved, that consciousness is saved, would I resign myself to make the sacrifice of this poor I, by which and by which alone I know this finality and this consciousness?

And here, facing this supreme religious sacrifice, we reach the summit of the tragedy, the very heart of it— the sacrifice of our own individual consciousness upon the altar of the perfected Human Consciousness, of the Divine Consciousness.

But is there really a tragedy? If we could attain to a clear vision of this anacefaleosis, if we could succeed in understanding and feeling that we were going to enrich Christ, should we hesitate for a moment in surrendering ourselves utterly to Him? Would the stream that flows into the sea, and feels in the freshness of its waters the bitterness of the salt of the ocean, wish to flow back to its source? would it wish to return to the cloud which drew its life from the sea? is not its joy to feel itself absorbed?

And yet . . .

Yes, in spite of everything, this is the climax of the tragedy.

And the soul, my soul at least, longs for something else, not absorption, not quietude, not peace, not appeasement, it longs ever to approach and never to arrive, it longs for a never-ending longing, for an eternal hope which is eternally renewed but never wholly fulfilled. And together with all this, it longs for an eternal lack of something and an eternal suffering. A suffering, a pain, thanks to which it grows without ceasing in consciousness and in longing. Do not write upon the gate of heaven that sentence which Dante placed over the threshold of hell, *Lasciate ogni speranza!* Do not destroy time! Our life is a hope which is continually converting itself into memory and memory in its turn begets hope. Give us leave to live! The eternity that is like an eternal present, without memory and without hope, is death. Thus do ideas exist, but not thus do men live. Thus do ideas exist in the God-Idea, but not thus can men live in the living God, in the God-Man.

An eternal purgatory, then, rather than a heaven of glory; an eternal ascent. If there is an end of all suffering, however pure and spiritualized we may suppose it to be, if there is an end of all desire, what is it that makes the blessed in paradise go on living? If in paradise they do not suffer for want of God, how shall they love Him? And if even there, in the heaven of glory, while they behold God little by little and closer and closer, yet without ever wholly attaining to Him, there does not always remain something more for them to know and desire, if there does not always remain a substratum of doubt, how shall they not fall asleep?

Or, to sum up, if in heaven there does not remain something of this innermost tragedy of the soul, what sort of a life is that? Is there perhaps any greater joy than that of remembering misery—and to remember it is to feel it—in time of felicity? Does not the prison haunt the freed prisoner? Does he not miss his former dreams of liberty?

Mythological dreams! it will be said. And I have not pretended that they are anything else. But has not the mythological dream its content of truth? Are not dream and myth perhaps revelations of an inexpressible truth, of an irrational truth, of a truth that cannot be proven?

Mythology! Perhaps; but, as in the days of Plato, we must needs mythologize when we come to deal with the other life. But we have just seen that whenever we seek to give a form that is concrete, conceivable, or in other words, rational, to our primary, primordial, and fundamental longing for an eternal life conscious of itself and of its personal individuality, esthetic, logical, and ethical absurdities are multiplied and there is no way of conceiving the beatific vision and the apocatastasis that is free from contradictions and inconsistencies.

And nevertheless! . . .

Nevertheless, yes, we must needs long for it, however absurd it may appear to us; nay, more, we must needs believe in it, in some way or another, in order that we may live. In order that we may live, eh? not in order that we may understand the Universe. We must needs believe in it, and to believe in it is to be religious. Christianity, the only religion which we Europeans of the twentieth century are really capable of feeling, is, as Kierkegaard said, a desperate sortie (*Afsluttende uvidenskabelig Efterskrift,* ii., i., cap. i.), a sortie which can be successful only by means of the martyrdom of faith, which is, according to this same tragic thinker, the crucifixion of reason.

Not without reason did he who had the right to do so speak of the foolishness of the cross. Foolishness, without doubt, foolishness. And the American humorist, Oliver Wendell Holmes, was not altogether wide of the mark in making one of the characters in his ingenious

17

conversations say that he thought better of those who were confined in a lunatic asylum on account of religious mania than of those who, while professing the same religious principles, kept their wits and appeared to enjoy life very well outside of the asylums.[1]   But those who are at large, are they not really, thanks to God, mad too?   Are there not mild madnesses, which not only permit us to mix with our neighbours without danger to society, but which rather enable us to do so, for by means of them we are able to attribute a meaning and finality to life and society themselves?

And after all, what is madness and how can we distinguish it from reason, unless we place ourselves outside both the one and the other, which for us is impossible?

Madness perhaps it is, and great madness, to seek to penetrate into the mystery of the Beyond; madness to seek to superimpose the self-contradictory dreams of our imagination upon the dictates of a sane reason.   And a sane reason tells us that nothing can be built up without foundations, and that it is not merely an idle but a subversive task to fill the void of the unknown with fantasies. And nevertheless . . .

We must needs believe in the other life, in the eternal life beyond the grave, and in an individual and personal life, in a life in which each one of us may feel his consciousness and feel that it is united, without being confounded, with all other consciousnesses in the Supreme Consciousness, in God; we must needs believe in that other life in order that we may live this life, and endure it, and give it meaning and finality.   And we must needs believe in that other life, perhaps, in order that we may deserve it, in order that we may obtain it, for it may be that he neither deserves it nor will obtain it who does not passionately desire it above reason and, if need be, against reason.

[1] *The Autocrat of the Breakfast-table*

And above all, we must feel and act as if an endless continuation of our earthly life awaited us after death; and if it be that nothingness is the fate that awaits us we must not, in the words of *Obermann,* so act that it shall be a just fate.

And this leads us directly to the examination of the practical or ethical aspect of our sole problem.

# XI

## THE PRACTICAL PROBLEM

*L'homme est périssable. Il se peut ; mais périssons en résistant, et, si le néant nous est reservé, ne faisons pas que ce soit une justice.—*SÉNANCOUR *Obermann*, lettre xc.

SEVERAL times in the devious course of these essays I have defined, in spite of my horror of definitions, my own position with regard to the problem that I have been examining; but I know there will always be some dissatisfied reader, educated in some dogmatism or other, who will say : "This man comes to no conclusion, he vacillates—now he seems to affirm one thing and then its contrary—he is full of contradictions—I can't label him. What is he?" Just this—one who affirms contraries, a man of contradiction and strife, as Jeremiah said of himself; one who says one thing with his heart and the contrary with his head, and for whom this conflict is the very stuff of life. And that is as clear as the water that flows from the melted snow upon the mountain tops.

I shall be told that this is an untenable position, that a foundation must be laid upon which to build our action and our works, that it is impossible to live by contradictions, that unity and clarity are essential conditions of life and thought, and that it is necessary to unify thought. And this leaves us as we were before. For it is precisely this inner contradiction that unifies my life and gives it its practical purpose.

Or rather it is the conflict itself, it is this self-same passionate uncertainty, that unifies my action and makes me live and work.

We think in order that we may live, I have said; but perhaps it were more correct to say that we think because we live, and the form of our thought corresponds with that of our life. Once more I must repeat that our ethical and philosophical doctrines in general are usually merely the justification *a posteriori* of our conduct, of our actions. Our doctrines are usually the means we seek in order to explain and justify to others and to ourselves our own mode of action. And this, be it observed, not merely for others, but for ourselves. The man who does not really know why he acts as he does and not otherwise, feels the necessity of explaining to himself the motive of his action and so he forges a motive. What we believe to be the motives of our conduct are usually but the pretexts for it. The very same reason which one man may regard as a motive for taking care to prolong his life may be regarded by another man as a motive for shooting himself.

Nevertheless it cannot be denied that reasons, ideas, have an influence upon human actions, and sometimes even determine them, by a process analogous to that of suggestion upon a hypnotized person, and this is so because of the tendency in every idea to resolve itself into action—an idea being simply an inchoate or abortive act. It was this notion that suggested to Fouillée his theory of idea-forces. But ordinarily ideas are forces which we accommodate to other forces, deeper and much less conscious.

But putting all this aside for the present, what I wish to establish is that uncertainty, doubt, perpetual wrestling with the mystery of our final destiny, mental despair, and the lack of any solid and stable dogmatic foundation, may be the basis of an ethic.

He who bases or thinks that he bases his conduct—his inward or his outward conduct, his feeling or his action—upon a dogma or theoretical principle which he deems incontrovertible, runs the risk of becoming a fanatic, and moreover, the moment that this dogma is weakened or shattered, the morality based upon it gives way. If the earth that he thought firm begins to rock, he himself trembles at the earthquake, for we do not all come up to the standard of the ideal Stoic who remains undaunted among the ruins of a world shattered into atoms. Happily the stuff that is underneath a man's ideas will save him. For if a man should tell you that he does not defraud or cuckold his best friend only because he is afraid of hell, you may depend upon it that neither would he do so even if he were to cease to believe in hell, but that he would invent some other excuse instead. And this is all to the honour of the human race.

But he who believes that he is sailing, perhaps without a set course, on an unstable and sinkable raft, must not be dismayed if the raft gives way beneath his feet and threatens to sink. Such a one thinks that he acts, not because he deems his principle of action to be true, but in order to make it true, in order to prove its truth, in order to create his own spiritual world.

My conduct must be the best proof, the moral proof, of my supreme desire; and if I do not end by convincing myself, within the bounds of the ultimate and irremediable uncertainty, of the truth of what I hope for, it is because my conduct is not sufficiently pure. Virtue, therefore, is not based upon dogma, but dogma upon virtue, and it is not faith that creates martyrs but martyrs who create faith. There is no security or repose—so far as security and repose are obtainable in this life, so essentially insecure and unreposeful—save in conduct that is passionately good.

Conduct, practice, is the proof of doctrine, theory. "If any man will do His will—the will of Him that sent me," said Jesus, "he shall know of the doctrine, whether it be of God or whether I speak of myself" (John vii. 17); and there is a well-known saying of Pascal: "Begin by taking holy water and you will end

by becoming a believer." And pursuing a similar train
of thought, Johann Jakob Moser, the pietist, was of the
opinion that no atheist or naturalist had the right to
regard the Christian religion as void of truth so long as
he had not put it to the proof by keeping its precepts
and commandments (Ritschl, *Geschichte des Pietismus,*
book vii., 43).

What is our heart's truth, anti-rational though it be?
The immortality of the human soul, the truth of the
persistence of our consciousness without any termination
whatsoever, the truth of the human finality of the
Universe. And what is its moral proof? We may
formulate it thus: Act so that in your own judgement
and in the judgement of others you may merit eternity,
act so that you may become irreplaceable, act so that you
may not merit death. Or perhaps thus: Act as if you
were to die to-morrow, but to die in order to survive and
be eternalized. The end of morality is to give personal,
human finality to the Universe; to discover the finality
that belongs to it—if indeed it has any finality—and to
discover it by acting.

More than a century ago, in 1804, in Letter XC of that
series that constitutes the immense monody of his *Obermann,* Sénancour wrote the words which I have put at
the head of this chapter—and of all the spiritual
descendants of the patriarchal Rousseau, Sénancour
was the most profound and the most intense; of all the
men of heart and feeling that France has produced, not
excluding Pascal, he was the most tragic. "Man is
perishable. That may be; but let us perish resisting,
and if it is nothingness that awaits us, do not let us so
act that it shall be a just fate." Change this sentence
from its negative to the positive form—" And if it is
nothingness that awaits us, let us so act that it shall be
an unjust fate "—and you get the firmest basis of action
for the man who cannot or will not be a dogmatist.

That which is irreligious and demoniacal, that which

incapacitates us for action and leaves us without any ideal
defence against our evil tendencies, is the pessimism
that Goethe puts into the mouth of Mephistopheles when
he makes him say, " All that has achieved existence
deserves to be destroyed " (*denn alles was ensteht ist
wert dass es zugrunde geht*). This is the pessimism
which we men call evil, and not that other pessimism
that consists in lamenting what it fears to be true and
struggling against this fear—namely, that everything is
doomed to annihilation in the end. Mephistopheles
asserts that everything that exists deserves to be destroyed,
annihilated, but not that everything will be destroyed or
annihilated; and we assert that everything that exists
deserves to be exalted and eternalized, even though no
such fate is in store for it. The moral attitude is the
reverse of this.

Yes, everything deserves to be eternalized, absolutely
everything, even evil itself, for that which we call evil
would lose its evilness in being eternalized, because it
would lose its temporal nature. For the essence of evil
consists in its temporal nature, in its not applying itself
to any ultimate and permanent end.

And it might not be superfluous here to say something
about that distinction, more overlaid with confusion than
any other, between what we are accustomed to call
optimism and pessimism, a confusion not less than that
which exists with regard to the distinction between
individualism and socialism. Indeed, it is scarcely possible to form a clear idea as to what pessimism really is.

I have just this very day read in the *Nation* (July 6,
1912) an article, entitled " A Dramatic Inferno," that
deals with an English translation of the works of Strind-
berg, and it opens with the following judicious observa-
tions : " If there were in the world a sincere and total
pessimism, it would of necessity be silent. The despair
which finds a voice is a social mood, it is the cry of
misery which brother utters to brother when both are

stumbling through a valley of shadows which is peopled
with—comrades.  In its anguish it bears witness to
something that is good in life, for it presupposes sympathy. . . .  The real gloom, the sincere despair, is
dumb and blind; it writes no books, and feels no impulse
to burden an intolerable universe with a monument more
lasting than brass.''  Doubtless there is something of
sophistry in this criticism, for the man who is really in
pain weeps and even cries aloud, even if he is alone and
there is nobody to hear him, simply as a means of
alleviating his pain, although this perhaps may be a
result of social habits.  But does not the lion, alone in
the desert, roar if he has an aching tooth?  But apart
from this, it cannot be denied that there is a substance
of truth underlying these remarks.  The pessimism that
protests and defends itself cannot be truly said to be
pessimism.  And, in truth, still less is it pessimism to
hold that nothing ought to perish although all things
may be doomed to annihilation, while on the other hand
it is pessimism to affirm that all things ought to be
annihilated even though nothing may perish.

Pessimism, moreover, may possess different values.
There is a eudemonistic or economic pessimism, that
which denies happiness; there is an ethical pessimism,
that which denies the triumph of moral good; and there
is a religious pessimism, that which despairs of the
human finality of the Universe, of the eternal salvation
of the individual soul.

All men deserve to be saved, but, as I have said in the
previous chapter, he above all deserves immortality who
desires it passionately and even in the face of reason.
An English writer, H. G. Wells, who has taken upon
himself the rôle of the prophet (a thing not uncommon in
his country), tells us in *Anticipations* that ''active and
capable men of all forms of religious profession tend in
practice to disregard the question of immortality
altogether.''  And this is because the religious professions

of these active and capable men to whom Wells refers are usually simply a lie, and their lives are a lie, too, if they seek to base them upon religion. But it may be that at bottom there is not so much truth in what Wells asserts as he and others imagine. These active and capable men live in the midst of a society imbued with Christian principles, surrounded by institutions and social feelings that are the product of Christianity, and faith in the immortality of the soul exists deep down in their own souls like a subterranean river, neither seen nor heard, but watering the roots of their deeds and their motives.

It must be admitted that there exists in truth no more solid foundation for morality than the foundation of the Catholic ethic. The end of man is eternal happiness, which consists in the vision and enjoyment of God *in sæcula sæculorum*. Where it errs, however, is in the choice of the means conducive to this end; for to make the attainment of eternal happiness dependent upon believing or not believing in the Procession of the Holy Ghost from the Father and the Son and not from the Father alone, or in the Divinity of Jesus, or in the theory of the Hypostatic Union, or even in the existence of God, is, as a moment's reflection will show, nothing less than monstrous. A human God—and that is the only kind of God we are able to conceive—would never reject him who was unable to believe in Him with his head, and it is not in his head but in his heart that the wicked man says that there is no God, which is equivalent to saying that he wishes that there may not be a God. If any belief could be bound up with the attainment of eternal happiness it would be the belief in this happiness itself and in the possibility of it.

And what shall we say of that other proposition of the king of pedants, to the effect that we have not come into the world to be happy but to fulfil our duty (*Wir sind nicht auf der Welt, um glucklich zu sein, sondern um unsere Schuldigkeit zu tun*)? If we are in the world *for*

something (*um etwas*), whence can this *for* be derived
but from the very essence of our own will, which asks for
happiness and not duty as the ultimate end? And if it
is sought to attribute some other value to this *for*, an
objective value, as some Sadducean pedant would say,
then it must be recognized that the objective reality, that
which would remain even though humanity should disappear, is as indifferent to our duty as to our happiness,
is as little concerned with our morality as with our
felicity. I am not aware that Jupiter, Uranus, or Sirius
would allow their course to be affected by the fact that
we are or are not fulfilling our duty any more than by the
fact that we are or are not happy.

Such considerations must appear to these pedants to
be characterized by a ridiculous vulgarity and a dilettante
superficiality. (The intellectual world is divided into
two classes—dilettanti on the one hand, and pedants on
the other.) What choice, then, have we? The modern
man is he who resigns himself to the truth and is content
to be ignorant of the synthesis of culture—witness what
Windelband says on this head in his study of the fate
of Hölderlin (*Praeludien,* i.). Yes, these men of culture
are resigned, but there remain a few poor savages like
ourselves for whom resignation is impossible. We do
not resign ourselves to the idea of having one day to
disappear, and the criticism of the great Pedant does not
console us.

The quintessence of common sense was expressed by
Galileo Galilei when he said : "Some perhaps will say
that the bitterest pain is the loss of life, but I say that
there are others more bitter ; for whosoever is deprived of
life is deprived at the same time of the power to lament,
not only this, but any other loss whatsoever." Whether
Galileo was conscious or not of the humour of this sentence I do not know, but it is a tragic humour.

But, to turn back, I repeat that if the attainment of
eternal happiness could be bound up with any particular

belief, it would be with the belief in the possibility of its
realization.   And yet, strictly speaking, not even with
this.   The reasonable man says in his head, "There is
no other life after this," but only the wicked says it in
his heart.   But since the wicked man is possibly only a
man who has been driven to despair, will a human God
condemn him because of his despair?   His despair alone
is misfortune enough.

But in any event let us adopt the Calderónian formula
in *La Vida es Sueño*:

> *Que estoy soñando y que quiero*
> *obrar hacer bien, pues no se pierde*
> *el hacer bien aun en sueños*[1]

But are good deeds really not lost?   Did Calderón know?
And he added:

> *Acudamos a lo eterno*
> *que es la fama vividora*
> *donde ni duermen las dichas*
> *no las grandezas reposan.*[2]

Is it really so?   Did Calderón know?

Calderón had faith, robust Catholic faith; but for him
who lacks faith, for him who cannot believe in what
Don Pedro Calderón de la Barca believed, there always
remains the attitude of *Obermann*.

If it is nothingness that awaits us, let us make an injustice of it; let us fight against destiny, even though without hope of victory; let us fight against it quixotically.

And not only do we fight against destiny in longing
for what is irrational, but in acting in such a way that
we make ourselves irreplaceable, in impressing our seal
and mark upon others, in acting upon our neighbours in
order to dominate them, in giving ourselves to them in
order that we may eternalize ourselves so far as we can.

---

[1] Act II., Scene 4: "I am dreaming and I wish to act rightly, for good
deeds are not lost, though they be wrought in dreams "

[2] Act III., Scene 10: "Let us aim at the eternal, the glory that does not
wane, where bliss slumbers not and where greatness does not repose."

Our greatest endeavour must be to make ourselves
irreplaceable; to make the theoretical fact—if this expression does not involve a contradiction in terms—the
fact that each one of us is unique and irreplaceable, that
no one else can fill the gap that will be left when we die,
a practical truth.

For in fact each man is unique and irreplaceable; there
cannot be any other I; each one of us—our soul, that is,
not our life—is worth the whole Universe. I say the
spirit and not the life, for the ridiculously exaggerated
value which those attach to human life who, not really
believing in the spirit—that is to say, in their personal
immortality—tirade against war and the death penalty,
for example, is a value which they attach to it precisely
because they do not really believe in the spirit of which
life is the servant. For life is of use only in so far as it
serves its lord and master, spirit, and if the master
perishes with the servant, neither the one nor the other
is of any great value.

And to act in such a way as to make our annihilation
an injustice, in such a way as to make our brothers, our
sons, and our brothers' sons, and their sons' sons, feel
that we ought not to have died, is something that is
within the reach of all.

The essence of the doctrine of the Christian redemption is in the fact that he who suffered agony and death
was the unique man—that is, Man, the Son of Man, or
the Son of God; that he, because he was sinless, did not
deserve to have died; and that this propitiatory divine
victim died in order that he might rise again and that
he might raise us up from the dead, in order that he
might deliver us from death by applying his merits to
us and showing us the way of life. And the Christ who
gave himself for his brothers in humanity with an
absolute self-abnegation is the pattern for our action to
shape itself on.

All of us, each one of us, can and ought to determine

to give as much of himself as he possibly can—nay, to
give more than he can, to exceed himself, to go beyond
himself, to make himself irreplaceable, to give himself
to others in order that he may receive himself back again
from them.   And each one in his own civil calling or
office.   The word office, *officium,* means obligation,
debt, but in the concrete, and that is what it always
ought to mean in practice.   We ought not so much to
try to seek that particular calling which we think most
fitting and suitable for ourselves, as to make a calling of
that employment in which chance, Providence, or our
own will has placed us.

Perhaps Luther rendered no greater service to Christian
civilization than that of establishing the religious value
of the civil occupation, of shattering the monastic and
medieval idea of the religious calling, an idea involved in
the mist of human passions and imaginations and the
cause of terrible life tragedies.   If we could but enter into
the cloister and examine the religious vocation of those
whom the self-interest of their parents had forced as
children into a novice's cell and who had suddenly
awakened to the life of the world—if indeed they ever do
awake !—or of those whom their own self-delusions had
led into it !   Luther saw this life of the cloister at close
quarters and suffered it himself, and therefore he was
able to understand and feel the religious value of the
civil calling, to which no man is bound by perpetual vows.

All that the Apostle said in the fourth chapter of his
Epistle to the Ephesians with regard to the respective
functions of Christians in the Church must be transferred
and applied to the civil or non-ecclesiastical life, for
to-day among ourselves the Christian—whether he know
it or not, and whether he like it or not—is the citizen, and
just as the Apostle exclaimed, " I am a Roman citizen !"
each one of us, even the atheist, might exclaim " I am a
Christian !"   And this demands the *civilizing,* in the
sense of dis-ecclesiasticizing, of Christianity, which was

Luther's task, although he himself eventually became the founder of a Church.

There is a common English phrase, " the right man in the right place." To which we might rejoin, " Cobbler, to thy last!" Who knows what is the post that suits him best and for which he is most fitted? Does a man himself know it better than others or do they know it better than he? Who can measure capacities and aptitudes? The religious attitude, undoubtedly, is to endeavour to make the occupation in which we find ourselves our vocation, and only in the last resort to change it for another.

This question of the proper vocation is possibly the gravest and most deep-seated of social problems, that which is at the root of all the others. That which is known *par excellence* as the social question is perhaps not so much a problem of the distribution of wealth, of the products of labour, as a problem of the distribution of avocations, of the modes of production. It is not aptitude—a thing impossible to ascertain without first putting it to the test and not always clearly indicated in a man, for with regard to the majority of callings a man is not born but made—it is not special aptitude, but rather social, political, and customary reasons that determine a man's occupation. At certain times and in certain countries it is caste and heredity; at other times and in other places, the guild or corporation; in later times machinery—in almost all cases necessity; liberty scarcely ever. And the tragedy of it culminates in those occupations, pandering to evil, in which the soul is sacrificed for the sake of the livelihood, in which the workman works with the consciousness, not of the uselessness merely, but of the social perversity, of his work, manufacturing the poison that will kill him, the weapon, perchance, with which his children will be murdered. This, and not the question of wages, is the gravest problem.

I shall never forget a scene of which I was a witness

that took place on the banks of the river that flows through Bilbao, my native town. A workman was hammering at something in a shipwright's yard, working without putting his heart into his work, as if he lacked energy or worked merely for the sake of getting a wage, when suddenly a woman's voice was heard crying, "Help! help!" A child had fallen into the river. Instantly the man was transformed. With an admirable energy, promptitude, and sang-froid he threw off his clothes and plunged into the water to rescue the drowning infant.

Possibly the reason why there is less bitterness in the agrarian socialist movement than in that of the towns is that the field labourer, although his wages and his standard of living are no better than those of the miner or artisan, has a clearer consciousness of the social value of his work. Sowing corn is a different thing from extracting diamonds from the earth.

And it may be that the greatest social progress consists in a certain indifferentiation of labour, in the facility for exchanging one kind of work for another, and that other not perhaps a more lucrative, but a nobler one—for there are degrees of nobility in labour. But unhappily it is only too seldom that a man who keeps to one occupation without changing is concerned with making a religious vocation of it, or that the man who changes his occupation for another does so from any religious motive.

And do you not know cases in which a man, justifying his action on the ground that the professional organism to which he belongs and in which he works is badly organized and does not function as it ought, will evade the strict performance of his duty on the pretext that he is thereby fulfilling a higher duty? Is not this insistence upon the literal carrying out of orders called disciplinarianism, and do not people speak disparagingly of bureaucracy and the Pharisaism of public officials? And cases occur not unlike that of an intelligent and studious military officer who should discover the deficiencies of

his country's military organization and denounce them to
his superiors and perhaps to the public—thereby fulfilling
his duty—and who, when on active service, should refuse
to carry out an operation which he was ordered to undertake, believing that there was but scant probability of
success or rather certainty of failure, so long as these
deficiencies remained unremedied.  He would deserve to
be shot.  And as for this question of Pharisaism . . .

And there is always a way of obeying an order while
yet retaining the command, a way of carrying out what
one believes to be an absurd operation while correcting
its absurdity, even though it involve one's own death.
When in my bureaucratic capacity I have come across
some legislative ordinance that has fallen into desuetude
because of its manifest absurdity, I have always
endeavoured to apply it.  There is nothing worse than a
loaded pistol which nobody uses left lying in some corner
of the house; a child finds it, begins to play with it, and
kills its own father.  Laws that have fallen into desuetude
are the most terrible of all laws, when the cause of the
desuetude is the badness of the law.

And these are not groundless suppositions, and least
of all in our country.  For there are many who, while
they go about looking out for I know not what ideal—
that is to say, fictitious duties and responsibilities—neglect the duty of putting their whole soul into the immediate and concrete business which furnishes them with a
living; and the rest, the immense majority, perform their
task perfunctorily, merely for the sake of nominally com-
plying with their duty—*para cumplir*, a terribly immoral
phrase—in order to get themselves out of a difficulty, to
get the job done, to qualify for their wages without earning them, whether these wages be pecuniary or otherwise.

Here you have a shoemaker who lives by making shoes,
and makes them with just enough care and attention to
keep his clientèle together without losing custom.
Another shoemaker lives on a somewhat higher spiritual

plane, for he has a proper love for his work, and out of pride or a sense of honour strives for the reputation of being the best shoemaker in the town or in the kingdom, even though this reputation brings him no increase of custom or profit, but only renown and prestige. But there is a still higher degree of moral perfection in this business of shoemaking, and that is for the shoemaker to aspire to become for his fellow-townsmen the one and only shoemaker, indispensable and irreplaceable, the shoemaker who looks after their footgear so well that they will feel a definite loss when he dies—when he is " dead to them," not merely " dead "[1]—and they will feel that he ought not to have died. And this will result from the fact that in working for them he was anxious to spare them any discomfort and to make sure that it should not be any preoccupation with their feet that should prevent them from being at leisure to contemplate the higher truths; he shod them for the love of them and for the love of God in them—he shod them religiously.

I have chosen this example deliberately, although it may perhaps appear to you somewhat pedestrian. For the fact is that in this business of shoemaking, the religious, as opposed to the ethical, sense is at a very low ebb.

Working men group themselves in associations, they form co-operative societies and unions for defence, they fight very justly and nobly for the betterment of their class; but it is not clear that these associations have any great influence on their moral attitude towards their work. They have succeeded in compelling employers to employ only such workmen, and no others, as the respective unions shall designate in each particular case; but in the selection of those designated they pay little heed to their technical fitness. Often the employer finds it almost impossible to dismiss an inefficient workman on account of his inefficiency, for his fellow-workers take his part. Their work,

[1] "Se les muera," y no sólo "se muera."

moreover, is often perfunctory, performed merely as a
pretext for receiving a wage, and instances even occur
when they deliberately mishandle it in order to injure
their employer.

In attempting to justify this state of things, it may be
said that the employers are a hundred times more blame-
worthy than the workmen, for they are not concerned to
give a better wage to the man who does better work, or
to foster the general education and technical proficiency
of the workman, or to ensure the intrinsic goodness of
the article produced.   The improvement of the product—
which, apart from reasons of industrial and mercantile
competition, ought to be in itself and for the good of the
consumers, for charity's sake, the chief end of the business—is not so regarded either by employers or employed,
and this is because neither the one nor the other have any
religious sense of their social function.   Neither of them
seek to make themselves irreplaceable.   The evil is
aggravated when the business takes the unhappy form of
the impersonal limited company, for where there is no
longer any personal signature there is no longer any of
that pride which seeks to give the signature prestige, a
pride which in its way is a substitute for the craving for
eternalization.   With the disappearance of the concrete
individuality, the basis of all religion, the religious sense
of the business calling disappears also.

And what has been said of employers and workmen
applies still more to members of the liberal professions
and public functionaries.   There is scarcely a single servant of the State who feels the religious bearing of his
official and public duties.   Nothing could be more un-
satisfactory, nothing more confused, than the feeling
among our people with regard to their duties towards the
State, and this sense of duty is still further obliterated by
the attitude of the Catholic Church, whose action so far
as the State is concerned is in strict truth anarchical.   It
is no uncommon thing to find among its ministers

upholders of the moral lawfulness of smuggling and con-
traband as if in disobeying the legally constituted
authority the smuggler and contrabandist did not sin
against the Fourth Commandment of the law of God,
which in commanding us to honour our father and
mother commands us to obey all lawful authority in so
far as the ordinances of such authority are not contrary
(and the levying of these contributions is certainly not
contrary) to the law of God.

There are many who, since it is written " In the sweat
of thy face shalt thou eat bread," regard work as a
punishment, and therefore they attribute merely an
economico-political, or at best an esthetic, value to the
work of everyday life.  For those who take this view—
and it is the view principally held by the Jesuits—the
business of life is twofold : there is the inferior and
transitory business of winning a livelihood, of winning
bread for ourselves and our children in an honourable
manner—and the elasticity of this honour is well known ;
and there is the grand business of our salvation, of winning eternal glory.  This inferior or worldly business
is to be undertaken not only so as to permit us, without
deceiving or seriously injuring our neighbours, to live
decently in accordance with our social position, but also
so as to afford us the greatest possible amount of time
for attending to the other main business of our life.
And there are others who, rising somewhat above this
conception of the work of our civil occupation, a conception which is economical rather than ethical, attain to
an esthetic conception and sense of it, and this involves
endeavouring to acquire distinction and renown in our
occupation, the converting of it into an art for art's sake,
for beauty's sake.  But it is necessary to rise still higher
than this, to attain to an ethical sense of our civil calling,
to a sense which derives from our religious sense, from
our hunger of eternalization.  To work at our ordinary
civil occupation, with eyes fixed on God, for the love of

God, which is equivalent to saying for the love of our eternalization, is to make of this work a work of religion.

That saying, " In the sweat of thy face shalt thou eat bread," does not mean that God condemned man to work, but to the painfulness of it. It would have been no condemnation to have condemned man to work itself, for work is the only practical consolation for having been born. And, for a Christian, the proof that God did not condemn man to work itself consists in the saying of the Scripture that, before the Fall, while he was still in a state of innocence, God took man and put him in the garden " to dress it and to keep it " (Gen. ii. 15). And how, in fact, would man have passed his time in Paradise if he had had no work to do in keeping it in order? And may it not be that the beatific vision itself is a kind of work?

And even if work were our punishment, we ought to strive to make it, the punishment itself, our consolation and our redemption; and if we must needs embrace some cross or other, there is for each one of us no better cross than the cross of our own civil calling. For Christ did not say, " Take up my cross and follow me," but " Take up thy cross and follow me ": every man his own cross, for the Saviour's cross the Saviour alone can bear. And the imitation of Christ, therefore, does not consist in that monastic ideal so shiningly set forth in the book that commonly bears the name of à Kempis, an ideal only applicable to a very limited number of persons and therefore anti-Christian; but to imitate Christ is to take up each one his own cross, the cross of his own civil occupation—civil and not merely religious—as Christ took up his cross, the cross of his calling, and to embrace it and carry it, looking towards God and striving to make each act of this calling a true prayer. In making shoes and because he makes them a man can gain heaven, provided that the shoemaker strives to be perfect, as a shoemaker, as our Father in heaven is perfect.

Fourier, the socialist dreamer, dreamed of making work attractive in his phalansteries by the free choice of vocations and in other ways. There is no other way than that of liberty. Wherein consists the charm of the game of chance, which is a kind of work, if not in the voluntary submission of the player to the liberty of Nature—that is, to chance? But do not let us lose ourselves in a comparison between work and play.

And the sense of making ourselves irreplaceable, of not meriting death, of making our annihilation, if it is annihilation that awaits us, an injustice, ought to impel us not only to perform our own occupation religiously, from love of God and love of our eternity and eternalization, but to perform it passionately, tragically if you like. It ought to impel us to endeavour to stamp others with our seal, to perpetuate ourselves in them and in their children by dominating them, to leave on all things the imperishable impress of our signature. The most fruitful ethic is the ethic of mutual imposition.

Above all, we must recast in a positive form the negative commandments which we have inherited from the Ancient Law. Thus where it is written, " Thou shalt not lie!" let us understand, "Thou shalt always speak the truth, in season and out of season!" although it is we ourselves, and not others, who are judges in each case of this seasonableness. And for " Thou shalt not kill!" let us understand, " Thou shalt give life and increase it!" And for " Thou shalt not steal!" let us say, " Thou shalt increase the general wealth!" And for " Thou shalt not commit adultery!" " Thou shalt give children, healthy, strong, and good, to thy country and to heaven!" And thus with all the other commandments.

He who does not lose his life shall not find it. Give yourself then to others, but in order to give yourself to

them, first dominate them. For it is not possible to
dominate except by being dominated. Everyone
nourishes himself upon the flesh of that which he
devours. In order that you may dominate your neighbour you must know and love him. It is by attempting
to impose my ideas upon him that I become the recipient
of his ideas. To love my neighbour is to wish that he
may be like me, that he may be another I—that is to say,
it is to wish that I may be he; it is to wish to obliterate
the division between him and me, to suppress the evil.
My endeavour to impose myself upon another, to be and
live in him and by him, to make him mine—which is the
same as making myself his—is that which gives religious
meaning to human collectivity, to human solidarity.

The feeling of solidarity originates in myself; since I
am a society, I feel the need of making myself master of
human society; since I am a social product, I must
socialize myself, and from myself I proceed to God—
who is I projected to the All—and from God to each of
my neighbours.

My immediate first impulse is to protest against the
inquisitor and to prefer the merchant who comes to offer
me his wares. But when my impressions are clarified
by reflection, I begin to see that the inquisitor, when he
acts from a right motive, treats me as a man, as an end
in myself, and if he molests me it is from a charitable
wish to save my soul; while the merchant, on the other
hand, regards me merely as a customer, as a means to an
end, and his indulgence and tolerance is at bottom
nothing but a supreme indifference to my destiny.
There is much more humanity in the inquisitor.

Similarly there is much more humanity in war than
in peace. Non-resistance to evil implies resistance to
good, and to take the offensive, leaving the defensive
out of the question, is perhaps the divinest thing in
humanity. War is the school of fraternity and the bond
of love; it is war that has brought peoples into touch

with one another, by mutual aggression and collision, and has been the cause of their knowing and loving one another. Human love knows no purer embrace, or one more fruitful in its consequences, than that between victor and vanquished on the battlefield. And even the purified hate that springs from war is fruitful. War is, in its strictest sense, the sanctification of homicide; Cain is redeemed as a leader of armies. And if Cain had not killed his brother Abel, perhaps he would have died by the hand of Abel. God revealed Himself above all in war; He began by being the God of battles: and one of the greatest services of the Cross is that, in the form of the sword-hilt, it protects the hand that wields the sword.

The enemies of the State say that Cain, the fratricide, was the founder of the State. And we must accept the fact and turn it to the glory of the State, the child of war. Civilization began on the day on which one man, by subjecting another to his will and compelling him to do the work of two, was enabled to devote himself to the contemplation of the world and to set his captive upon works of luxury. It was slavery that enabled Plato to speculate upon the ideal republic, and it was war that brought slavery about. Not without reason was Athena the goddess of war and of wisdom. But is there any need to repeat once again these obvious truths, which, though they have continually been forgotten, are continually rediscovered?

And the supreme commandment that arises out of love towards God, and the foundation of all morality, is this : Yield yourself up entirely, give your spirit to the end that you may save it, that you may eternalize it. Such is the sacrifice of life.

The individual *quâ* individual, the wretched captive of the instinct of preservation and of the senses, cares only about preserving himself, and all his concern is that others should not force their way into his sphere, should not disturb him, should not interrupt his idleness; and in return for their abstention or for the sake of example he refrains from forcing himself upon them, from interrupting their idleness, from disturbing them, from taking possession of them. " Do not do unto others what you would not have them do unto you," he translates thus : I do not interfere with others—let them not interfere with me. And he shrinks and pines and perishes in this spiritual avarice and this repellent ethic of anarchic individualism : each one for himself. And as each one is not himself, he can hardly live for himself.

But as soon as the individual feels himself in society, he feels himself in God, and kindled by the instinct of perpetuation he glows with love towards God, and with a dominating charity he seeks to perpetuate himself in others, to perennialize his spirit, to eternalize it, to unnail God, and his sole desire is to seal his spirit upon other spirits and to receive their impress in return. He has shaken off the yoke of his spiritual sloth and avarice.

Sloth, it is said, is the mother of all the vices; and in fact sloth does engender two vices—avarice and envy—which in their turn are the source of all the rest. Sloth is the weight of matter, in itself inert, within us, and this sloth, while it professes to preserve us by economizing our forces, in reality attenuates us and reduces us to nothing.

In man there is either too much matter or too much spirit, or to put it better, either he feels a hunger for spirit—that is, for eternity—or he feels a hunger for matter—that is, submission to annihilation. When spirit is in excess and he feels a hunger for yet more of it, he pours it forth and scatters it abroad, and in scattering it abroad he amplifies it with that of others; and on the contrary, when a man is avaricious of himself and thinks that he will preserve himself better by withdrawing within himself, he ends by losing all—he is like the

man who received the single talent : he buried it in order
that he might not lose it, and in the end he was bereft
of it.   For to him that hath shall be given, but from
him that hath but a little shall be taken away even the
little that he hath.

Be ye perfect even as your Father in heaven is perfect, we are bidden, and this terrible precept—terrible
because for us the infinite perfection of the Father is
unattainable—must be our supreme rule of conduct.
Unless a man aspires to the impossible, the possible
that he achieves will be scarcely worth the trouble of
achieving.   It behoves us to aspire to the impossible, to
the absolute and infinite perfection, and to say to the
Father, " Father, I cannot—help Thou my impotence."
And He acting in us will achieve it for us.

And to be perfect is to be all, it is to be myself and
to be all else, it is to be humanity, it is to be the Universe.
And there is no other way of being all but to give oneself
to all, and when all shall be in all, all will be in each one
of us.   The apocatastasis is more than a mystical dream :
it is a rule of action, it is a beacon beckoning us to high
exploits.

And from it springs the ethic of invasion, of domination, of aggression, of inquisition if you like.   For true
charity is a kind of invasion—it consists in putting my
spirit into other spirits, in giving them my suffering as
the food and consolation for their sufferings, in awakening their unrest with my unrest, in sharpening their hunger
for God with my hunger for God.   It is not charity to
rock and lull our brothers to sleep in the inertia and
drowsiness of matter, but rather to awaken them to the
uneasiness and torment of spirit.

To the fourteen works of mercy which we learnt in the
Catechism of Christian Doctrine there should sometimes be added yet another, that of awakening the sleeper.
Sometimes, at any rate, and surely when the sleeper
sleeps on the brink of a precipice, it is much more merciful

to awaken him than to bury him after he is dead—let us
leave the dead to bury their dead.   It has been well said,
"Whosoever loves thee dearly will make thee weep,"
and charity often causes weeping.   "The love that does
not mortify does not deserve so divine a name," said that
ardent Portuguese apostle, Fr. Thomé de Jesús,[1] who
was also the author of this ejaculation—"O infinite fire,
O eternal love, who weepest when thou hast naught to
embrace and feed upon and many hearts to burn!"   He
who loves his neighbour burns his heart, and the heart,
like green wood, in burning groans and distils itself in
tears.

And to do this is generosity, one of the two mother
virtues which are born when inertia, sloth, is overcome.
Most of our miseries come from spiritual avarice.

The cure for suffering—which, as we have said, is the
collision of consciousness with unconsciousness—is not
to be submerged in unconsciousness, but to be raised to
consciousness and to suffer more.   The evil of suffering
is cured by more suffering, by higher suffering.   Do not
take opium, but put salt and vinegar in the soul's wound,
for when you sleep and no longer feel the suffering, you
are not.   And to be, that is imperative.   Do not then
close your eyes to the agonizing Sphinx, but look her in
the face and let her seize you in her mouth and crunch you
with her hundred thousand poisonous teeth and swallow
you.   And when she has swallowed you, you will know
the sweetness of the taste of suffering.

The way thereto in practice is by the ethic of mutual
imposition.   Men should strive to impose themselves
upon one another, to give their spirits to one another,
to seal one another's souls.

There is matter for thought in the fact that the
Christian ethic has been called an ethic of slaves.   By
whom?   By anarchists!   It is anarchism that is an
ethic of slaves, for it is only the slave that chants the

---

[1] *Trabalhos de Jesus*, part i

praises of anarchical liberty. Anarchism, no! but
*panarchism;* not the creed of "Nor God nor master!"
but that of "All gods and all masters!" all striving to
become gods, to become immortal, and achieving this
by dominating others.

And there are so many ways of dominating. There is
even a passive way, or one at least that is apparently
passive, of fulfilling at times this law of life. Adaptation to environment, imitation, putting oneself in
another's place, sympathy, in a word, besides being a
manifestation of the unity of the species, is a mode of
self-expansion, of being another. To be conquered, or
at least to seem to be conquered, is often to conquer; to
take what is another's is a way of living in him.

And in speaking of domination, I do not mean the
domination of the tiger. The fox also dominates by
cunning, and the hare by flight, and the viper by poison,
and the mosquito by its smallness, and the squid by the
inky fluid with which it darkens the water and under
cover of which it escapes. And no one is scandalized at
this, for the same universal Father who gave its fierce-
ness, its talons, and its jaws to the tiger, gave cunning
to the fox, swift feet to the hare, poison to the viper,
diminutiveness to the mosquito, and its inky fluid to the
squid. And nobleness or ignobleness does not consist
in the weapons we use, for every species and even every
individual possesses its own, but rather in the way in
which we use them, and above all in the cause in which
we wield them.

And among the weapons of conquest must be included
the weapon of patience and of resignation, but a
passionate patience and a passionate resignation, con-
taining within itself an active principle and antecedent
longings. You remember that famous sonnet of Milton
—Milton, the great fighter, the great Puritan disturber
of the spiritual peace, the singer of Satan—who, when
he considered how his light was spent and that one talent

which it is death to hide lodged with him useless, heard
the voice of Patience saying to him,

> God doth not need
> Either man's work, or his own gifts ; who best
> Bear his mild yoke, they serve Him best . his state
> Is kingly , thousands at his bidding speed,
> And post o'er land and ocean without rest ,
> They also serve who only stand and wait.

They also serve who only stand and wait—yes, but it
is when they wait for Him passionately, hungeringly,
full of longing for immortality in Him.

And we must impose ourselves, even though it be by
our patience. " My cup is small, but I drink out of my
cup," said the egoistical poet of an avaricious people.[1]
No, out of my cup all drink, for I wish all to drink out
of it; I offer it to them, and my cup grows according to
the number of those who drink out of it, and all, in putting it to their lips, leave in it something of their spirit.
And while they drink out of my cup, I also drink out of
theirs.   For the more I belong to myself, and the more
I am myself, the more I belong to others; out of the fullness of myself I overflow upon my brothers, and as I
overflow upon them they enter into me.

" Be ye perfect, as your Father is perfect," we are
bidden, and our Father is perfect because He is Himself
and because He is in each one of His children who live
and move and have their being in Him.   And the end
of perfection is that we all may be one (John xvii. 21),
all one body in Christ (Rom. xii. 5), and that, at the last,
when all things are subdued unto the Son, the Son himself may be subject to Him that put all things under
him, that God may be all in all.   And this is to make the
Universe consciousness, to make Nature a society, and
a human society.   And then shall we be able confidently
to call God Father.

[1] De Musset.

I am aware that those who say that ethics is a science will say that all this commentary of mine is nothing but rhetoric; but each man has his own language and his own passion—that is to say, each man who knows what passion is—and as for the man who knows it not, nothing will it avail him to know science.

And the passion that finds its expression in this rhetoric, the devotees of ethical science call egotism. But this egotism is the only true remedy for egoism, spiritual avarice, the vice of preserving and reserving oneself and of not striving to perennialize oneself by giving oneself.

"Be not, and ye shall be mightier than all that is," said Fr. Juan de los Angeles in one of his *Diálogos de la Conquista del Reina de Dios* (*Dial.*, iii., 8); but what does this "Be not" mean? May it not mean paradoxically—and such a mode of expression is common with the mystics—the contrary of that which, at a first and literal reading, it would appear to mean? Is not the whole ethic of submission and quietism an immense paradox, or rather a great tragic contradiction? Is not the monastic, the strictly monastic, ethic an absurdity? And by the monastic ethic I mean that of the solitary Carthusian, that of the hermit, who flees from the world—perhaps carrying it with him nevertheless—in order that he may live quite alone with a God who is lonely as himself; not that of the Dominican inquisitor who scoured Provence in search of Albigensian hearts to burn.

"Let God do it all," someone will say; but if man folds his arms, God will go to sleep.

This Carthusian ethic and that scientific ethic which is derived from ethical science—oh, this science of ethics! rational and rationalistic ethics! pedantry of pedantry, all is pedantry!—yes, this perhaps is egoism and coldness of heart.

There are some who say that they isolate themselves

with God in order that they may the better work out
their salvation, their redemption; but since sin is collective, redemption must be collective also. "The
religious is the determination of the whole, and everything outside this is an illusion of the senses, and that is
why the greatest criminal is at bottom innocent, a good-
natured man and a saint" (Kierkegaard, *Afsluttende*,
etc., ii., ii., cap. iv., sect. 2, *a*).

Are we to understand, on the other hand, that men
seek to gain the other, the eternal life, by renouncing
this the temporal life? If the other life is anything, it
must be a continuation of this, and only as such a continuation, more or less purified, is it mirrored in our
desire; and if this is so, such as is this life of time, so will
be the life of eternity.

"This world and the other are like the two wives of
one husband—if he pleases one he makes the other
envious," said an Arab thinker, quoted by Windelband
(*Das Heilige*, in vol. ii. of *Präludien*); but such a
thought could only have arisen in the mind of one who
had failed to resolve the tragic conflict between his spirit
and the world in a fruitful warfare, a practical contradiction. "Thy kingdom come" to us; so Christ taught
us to pray to the Father, not "May we come to Thy
kingdom"; and according to the primitive Christian
belief the eternal life was to be realized on this earth itself
and as a continuation of the earthly life. We were made
men and not angels in order that we might seek our
happiness through the medium of this life, and the Christ
of the Christian Faith became, not an angelic, but a
human, being, redeeming us by taking upon himself a
real and effective body and not an appearance of one
merely. And according to this same Faith, even the
highest of the angelical hierarchy adore the Virgin, the
supreme symbol of terrestrial Humanity. The angelical
ideal, therefore, is not the Christian ideal, and still less
is it the human ideal, nor can it be. An angel, more-

over, is a neutral being, without sex and without country.

It is impossible for us to feel the other life, the eternal life, I have already repeated more than once, as a life of angelical contemplation; it must be a life of action. Goethe said that "man must believe in immortality, since in his nature he has a right to it." And he added: "The conviction of our persistence arises in me from the concept of activity. If I work without ceasing to the end, Nature is obliged (*so ist die Natur verpflichtet*) to provide me with another form of existence, since my actual spirit can bear no more." Change Nature to God, and you have a thought that remains Christian in character, for the first Fathers of the Church did not believe that the immortality of the soul was a natural gift—that is to say, something rational—but a divine gift of grace. And that which is of grace is usually, in its essence, of justice, since justice is divine and gratuitous, not natural. And Goethe added: "I could begin nothing with an eternal happiness before me, unless new tasks and new difficulties were given me to overcome." And true it is that there is no happiness in a vacuity of contemplation.

But may there not be some justification for the morality of the hermit, of the Carthusian, the ethic of the Thebaid? Might we not say, perhaps, that it is necessary to preserve these exceptional types in order that they may stand as everlasting patterns for mankind? Do not men breed racehorses, which are useless for any practical kind of work, but which preserve the purity of the breed and become the sires of excellent hackneys and hunters? Is there not a luxury of ethics, not less justifiable than any other sort of luxury? But, on the other hand, is not all this substantially esthetics, and not ethics, still less religion? May not the contemplative, medieval, monastic ideal be esthetical, and not religious nor even ethical? And after all, those of the seekers after solitude who have related to us their conversation when they were alone with God have performed an eternalizing work, they have concerned themselves with the souls of others. And by this alone, that it has given us an Eckhart, a Seuse, a Tauler, a Ruysbroek, a Juan de la Cruz, a Catherine of Siena, an Angela of Foligno, a Teresa de Jesús, is the cloister justified.

But the chief of our Spanish Orders are the Predicadores, founded by Domingo de Guzmán for the aggressive work of extirpating heresy; the Company of Jesus, a militia with the world as its field of operations (which explains its history); the order of the Escuelas Pías, also devoted to a work of an aggressive or invasive nature, that of instruction. I shall certainly be reminded that the reform of the contemplative Order of the Carmelites which Teresa de Jesús undertook was a Spanish work. Yes, Spanish it was, and in it men sought liberty.

It was, in fact, the yearning for liberty, for inward liberty, which, in the troubled days of the Inquisition, led many choice spirits to the cloister. They imprisoned themselves in order that they might be more free. " Is it not a fine thing that a poor nun of San José can attain to sovereignty over the whole earth and the elements ?" said St. Teresa in her *Life*. It was the Pauline yearning for liberty, the longing to shake off the bondage of the external law, which was then very severe, and, as Maestro Fray Luis de León said, very stubborn.

But did they actually find liberty in the cloister? It is very doubtful if they did, and to-day it is impossible. For true liberty is not to rid oneself of the external law; liberty is consciousness of the law. Not he who has shaken off the yoke of the law is free, but he who has made himself master of the law. Liberty must be sought in the midst of the world, which is the domain of the law, and of sin, the offspring of the law. That which we must be freed from is sin, which is collective.

Instead of renouncing the world in order that we may

19

dominate it—and who does not know the collective instinct of domination of those religious Orders whose members renounce the world?—what we ought to do is to dominate the world in order that we may be able to renounce it. Not to seek poverty and submission, but to seek wealth in order that we may use it to increase human consciousness, and to seek power for the same end.

It is curious that monks and anarchists should be at enmity with each other, when fundamentally they both profess the same ethic and are related by close ties of kinship. Anarchism tends to become a kind of atheistic monachism and a religious, rather than an ethical or economico-social, doctrine. The one party starts from the assumption that man is naturally evil, born in original sin, and that it is through grace that he becomes good, if indeed he ever does become good; and the other from the assumption that man is naturally good and is subsequently perverted by society. And these two theories really amount to the same thing, for in both the individual is opposed to society, as if the individual had preceded society and therefore were destined to survive it. And both ethics are ethics of the cloister.

And the fact that guilt is collective must not actuate me to throw mine upon the shoulders of others, but rather to take upon myself the burden of the guilt of others, the guilt of all men; not to merge and sink my guilt in the total mass of guilt, but to make this total guilt my own; not to dismiss and banish my own guilt, but to open the doors of my heart to the guilt of all men, to centre it within myself and appropriate it to myself. And each one of us ought to help to remedy the guilt, and just because others do not do so. The fact that society is guilty aggravates the guilt of each member of it. "Someone ought to do it, but why should I? is the ever re-echoed phrase of weak-kneed amiability. Someone ought to do it, so why not I? is the cry of some earnest servant of man, eagerly forward springing to face some perilous duty. Between these two sentences lie whole centuries of moral evolution.'' Thus spoke Mrs. Annie Besant in her autobiography. Thus spoke theosophy.

The fact that society is guilty aggravates the guilt of each one, and he is most guilty who most is sensible of the guilt. Christ, the innocent, since he best knew the intensity of the guilt, was in a certain sense the most guilty. In him the culpability, together with the divinity, of humanity arrived at the consciousness of itself. Many are wont to be amused when they read how, because of the most trifling faults, faults at which a man of the world would merely smile, the greatest saints counted themselves the greatest sinners. But the intensity of the fault is not measured by the external act, but by the consciousness of it, and an act for which the conscience of one man suffers acutely makes scarcely any impression on the conscience of another. And in a saint, conscience may be developed so fully and to such a degree of sensitiveness that the slightest sin may cause him more remorse than his crime causes the greatest criminal. And sin rests upon our consciousness of it, it is in him who judges and in so far as he judges. When a man commits a vicious act believing in good faith that he is doing a virtuous action, we cannot hold him morally guilty, while on the other hand that man is guilty who commits an act which he believes to be wrong, even though in itself the act is indifferent or perhaps beneficent. The act passes away, the intention remains, and the evil of the evil act is that it corrupts the intention, that in knowingly doing wrong a man is predisposed to go on doing it, that it blurs the conscience. And doing evil is not the same as being evil. Evil blurs the conscience, and not only the moral conscience but the general, psychical consciousness. And everything that exalts and expands consciousness is good, while that which depresses and diminishes it is evil.

And here we might raise the question which, according to Plato, was propounded by Socrates, as to whether virtue is knowledge, which is equivalent to asking whether virtue is rational.

The ethicists—those who maintain that ethics is a science, those whom the reading of these divagations will provoke to exclaim, " Rhetoric, rhetoric, rhetoric !"—would appear to think that virtue is the fruit of know-ledge, of rational study, and that even mathematics help us to be better men. I do not know, but for my part I feel that virtue, like religion, like the longing never to die—and all these are fundamentally the same thing—is the fruit of passion.

But, I shall be asked, What then is passion? I do not know, or rather, I know full well, because I feel it, and since I feel it there is no need for me to define it to myself. Nay, more ; I fear that if I were to arrive at a definition of it, I should cease to feel it and to possess it. Passion is like suffering, and like suffering it creates its object. It is easier for the fire to find something to burn than for something combustible to find the fire.

That this may appear empty and sophistical well I know. And I shall also be told that there is the science of passion and the passion of science, and that it is in the moral sphere that reason and life unite together.

I do not know, I do not know, I do not know. . . . And perhaps I may be saying fundamentally the same thing, although more confusedly, that my imaginary adversaries say, only more clearly, more definitely, and more rationally, those adversaries whom I imagine in order that I may have someone to fight. I do not know, I do not know. . . . But what they say freezes me and sounds to me as though it proceeded from emptiness of feeling.

And, returning to our former question, Is virtue know-ledge ?—Is knowledge virtue ? For they are two dis-tinct questions. Virtue may be a science, the science of

acting rightly, without every other science being therefore virtue. The virtue of Machiavelli is a science, and
it cannot be said that his *virtu* is always moral virtue.
It is well known, moreover, that the cleverest and the
most learned men are not the best.

No, no, no ! Physiology does not teach us how to
digest, nor logic how to discourse, nor esthetics how to
feel beauty or express it, nor ethics how to be good. And
indeed it is well if they do not teach us how to be hypocrites; for pedantry, whether it be the pedantry of logic,
or of esthetics, or of ethics, is at bottom nothing but
hypocrisy.

Reason perhaps teaches certain bourgeois virtues, but
it does not make either heroes or saints. Perhaps the
saint is he who does good not for good's sake, but for
God's sake, for the sake of eternalization.

Perhaps, on the other hand, culture, or as I should say
Culture—oh, this culture !—which is primarily the work
of philosophers and men of science, is a thing which
neither heroes nor saints have had any share in the
making of. For saints have concerned themselves very
little with the progress of human culture; they have concerned themselves rather with the salvation of the
individual souls of those amongst whom they lived. Of
what account in the history of human culture is our
San Juan de la Cruz, for example—that fiery little monk,
as culture, in perhaps somewhat uncultured phrase, has
called him—compared with Descartes ?

All those saints, burning with religious charity towards
their neighbours, hungering for their own and others'
eternalization, who went about burning hearts, inquisi-
tors, it may be—what have all those saints done for the
progress of the science of ethics ? Did any of them discover the categorical imperative, like the old bachelor of
Königsberg, who, if he was not a saint, deserved to
be one ?

The son of a famous professor of ethics, one who

scarcely ever opened his lips without mentioning the categorical imperative, was lamenting to me one day the fact that he lived in a desolating dryness of spirit, in a state of inward emptiness. And I was constrained to answer him thus: " My friend, your father had a subterranean river flowing through his spirit, a fresh current fed by the beliefs of his early childhood, by hopes in the beyond; and while he thought that he was nourishing his soul with this categorical imperative or something of that sort, he was in reality nourishing it with those waters which had their spring in his childish days. And it may be that to you he has given the flower of his spirit, his rational doctrines of ethics, but not the root, not the subterranean source, not the irrational substratum."

How was it that Krausism took root here in Spain, while Kantism and Hegelianism did not, although the two latter systems are much more profound, morally and philosophically, than the first? Because in transplanting the first, its roots were transplanted with it. The philosophical thought of a people or a period is, as it were, the flower, the thing that is external and above ground; but this flower, or fruit if you prefer it, draws its sap from the root of the plant, and this root, which is in and under the ground, is the religious sense. The philosophical thought of Kant, the supreme flower of the mental evolution of the Germanic people, has its roots in the religious feeling of Luther, and it is not possible for Kantism, especially the practical part of it, to take root and bring forth flower and fruit in peoples who have not undergone the experience of the Reformation and who perhaps were incapable of experiencing it. Kantism is Protestant, and we Spaniards are fundamentally Catholic. And if Krause struck some roots here—more numerous and more permanent than is commonly supposed—it is because Krause had roots in pietism, and pietism, as Ritschl has demonstrated in his *Geschichte*

*des Pietismus,* has specifically Catholic roots and may
be described as the irruption, or rather the persistence,
of Catholic mysticism in the heart of Protestant
rationalism.   And this explains why not a few Catholic
thinkers in Spain became followers of Krause.

And since we Spaniards are Catholic—whether we
know it or not, and whether we like it or not—and
although some of us may claim to be rationalists or
atheists, perhaps the greatest service we can render to
the cause of culture, and of what is of more value than
culture, religiousness—if indeed they are not the same
thing—is in endeavouring to formulate clearly to ourselves this subconscious, social, or popular Catholicism
of ours.   And that is what I have attempted to do in this
work.

What I call the tragic sense of life in men and peoples
is at any rate our tragic sense of life, that of Spaniards
and the Spanish people, as it is reflected in my consciousness, which is a Spanish consciousness, made in Spain.
And this tragic sense of life is essentially the Catholic
sense of it, for Catholicism, and above all popular
Catholicism, is tragic.   The people abhors comedy.
When Pilate—the type of the refined gentleman, the
superior person, the esthete, the rationalist if you like—
proposes to give the people comedy and mockingly presents Christ to them, saying, " Behold the man !" the
people mutinies and shouts " Crucify him ! Crucify
him !"   The people does not want comedy but tragedy.
And that which Dante, the great Catholic, called the
Divine Comedy, is the most tragical tragedy that has
ever been written.

And as I have endeavoured in these essays to exhibit
the soul of a Spaniard, and therewithal the Spanish soul,
I have curtailed the number of quotations from Spanish
writers, while scattering with perhaps too lavish a hand
those from the writers of other countries.   For all human
souls are brother-souls.

And there is one figure, a comically tragic figure, a figure in which is revealed all that is profoundly tragic in the human comedy, the figure of Our Lord Don Quixote, the Spanish Christ, who resumes and includes in himself the immortal soul of my people. Perhaps the passion and death of the Knight of the Sorrowful Countenance is the passion and death of the Spanish people, its death and resurrection. And there is a Quixotesque philosophy and even a Quixotesque metaphysic, there is a Quixotesque logic, and also a Quixotesque ethic and a Quixotesque religious sense— the religious sense of Spanish Catholicism. This is the philosophy, this is the logic, this is the ethic, this is the religious sense, that I have endeavoured to outline, to suggest rather than to develop, in this work. To develop it rationally, no; the Quixotesque madness does not submit to scientific logic.

And now, before concluding and bidding my readers farewell, it remains for me to speak of the rôle that is reserved for Don Quixote in the modern European tragicomedy.

Let us see, in the next and last essay, what this may be.

# CONCLUSION

## DON QUIXOTE IN THE CONTEMPORARY EUROPEAN TRAGI-COMEDY

"A voice crying in the wilderness !"—Isa. xl. 3.

NEED is that I bring to a conclusion, for the present at any rate, these essays that threaten to become like a tale that has no ending. They have gone straight from my hands to the press in the form of a kind of improvization upon notes collected during a number of years, and in writing each essay I have not had before me any of those that preceded it. And thus they will go forth full of inward contradictions—apparent contradictions, at any rate—like life and like me myself.

My sin, if any, has been that I have embellished them to excess with foreign quotations, many of which will appear to have been dragged in with a certain degree of violence. But I will explain this another time.

A few years after Our Lord Don Quixote had journeyed through Spain, Jacob Böhme declared in his *Aurora* (chap xi., § 142) that he did not write a story or history related to him by others, but that he himself had had to stand in the battle, which he found to be full of heavy strivings, and wherein he was often struck down to the ground like all other men ; and a little further on (§ 152) he adds : " Although I must become a spectacle of scorn to the world and the devil, yet my hope is in God concerning the life to come; in Him will I venture to hazard it and not resist or strive against the Spirit. Amen." And like this Quixote of the German intellectual world, neither will I resist the Spirit.

297

And therefore I cry with the voice of one crying in the wilderness, and I send forth my cry from this University of Salamanca, a University that arrogantly styled itself *omnium scientiarum princeps,* and which Carlyle called a stronghold of ignorance and which a French man of letters recently called a phantom University; I send it forth from this Spain—'' the land of dreams that become realities, the rampart of Europe, the home of the knightly ideal,'' to quote from a letter which the American poet Archer M. Huntington sent me the other day —from this Spain which was the head and front of the Counter-Reformation in the sixteenth century. And well they repay her for it !

In the fourth of these essays I spoke of the essence of Catholicism. And the chief factors in *de-essentializing* it—that is, in de-Catholicizing Europe—have been the Renaissance, the Reformation, and the Revolution, which for the ideal of an eternal, ultra-terrestrial life, have substituted the ideal of progress, of reason, of science, or, rather, of Science with the capital letter. And last of all, the dominant ideal of to-day, comes Culture.

And in the second half of the nineteenth century, an age essentially unphilosophical and technical, dominated by a myopic specialism and by historical materialism, this ideal took a practical form, not so much in the popularization as in the vulgarization of science—or, rather, of pseudo-science—venting itself in a flood of cheap, popular, and propagandist literature. Science sought to popularize itself as if it were its function to come down to the people and subserve their passions, and not the duty of the people to rise to science and through science to rise to higher heights, to new and profounder aspirations.

All this led Brunetière to proclaim the bankruptcy of science, and this science—if you like to call it science— did in effect become bankrupt. And as it failed to satisfy, men continued their quest for happiness, but without finding it, either in wealth, or in knowledge, or in power, or in pleasure, or in resignation, or in a good conscience, or in culture. And the result was pessimism.

Neither did the gospel of progress satisfy. What end did progress serve? Man would not accommodate himself to rationalism; the *Kulturkampf* did not suffice him; he sought to give a final finality to life, and what I call the final finality is the real ὄντως ὄν. And the famous *maladie du siècle,* which announced itself in Rousseau and was exhibited more plainly in Sénancour's *Obermann* than in any other character, neither was nor is anything else but the loss of faith in the immortality of the soul, in the human finality of the Universe.

The truest symbol of it is to be found in a creation of fiction, Dr. Faustus.

This immortal Dr. Faustus, the product of the Renaissance and the Reformation, first comes into our ken at the beginning of the seventeenth century, when in 1604 he is introduced to us by Christopher Marlowe. This is the same character that Goethe was to rediscover two centuries later, although in certain respects the earlier Faust was the fresher and more spontaneous. And side by side with him Mephistopheles appears, of whom Faust asks: "What good will my soul do thy lord?" "Enlarge his kingdom," Mephistopheles replies. "Is that the reason why he tempts us thus?" the Doctor asks again, and the evil spirit answers: "*Solamen miseris socios habuisse doloris,*" which, mistranslated into Romance, is the equivalent of our proverb—"The misfortune of many is the consolation of fools." "Where we are is hell, and where hell is there must we ever be," Mephistopheles continues, to which Faust answers that he thinks hell's a fable and asks him who made the world. And finally this tragic Doctor, tortured with our torture, meets Helen, who, although no doubt Marlowe never suspected it, is none other than renascent Culture. And in Marlowe's *Faust* there is a scene that is worth the whole of the second part of the *Faust* of Goethe. Faust says to Helen : "Sweet Helen, make me immortal with a kiss "—and he kisses her—

> Her lips suck forth my soul ; see where it flies !
> Come, Helen, come, give me my soul again.
> Here will I dwell, for Helen is in these lips,
> And all is dross that is not Helena.

Give me my soul again !—the cry of Faust, the Doctor, when, after having kissed Helen, he is about to be lost eternally. For the primitive Faust has no ingenuous Margaret to save him. This idea of his salvation was the invention of Goethe. And is there not a Faust whom we all know, our own Faust? This Faust has studied·Philosophy, Jurisprudence, Medicine, and even Theology, only to find that we can know nothing, and he has sought escape in the open country (*hinaus ins weite Land*) and has encountered Mephistopheles, the embodiment of that force which, ever willing evil, ever achieves good in its own despite. This Faust has been led by Mephistopheles to the arms of Margaret, child of the simple-hearted people, she whom Faust, the over-wise, had lost. And thanks to her—for she gave herself to him—this Faust is saved, redeemed by the people that believes with a simple faith. But there was a second part, for that Faust was the anecdotical Faust and not the categorical Faust of Goethe, and he gave himself again to Culture, to Helen, and begot Euphorion upon her, and everything ends among mystical choruses with the discovery of the eternal feminine. Poor Euphorion !

And this Helen is the spouse of the fair Menelaus, the Helen whom Paris bore away, who was the cause of the war of Troy, and of whom the ancient Trojans said that no one should be incensed because men fought for a woman who bore so terrible a likeness to the immortal gods. But I rather think that Faust's Helen was that other Helen who accompanied Simon Magus, and whom he declared to be the divine wisdom. And Faust can say to her : Give me my soul again !

For Helen with her kisses takes away our soul. And what we long for and have need of is soul—soul of bulk and substance.

But the Renaissance, the Reformation, and the Revolution came, bringing Helen to us, or, rather, urged on by Helen, and now they talk to us about Culture and Europe.

Europe ! This idea of Europe, primarily and immediately of geographical significance, has been converted for us by some magical process into a kind of metaphysical category. Who can say to-day—in Spain, at any rate—what Europe is ? I only know that it is a shibboleth (*vide* my *Tres Ensayos*). And when I proceed to examine what it is that our Europeanizers call Europe, it sometimes seems to me that much of its periphery remains outside of it—Spain, of course, and also England, Italy, Scandinavia, Russia—and hence it is reduced to the central portion, Franco-Germany, with its annexes and dependencies.

All this is the consequence, I repeat, of the Renaissance and the Reformation, which, although apparently they lived in a state of internecine war, were twin-brothers. The Italians of the Renaissance were all of them Socinians; the humanists, with Erasmus at their head, regarded Luther, the German monk, as a barbarian, who derived his driving force from the cloister, as did Bruno and Campanella. But this barbarian was their twin-brother, and though their antagonist he was also the antagonist of the common enemy. All this, I say, is due to the Renaissance and the Reformation, and to what was the offspring of these two, the Revolution, and to them we owe also a new Inquisition, that of science or culture, which turns against those who refuse

to submit to its orthodoxy the weapons of ridicule and
contempt.

When Galileo sent his treatise on the earth's motion
to the Grand Duke of Tuscany, he told him that it was
meet that that which the higher authorities had deter-
mined should be believed and obeyed, and that he considered his treatise "as poetry or as a dream, and as
such I desire your highness to receive it." And at
other times he calls it a "chimera" or a "mathematical
caprice." And in the same way in these essays, for
fear also—why not confess it?—of the Inquisition, of
the modern, the scientific, Inquisition, I offer as a
poetry, dream, chimera, mystical caprice, that which
springs from what is deepest in me. And I say with
Galileo, *Eppur si muove!* But is it only because of
this fear? Ah, no! for there is another, more tragic
Inquisition, and that is the Inquisition which the modern
man, the man of culture, the European—and such am I,
whether I will or not—carries within him. There is a
more terrible ridicule, and that is the ridicule with which
a man contemplates his own self. It is my reason that
laughs at my faith and despises it.

And it is here that I must betake me to my Lord Don
Quixote in order that I may learn of him how to confront ridicule and overcome it, and a ridicule which
perhaps—who knows?—he never knew.

Yes, yes—how shall my reason not smile at these
dilettantesque, would-be mystical, pseudo-philosophical
interpretations, in which there is anything rather than
patient study and—shall I say scientific?—objectivity
and method? And nevertheless . . . *eppur si muove!*

*Eppur si muove!* And I take refuge in dilettantism,
in what a pedant would call *demi-mondaine* philosophy,
as a shelter against the pedantry of specialists, against
the philosophy of the professional philosophers. And
who knows? . . . Progress usually comes from the
barbarian, and there is nothing more stagnant than the

philosophy of the philosophers and the theology of the theologians.

Let them talk to us of Europe! The civilization of Thibet is parallel with ours, and men who disappear like ourselves have lived and are living by it. And over all civilizations there hovers the shadow of Ecclesiastes, with his admonition, "How dieth the wise man?—as the fool " (ii. 16).

Among the people of my country there is an admirable reply to the customary interrogation, "How are you?"[1] and it is "Living." And that is the truth—we are living, and living as much as all the rest. What can a man ask for more? And who does not recollect the verse?—

> Cada vez que considero
> que me tengo de morir,
> tiendo la capa en el suelo
> y no me harto de dormir.[2]

But no, not sleeping, but dreaming—dreaming life, since life is a dream.

Among us Spaniards another phrase has very rapidly passed into current usage, the expression " It's a question of passing the time," or " killing the time." And, in fact, we make time in order to kill it. But there is something that has always preoccupied us as much as or more than passing the time—a formula which denotes an esthetical attitude—and that is, gaining eternity, which is the formula of the religious attitude. The truth is, we leap from the esthetic and the economic to the religious, passing over the logical and the ethical; we jump from art to religion.

One of our younger novelists, Ramón Pérez de Ayala, in his recent novel, La Pata de la Raposa, has told us that the idea of death is the trap, and spirit

---

[1] " Que tal ?" o " como va?" y es aquella que responde : " se vive !"

[2] Whenever I consider that I needs must die, I stretch my cloak upon the ground and am not surfeited with sleeping.

the fox or the wary virtue with which to circumvent the
ambushes set by fatality, and he continues: "Caught
in the trap, weak men and weak peoples lie prone on the
ground . . .; to robust spirits and strong peoples the
rude shock of danger gives clear-sightedness; they
quickly penetrate into the heart of the immeasurable
beauty of life, and renouncing for ever their original
hastiness and folly, emerge from the trap with muscles
taut for action and with the soul's vigour, power, and
efficiency increased a hundredfold." But let us see;
weak men . . . weak peoples . . . robust spirits . . .
strong peoples . . . what does all this mean? I do not
know. What I think I know is that some individuals
and peoples have not yet really thought about death and
immortality, have not felt them, and that others have
ceased to think about them, or rather ceased to feel them.
And the fact that they have never passed through the
religious period is not, I think, a matter for either men
or peoples to boast about.

The immeasurable beauty of life is a very fine thing to
write about, and there are, indeed, some who resign
themselves to it and accept it as it is, and even some who
would persuade us that there is no problem in the
"trap." But it has been said by Calderón that "to
seek to persuade a man that the misfortunes which he
suffers are not misfortunes, does not console him for
them, but is another misfortune in addition."[1]    And,
furthermore, "only the heart can speak to the heart,"
as Fray Diego de Estella said (*Vanidad del Mundo*,
cap. xxi.).

A short time ago a reply that I made to those who
reproached us Spaniards for our scientific incapacity
appeared to scandalize some people. After having remarked that the electric light and the steam engine func-

___
[1] No es consuelo de desdichas—es otra desdicha aparte—querer a quien las
padece—persuadir que no son tales (*Gustos y disgustos no son más que imagina-
ción*, Act I., Scene 4).

tion here in Spain just as well as in the countries where
they were invented, and that we make use of logarithms
as much as they do in the country where the idea of them
was first conceived, I exclaimed, " Let others invent!"
—a paradoxical expression which I do not retract. We
Spaniards ought to appropriate to ourselves some of
those sage counsels which Count Joseph de Maistre gave
to the Russians, a people not unlike ourselves. In his
admirable letters to Count Rasoumowski on public
education in Russia, he said that a nation should not
think the worse of itself because it was not made for
science; that the Romans had no understanding of the
arts, neither did they possess a mathematician, which,
however, did not prevent them from playing their part
in the world; and in particular we should take to heart
everything that he said about that crowd of arrogant
sciolists who idolize the tastes, the fashions, and the
languages of foreign countries, and are ever ready to
pull down whatever they despise—and they despise
everything.

We have not the scientific spirit? And what of that,
if we have some other spirit? And who can tell if the
spirit that we have is or is not compatible with the
scientific spirit?

But in saying " Let others invent!" I did not mean to
imply that we must be content with playing a passive
rôle. No. For them their science, by which we shall
profit; for us, our own work. It is not enough to be on
the defensive, we must attack.

But we must attack wisely and cautiously. Reason
must be our weapon. It is the weapon even of the fool.
Our sublime fool and our exemplar, Don Quixote, after
he had destroyed with two strokes of his sword that
pasteboard visor " which he had fitted to his head-piece,
made it anew, placing certain iron bars within it, in such
a manner that he rested satisfied with its solidity, and
without wishing to make a second trial of it, he deputed

20

and held it in estimation of a most excellent visor.''[1]  And
with the pasteboard visor on his head he made himself
immortal—that is to say, he made himself ridiculous
For it was by making himself ridiculous that Don
Quixote achieved his immortality.

And there are so many ways of making ourselves
ridiculous! . . .  Cournot said (*Traité de l'enchaînement des idées fondamentales*, etc., § 510) : " It is best
not to speak to either princes or peoples of the probabili-
ties of death ; princes will punish this temerity with dis-
grace ; the public will revenge itself with ridicule." True,
and therefore it is said that we must live as the age lives.
*Corrumpere et corrumpi sæculum vocatur* (Tacitus:
*Germania* 19).

It is necessary to know how to make ourselves ridiculous, and not only to others but to ourselves.   And more
than ever to-day, when there is so much chatter about
our backwardness compared with other civilized peoples,
to-day when a parcel of shallow-brained critics say that
we have had no science, no art, no philosophy, no Renaissance, (of this we had perhaps too much), no anything, these same critics being ignorant of our real
history, a history that remains yet to be written, the first
task being to undo the web of calumniation and protest
that has been woven around it.

Carducci, the author of the phrase about the *con-
torcimenti dell'affannosa grandiosità spagnola*, has
written (in *Mosche Cochiere*) that " even Spain, which
never attained the hegemony of the world of thought,
had her Cervantes."   But was Cervantes a solitary and
isolated phenomenon, without roots, without ancestry,
without a foundation ?  That an Italian rationalist, remembering that it was Spain that reacted against the
Renaissance in his country, should say that Spain *non
ebbe egemonia mai di pensiero* is, however, readily comprehended.   Was there no importance, was there nothing

----

[1] *Don Quijote*, part i., chap. i.

akin to cultural hegemony, in the Counter-Reformation, of which Spain was the champion, and which in point of fact began with the sack of Rome by the Spaniards, a providential chastisement of the city of the pagan popes of the pagan Renaissance? Apart from the question as to whether the Counter-Reformation was good or bad, was there nothing akin to hegemony in Loyola or the Council of Trent? Previous to this Council, Italy witnessed a nefarious and unnatural union between Christianity and Paganism, or rather, between immortalism and mortalism, a union to which even some of the Popes themselves consented in their souls; theological error was philosophical truth, and all difficulties were solved by the accommodating formula *salva fide*. But it was otherwise after the Council; after the Council came the open and avowed struggle between reason and faith, science and religion. And does not the fact that this change was brought about, thanks principally to Spanish obstinacy, point to something akin to hegemony?

Without the Counter-Reformation, would the Reformation have followed the course that it did actually follow? without the Counter-Reformation might not the Reformation, deprived of the support of pietism, have perished in the gross rationalism of the *Aufklärung*, of the age of Enlightenment? Would nothing have been changed had there been no Charles I., no Philip II., our great Philip?

A negative achievement, it will be said. But what is that? What is negative? what is positive? At what point in time—a line always continuing in the same direction, from the past to the future—does the zero occur which denotes the boundary between the positive and the negative? Spain, which is said to be the land of knights and rogues—and all of them rogues—has been the country most slandered by history precisely because it championed the Counter-Reformation. And because its arrogance has prevented it from stepping down into the public forum, into the world's vanity fair, and publishing its own justification.

Let us leave on one side Spain's eight centuries of warfare against the Moors, during which she defended Europe from Mohammedanism, her work of internal unification, her discovery of America and the Indies— for this was the achievement of Spain and Portugal, and not of Columbus and Vasco da Gama—let us leave all this, and more than this, on one side, and it is not a little thing. Is it not a cultural achievement to have created a score of nations, reserving nothing for herself, and to have begotten, as the Conquistadores did, free men on poor Indian slaves? Apart from all this, does our mysticism count for nothing in the world of thought? Perhaps the peoples whose souls Helen will ravish away with her kisses may some day have to return to this mysticism to find their souls again.

But, as everybody knows, Culture is composed of ideas and only of ideas, and man is only Culture's instrument. Man for the idea, and not the idea for man; the substance for the shadow. The end of man is to create science, to catalogue the Universe, so that it may be handed back to God in order, as I wrote years ago in my novel, *Amor y Pedagogía*. Man, apparently, is not even an idea. And at the end of all, the human race will fall exhausted at the foot of a pile of libraries—whole woods rased to the ground to provide the paper that is stored away in them—museums, machines, factories, laboratories . . . in order to bequeath them—to whom? For God will surely not accept them.

That horrible regenerationist literature, almost all of it an imposture, which the loss of our last American colonies provoked, led us into the pedantry of extolling persevering and silent effort — and this with great vociferation, vociferating silence—of extolling prudence, exactitude, moderation, spiritual fortitude, synteresis,

equanimity, the social virtues, and the chiefest advocates
of them were those of us who lacked them most. Almost
all of us Spaniards fell into this ridiculous mode of literature, some more and some less. And so it befell that
that arch-Spaniard Joaquín Costa, one of the least
European spirits we ever had, invented his famous saying that we must Europeanize Spain, and, while pro-
claiming that we must lock up the sepulchre of the Cid
with a sevenfold lock, Cid-like urged us to—conquer
Africa! And I myself uttered the cry, "Down with
Don Quixote!" and from this blasphemy, which meant
the very opposite of what it said—such was the fashion
of the hour—sprang my *Vida de Don Quijote y Sancho*
and my cult of Quixotism as the national religion.

I wrote that book in order to rethink *Don Quixote* in
opposition to the Cervantists and erudite persons, in
order to make a living work of what was and still is for
the majority a dead letter. What does it matter to me
what Cervantes intended or did not intend to put into it
and what he actually did put into it? What is living in
it is what I myself discover in it, whether Cervantes put
it there or not, what I myself put into and under and
over it, and what we all put into it. I wanted to hunt
down our philosophy in it.

For the conviction continually grows upon me that
our philosophy, the Spanish philosophy, is liquescent
and diffused in our literature, in our life, in our action,
in our mysticism, above all, and not in philosophical
systems. It is concrete. And is there not perhaps as
much philosophy or more in Goethe, for example, as in
Hegel? The poetry of Jorge Manrique, the Romancero,
*Don Quijote, La Vida es Sueño*, the *Subida al Monte
Carmelo*, imply an intuition of the world and a concept
of life (*Weltanschauung und Lebensansicht*). And it
was difficult for this philosophy of ours to formulate itself
in the second half of the nineteenth century, a period that
was aphilosophical, positivist, technicist, devoted to

pure history and the natural sciences, a period essentially materialist and pessimist.

Our language itself, like every cultured language, contains within itself an implicit philosophy.

A language, in effect, is a potential philosophy. Platonism is the Greek language which discourses in Plato, unfolding its secular metaphors; scholasticism is the philosophy of the dead Latin of the Middle Ages wrestling with the popular tongues; the French language discourses in Descartes, the German in Kant and in Hegel, and the English in Hume and in Stuart Mill. For the truth is that the logical starting-point of all philosophical speculation is not the I, neither is it representation (*Vorstellung*), nor the world as it presents itself immediately to the senses; but it is mediate or historical representation, humanly elaborated and such as it is given to us principally in the language by means of which we know the world; it is not psychical but spiritual representation. When we think, we are obliged to set out, whether we know it not and whether we will or not, from what has been thought by others who came before us and who environ us. Thought is an inheritance. Kant thought in German, and into German he translated Hume and Rousseau, who thought in English and French respectively. And did not Spinoza think in Judeo-Portuguese, obstructed by and contending with Dutch?

Thought rests upon prejudgements, and prejudgements pass into language. To language Bacon rightly ascribed not a few of the errors of the *idola fori*. But is it possible to philosophize in pure algebra or even in Esperanto? In order to see the result of such an attempt one has only to read the work of Avenarius on the criticism of pure experience (*reine Erfahrung*), of this prehuman or inhuman experience. And even Avenarius, who was obliged to invent a language, invented one that was based upon the Latin tradition, with roots which

carry in their metaphorical implications a content of
impure experience, of human social experience.

All philosophy is, therefore, at bottom philology.
And philology, with its great and fruitful law of
analogical formations, opens wide the door to chance, to
the irrational, to the absolutely incommensurable. History is not mathematics, neither is philosophy. And
how many philosophical ideas are not strictly owing to
something akin to rhyme, to the necessity of rightly
placing a consonant! In Kant himself there is a great
deal of this, of esthetic symmetry, rhyme.

Representation is, therefore, like language, like reason
itself—which is simply internal language—a social and
racial product, and race, the blood of the spirit, is language, as Oliver Wendell Holmes has said, and as I
have often repeated.

It was in Athens and with Socrates that our Western
philosophy first became mature, conscious of itself, and
it arrived at this consciousness by means of the dialogue,
of social conversation. And it is profoundly significant
that the doctrine of innate ideas, of the objective and
normative value of ideas, of what Scholasticism afterwards knew as Realism, should have formulated itself in
dialogues. And these ideas, which constitute reality,
are names, as Nominalism showed. Not that they may
not be more than names (*flatus vocis*), but that they are
nothing less than names. Language is that which gives
us reality, and not as a mere vehicle of reality, but as
its true flesh, of which all the rest, dumb or inarticulate
representation, is merely the skeleton. And thus logic
operates upon esthetics, the concept upon the expression,
upon the word, and not upon the brute perception.

And this is true even in the matter of love. Love
does not discover that it is love until it speaks, until it
says, I love thee! In Stendhal's novel, *La Chartreuse
de Parme*, it is with a very profound intuition that Count
Mosca, furious with jealousy because of the love which

he believes unites the Duchess of Sanseverina with his nephew Fabrice, is made to say, " I must be calm; if my manner is violent the duchess, simply because her vanity is piqued, is capable of following Belgirate, and then, during the journey, chance may lead to a word which will give a name to the feelings they bear towards each other, and thereupon in a moment all the consequences will follow."

Even so—all things were made by the word, and the word was in the beginning.

Thought, reason—that is, living language—is an inheritance, and the solitary thinker of Aben Tofail, the Arab philosopher of Guadix, is as absurd as the ego of Descartes. The real and concrete truth, not the methodical and ideal, is: *homo sum, ergo cogito.* To feel oneself a man is more immediate than to think. But, on the other hand, History, the process of culture, finds its perfection and complete effectivity only in the individual; the end of History and Humanity is man, each man, each individual. *Homo sum, ergo cogito; cogito ut sim Michael de Unamuno.* The individual is the end of the Universe.

And we Spaniards feel this very strongly, that the individual is the end of the Universe. The introspective individuality of the Spaniard was pointed out by Martin A. S. Hume in a passage in *The Spanish People,*[1] upon which I commented in an essay published in *La España Moderna.*[2]

And it is perhaps this same introspective individualism which has not permitted the growth on Spanish soil of strictly philosophical—or, rather, metaphysical—systems. And this in spite of Suárez, whose formal subtilties do not merit the name of philosophy.

Our metaphysics, if we can be said to possess such a thing, has been metanthropics, and our metaphysicians

---

[1] Preface
[2] *El individualismo español,* in vol. clxxi., March 1, 1903.

have been philologists—or, rather, humanists—in the most comprehensive sense of the term.

Menéndez de Pelayo, as Benedetto Croce very truly said (*Estetica*, bibliographical appendix), was inclined towards metaphysical idealism, but he appeared to wish to take something from other systems, even from empirical theories. For this reason Croce considers that his work (referring to his *Historia de las ideas estéticas de España*) suffers from a certain uncertainty, from the theoretical point of view of its author, Menéndez de Pelayo, which was that of a perfervid Spanish humanist, who, not wishing to disown the Renaissance, invented what he called Vivism, the philosophy of Luis Vives, and perhaps for no other reason than because he himself, like Vives, was an eclectic Spaniard of the Renaissance. And it is true that Menéndez de Pelayo, whose philosophy is certainly all uncertainty, educated in Barcelona in the timidities of the Scottish philosophy as it had been imported into the Catalan spirit—that creeping philosophy of common sense, which was anxious not to compromise itself and yet was all compromise, and which is so well exemplified in Balmes—always shunned all strenuous inward combat and formed his consciousness upon compromises.

Angel Ganivet, a man all divination and instinct, was more happily inspired, in my opinion, when he proclaimed that the Spanish philosophy was that of Seneca, the pagan Stoic of Cordoba, whom not a few Christians regarded as one of themselves, a philosophy lacking in originality of thought but speaking with great dignity of tone and accent. His accent was a Spanish, Latino-African accent, not Hellenic, and there are echoes of him in Tertullian—Spanish, too, at heart—who believed in the corporal and substantial nature of God and the soul, and who was a kind of Don Quixote in the world of Christian thought in the second century.

But perhaps we must look for the hero of Spanish

thought, not in any actual flesh-and-bone philosopher, but in a creation of fiction, a man of action, who is more real than all the philosophers—Don Quixote. There is undoubtedly a philosophical Quixotism, but there is also a Quixotic philosophy. May it not perhaps be that the philosophy of the Conquistadores, of the Counter-Reformers, of Loyola, and above all, in the order of abstract but deeply felt thought, that of our mystics, was, in its essence, none other than this? What was the mysticism of St. John of the Cross but a knight-errantry of the heart in the divine warfare?

And the philosophy of Don Quixote cannot strictly be called idealism; he did not fight for ideas. It was of the spiritual order; he fought for the spirit.

Imagine Don Quixote turning his heart to religious speculation—as he himself once dreamed of doing when he met those images in bas-relief which certain peasants were carrying to set up in the retablo of their village church[1]—imagine Don Quixote given up to meditation upon eternal truths, and see him ascending Mount Carmel in the middle of the dark night of the soul, to watch from its summit the rising of that sun which never sets, and, like the eagle that was St. John's companion in the isle of Patmos, to gaze upon it face to face and scrutinize its spots. He leaves to Athena's owl—the goddess with the glaucous, or owl-like, eyes, who sees in the dark but who is dazzled by the light of noon—he leaves to the owl that accompanied Athena in Olympus the task of searching with keen eyes in the shadows for the prey wherewith to feed its young.

And the speculative or meditative Quixotism is, like the practical Quixotism, madness, a daughter-madness to the madness of the Cross. And therefore it is despised by the reason. At bottom, philosophy abhors

[1] See *El ingenioso hidalgo Don Quijote de la Mancha*, part ii., chap. lviii., and the corresponding chapter in my *Vida de Don Quijote y Sancho*.

Christianity, and well did the gentle Marcus Aurelius prove it.

The tragedy of Christ, the divine tragedy, is the tragedy of the Cross. Pilate, the sceptic, the man of culture, by making a mockery of it, sought to convert it into a comedy; he conceived the farcical idea of the king with the reed sceptre and crown of thorns, and cried " Behold the man !" But the people, more human than he, the people that thirsts for tragedy, shouted, " Crucify him ! crucify him !" And the human, the intra-human, tragedy is the tragedy of Don Quixote, whose face was daubed with soap in order that he might make sport for the servants of the dukes and for the dukes themselves, as servile as their servants. " Behold the madman !" they would have said. And the comic, the irrational, tragedy is the tragedy of suffering caused by ridicule and contempt.

The greatest height of heroism to which an individual, like a people, can attain is to know how to face ridicule; better still, to know how to make oneself ridiculous and not to shrink from the ridicule.

I have already spoken of the forceful sonnets of that tragic Portuguese, Antero de Quental, who died by his own hand. Feeling acutely for the plight of his country on the occasion of the British ultimatum in 1890, he wrote as follows :[1] " An English statesman of the last century, who was also undoubtedly a perspicacious observer and a philosopher, Horace Walpole, said that for those who feel, life is a tragedy, and a comedy for those who think. Very well, then, if we are destined to end tragically, we Portuguese, we who *feel*, we would far rather prefer this terrible, but noble, destiny, to that which is reserved, and perhaps at no very remote future

[1] In an article which was to have been published on the occasion of the ultimatum, and of which the original is in the possession of the Conde do Ameal. This fragment appeared in the Portuguese review, *A Aguia* (No. 3), March, 1912.

date, for England, the country that *thinks* and *calculates*, whose destiny it is to finish miserably and comically." We may leave on one side the assertion that the English are a thinking and calculating people, implying thereby their lack of feeling, the injustice of which is explained by the occasion which provoked it, and also the assertion that the Portuguese feel, implying that they do not think or calculate—for we twin-brothers of the Atlantic sea-board have always been distinguished by a certain pedantry of feeling; but there remains a basis of truth underlying this terrible idea—namely, that some peoples, those who put thought above feeling, I should say reason above faith, die comically, while those die tragically who put faith above reason. For the mockers are those who die comically, and God laughs at their comic ending, while the nobler part, the part of tragedy, is theirs who endured the mockery.

The mockery that underlies the career of Don Quixote is what we must endeavour to discover.

And shall we be told yet again that there has never been any Spanish philosophy in the technical sense of the word? I will answer by asking, What is this sense? What does philosophy mean? Windelband, the historian of philosophy, in his essay on the meaning of philosophy (*Was ist Philosophie?* in the first volume of his *Praludien*) tells us that "the history of the word ' philosophy ' is the history of the cultural significance of science." He continues : " When scientific thought attains an independent existence as a desire for knowledge for the sake of knowledge, it takes the name of philosophy; when subsequently knowledge as a whole divides into its various branches, philosophy is the general knowledge of the world that embraces all other knowledge. As soon as scientific thought stoops again to becoming a means to ethics or religious contemplation, philosophy is transformed into an art of life or into a formulation of religious beliefs. And when afterwards

the scientific life regains its liberty, philosophy acquires
once again its character as an independent knowledge of
the world, and in so far as it abandons the attempt to
solve this problem, it is changed into a theory of knowledge itself." Here you have a brief recapitulation of
the history of philosophy from Thales to Kant, including
the medieval scholasticism upon which it endeavoured
to establish religious beliefs. But has philosophy no
other office to perform, and may not its office be to reflect
upon the tragic sense of life itself, such as we have been
studying it, to formulate this conflict between reason
and faith, between science and religion, and deliberately
to perpetuate this conflict?

Later on Windelband says : " By philosophy in the
systematic, not in the historical, sense, I understand the
critical knowledge of values of universal validity
(*allgemeingiltigen Werten*)." But what values are there
of more universal validity than that of the human will
seeking before all else the personal, individual, and concrete immortality of the soul—or, in other words, the
human finality of the Universe—and that of the human
reason denying the rationality and even the possibility
of this desire? What values are there of more universal
validity than the rational or mathematical value and the
volitional or teleological value of the Universe in conflict with one another?

For Windelband, as for Kantians and neo-Kantians
in general, there are only three normative categories,
three universal norms—those of the true or the false, the
beautiful or the ugly, and the morally good or evil.
Philosophy is reduced to logics, esthetics, and ethics,
accordingly as it studies science, art, or morality.
Another category remains excluded—namely, that of the
pleasing and the unpleasing, or the agreeable and the
disagreeable : in other words, the hedonic. The hedonic
cannot, according to them, pretend to universal validity,
it cannot be normative. " Whosoever throws upon

philosophy," wrote Windelband, " the burden of deciding the question of optimism and pessimism, whosoever demands that philosophy should pronounce judgement on the question as to whether the world is more adapted to produce pain than pleasure, or *vice versa*—such a one, if his attitude is not merely that of a dilettante, sets himself the fantastic task of finding an absolute determination in a region in which no reasonable man has ever looked for one." It remains to be seen, nevertheless, whether this is as clear as it seems, in the case of a man like myself, who am at the same time reasonable and yet nothing but a dilettante, which of course would be the abomination of desolation.

It was with a very profound insight that Benedetto Croce, in his philosophy of the spirit in relation to esthetics as the science of expression and to logic as the science of pure concept, divided practical philosophy into two branches—economics and ethics. He recognizes, in effect, the existence of a practical grade of spirit, purely economical, directed towards the singular and unconcerned with the universal. Its types of perfection, of economic genius, are Iago and Napoleon, and this grade remains outside morality. And every man passes through this grade, because before all else he must wish to be himself, as an individual, and without this grade morality would be inexplicable, just as without esthetics logic would lack meaning. And the discovery of the normative value of the economic grade, which seeks the hedonic, was not unnaturally the work of an Italian, a disciple of Machiavelli, who speculated so fearlessly with regard to *virtù*, practical efficiency, which is not exactly the same as moral virtue.

But at bottom this economic grade is but the rudimentary state of the religious grade. The religious is the transcendental economic or hedonic. Religion is a transcendental economy and hedonistic. That which man seeks in religion, in religious faith, is to save his own individuality, to eternalize it, which he achieves neither by science, nor by art, nor by ethics. God is a necessity neither for science, nor art, nor ethics; what necessitates God is religion. And with an insight that amounts to genius our Jesuits speak of the grand business of our salvation. Business—yes, business: something belonging to the economic, hedonistic order, although transcendental. We do not need God in order that He may teach us the truth of things, or the beauty of them, or in order that He may safeguard morality by means of a system of penalties and punishments, but in order that He may save us, in order that He may not let us die utterly. And because this unique longing is the longing of each and every normal man—those who are abnormal by reason of their barbarism or their hyperculture may be left out of the reckoning—it is universal and normative.

Religion, therefore, is a transcendental economy, or, if you like, metaphysic. Together with its logical, esthetic, and ethical values, the Universe has for man an economic value also, which, when thus made universal and normative, is the religious value. We are not concerned only with truth, beauty, and goodness: we are concerned also and above all with the salvation of the individual, with perpetuation, which those norms do not secure for us. That science of economy which is called political teaches us the most adequate, the most economical way of satisfying our needs, whether these needs are rational or irrational, beautiful or ugly, moral or immoral—a business economically good may be a swindle, something that in the long run kills the soul—and the supreme human *need* is the need of not dying, the need of enjoying for ever the plenitude of our own individual limitation. And if the Catholic eucharistic doctrine teaches that the substance of the body of Jesus Christ is present whole and entire in the consecrated Host, and in each part of it, this means that God is wholly and entirely in the whole Universe and also in each one of the individuals that compose it. And this is, fundamentally, not a logical, nor an esthetic, nor an ethical priciple, but a transcendental economic or religious principle. And with this norm, philosophy is able to judge of optimism and pessimism. *If the human soul is immortal, the world is economically or hedonistically good; if not, it is bad.* And the meaning which pessimism and optimism give to the categories of good and evil is not an ethical sense, but an economic or hedonistic sense. Good is that which satisfies our vital longing and evil is that which does not satisfy it.

Philosophy, therefore, is also the science of the tragedy of life, a reflection upon the tragic sense of it. An essay in this philosophy, with its inevitable internal contradictions and antinomies, is what I have attempted in these essays. And the reader must not overlook the fact that I have been operating upon myself; that this work partakes of the nature of a piece of self-surgery, and without any other anesthetic than that of the work itself. The enjoyment of operating upon myself has ennobled the pain of being operated upon.

And as for my other claim—the claim that this is a Spanish philosophy, perhaps *the* Spanish philosophy, that if it was an Italian who discovered the normative and universal value of the economic grade, it is a Spaniard who announces that this grade is merely the beginning of the religious grade, and that the essence of our religion, of our Spanish Catholicism, consists precisely in its being neither a science, nor an art, nor an ethic, but an economy of things eternal—that is to say, of things divine : as for this claim that all this is Spanish, I must leave the task of substantiating it to another and an historical work. But leaving aside the external and written tradition, that which can be demonstrated by reference to historical documents, is there not some present justification of this claim in the fact that I am a Spaniard—and a Spaniard who has scarcely ever been

outside Spain; a product, therefore, of the Spanish tradition, of the living tradition, of the tradition which is
transmitted in feelings and ideas that dream, and not in
texts that sleep?

The philosophy in the soul of my people appears to
me as the expression of an inward tragedy analogous to
the tragedy of the soul of Don Quixote, as the expression
of a conflict between what the world is as scientific reason
shows it to be, and what we wish that it might be, as our
religious faith affirms it to be. And in this philosophy
is to be found the explanation of what is usually said
about us—namely, that we are fundamentally irreducible
to *Kultur*—or, in other words, that we refuse to submit
to it. No, Don Quixote does not resign himself either
to the world, or to science or logic, or to art or esthetics,
or to morality or ethics.

" And the upshot of all this," so I have been told more
than once and by more than one person, " will be simply
that all you will succeed in doing will be to drive people
to the wildest Catholicism." And I have been accused
of being a reactionary and even a Jesuit. Be it so!
And what then?

Yes, I know, I know very well, that it is madness to
seek to turn the waters of the river back to their source,
and that it is only the ignorant who seek to find in the
past a remedy for their present ills; but I know too that
everyone who fights for any ideal whatever, although his
ideal may seem to lie in the past, is driving the world
on to the future, and that the only reactionaries are those
who find themselves at home in the present. Every supposed restoration of the past is a creation of the future,
and if the past which it is sought to restore is a dream,
something imperfectly known, so much the better. The
march, as ever, is towards the future, and he who
marches is getting there, even though he march walking
backwards. And who knows if that is not the better
way! . . .

21

I feel that I have within me a medieval soul, and I believe that the soul of my country is medieval, that it has perforce passed through the Renaissance, the Reformation, and the Revolution—learning from them, yes, but without allowing them to touch the soul, preserving the spiritual inheritance which has come down from what are called the Dark Ages. And Quixotism is simply the most desperate phase of the struggle between the Middle Ages and the Renaissance which was the offspring of the Middle Ages.

And if some accuse me of subserving the cause of Catholic reaction, others perhaps, the official Catholics. . . . But these, in Spain, trouble themselves little about anything, and are interested only in their own quarrels and dissensions. And besides, poor folk, they have neither eyes nor ears !

But the truth is that my work—I was going to say my mission—is to shatter the faith of men here, there, and everywhere, faith in affirmation, faith in negation, and faith in abstention from faith, and this for the sake of faith in faith itself; it is to war against all those who submit, whether it be to Catholicism, or to rationalism, or to agnosticism; it is to make all men live the life of inquietude and passionate desire.

Will this work be efficacious ? But did Don Quixote believe in the immediate apparential efficacy of his work ? It is very doubtful, and at any rate he did not by any chance put his visor to the test by slashing it a second time. And many passages in his history show that he did not look with much confidence to the immediate success of his design to restore knight-errantry. And what did it matter to him so long as thus he lived and immortalized himself ? And he must have surmised, and did in fact surmise, that his work would have another and a higher efficacy, and that was that it would ferment in the minds of all those who in a pious spirit read of his exploits.

Don Quixote made himself ridiculous; but did he know the most tragic ridicule of all, the inward ridicule, the ridiculousness of a man's self to himself, in the eyes of his own soul? Imagine Don Quixote's battlefield to be his own soul; imagine him to be fighting in his soul to save the Middle Ages from the Renaissance, to preserve the treasure of his infancy; imagine him an inward Don Quixote, with a Sancho, at his side, inward and heroical too—and tell me if you find anything comic in the tragedy.

And what has Don Quixote left, do you ask? I answer, he has left himself, and a man, a living and eternal man, is worth all theories and all philosophies. Other peoples have left chiefly institutions, books; we have left souls; St. Teresa is worth any institution, any *Critique of Pure Reason.*

But Don Quixote was converted. Yes—and died, poor soul. But the other, the real Don Quixote, he who remained on earth and lives amongst us, animating us with his spirit—this Don Quixote was not converted, this Don Quixote continues to incite us to make ourselves ridiculous, this Don Quixote must never die. And the conversion of the other Don Quixote—he who was converted only to die—was possible because he was mad, and it was his madness, and not his death nor his conversion that immortalized him, earning him forgiveness for the crime of having been born.[1] *Felix culpa!* And neither was his madness cured, but only transformed. His death was his last knightly adventure; in dying he stormed heaven, which suffereth violence.

This mortal Don Quixote died and descended into hell, which he entered lance on rest, and freed all the condemned, as he had freed the galley slaves, and he shut the gates of hell, and tore down the scroll that Dante saw there and replaced it by one on which was written " Long

[1] An allusion to the phrase in Calderón's *La Vida es Sueño,* " Que delito cometí contra vosotros naciendo ?"—J. E. C. F.

live hope !" and escorted by those whom he had freed, and they laughing at him, he went to heaven. And God laughed paternally at him, and this divine laughter filled his soul with eternal happiness.

And the other Don Quixote remained here amongst us, fighting with desperation. And does he not fight out of despair? How is it that among the words that English has borrowed from our language, such as *siesta*, *camarilla*, *guerrilla*, there is to be found this word *desperado*? Is not this inward Don Quixote that I spoke of, conscious of his own tragic comicness, a man of despair (*desesperado*). A *desperado*—yes, like Pizarro and like Loyola. But " despair is the master of impossibilities," as we learn from Salazar y Torres (*Elegir al enemigo*, Act I.), and it is despair and despair alone that begets heroic hope, absurd hope, mad hope. *Spero quia absurdum*, it ought to have been said, rather than *credo*.

And Don Quixote, who lived in solitude, sought more solitude still ; he sought the solitudes of the Peña Pobre, in order that there, alone, without witnesses, he might give himself up to greater follies with which to assuage his soul. But he was not quite alone, for Sancho accompanied him—Sancho the good, Sancho the believing, Sancho the simple. If, as some, say, in Spain Don Quixote is dead and Sancho lives, then we are saved, for Sancho, his master dead, will become a knight-errant himself. And at any rate he is waiting for some other mad knight to follow again.

And there is also a tragedy of Sancho. The other Sancho, the Sancho who journeyed with the mortal Don Quixote—it is not certain that he died, although some think that he died hopelessly mad, calling for his lance and believing in the truth of all those things which his dying and converted master had denounced and abominated as lies. But neither is it certain that the bachelor Sansón Carrasco, or the curate, or the barber, or the dukes and canons are dead, and it is with these that the heroical Sancho has to contend.

Don Quixote journeyed alone, alone with Sancho, alone with his solitude. And shall we not also journey alone, we his lovers, creating for ourselves a Quixotesque Spain which only exists in our imagination?

And again we shall be asked: What has Don Quixote bequeathed to *Kultur?* I answer: Quixotism, and that is no little thing! It is a whole method, a whole epistemology, a whole esthetic, a whole logic, a whole ethic—above all, a whole religion—that is to say, a whole economy of things eternal and things divine, a whole hope in what is rationally absurd.

For what did Don Quixote fight? For Dulcinea, for glory, for life, for survival. Not for Iseult, who is the eternal flesh; not for Beatrice, who is theology; not for Margaret, who is the people; not for Helen, who is culture. He fought for Dulcinea, and he won her, for he lives.

And the greatest thing about him was his having been mocked and vanquished, for it was in being overcome that he overcame; he overcame the world by giving the world cause to laugh at him.

And to-day? To-day he feels his own comicness and the vanity of his endeavours so far as their temporal results are concerned; he sees himself from without—culture has taught him to objectify himself, to alienate himself from himself instead of entering into himself—and in seeing himself from without he laughs at himself, but with a bitter laughter. Perhaps the most tragic character would be that of a Margutte of the inner man, who, like the Margutte of Pulci, should die of laughter, but of laughter at himself. *E riderá in eterno,* he will laugh for all eternity, said the Angel Gabriel of Margutte. Do you not hear the laughter of God?

The mortal Don Quixote, in dying, realized his own comicness and bewept his sins; but the immortal Quixote,

realizing his own comicness, superimposes himself upon
it and triumphs over it without renouncing it.

And Don Quixote does not surrender, because he is
not a pessimist, and he fights on.  He is not a pessimist,
because pessimism is begotten by vanity, it is a matter of
fashion, pure intellectual snobbism, and Don Quixote is
neither vain nor modern with any sort of modernity (still
less is he a modernist), and he does not understand the
meaning of the word " snob " unless it be explained to
him in old Christian Spanish.  Don Quixote is not a
pessimist, for since he does not understand what is meant
by the *joie de vivre* he does not understand its opposite.
Neither does he understand futurist fooleries.  In spite
of Clavileño,[1] he has not got as far as the aeroplane,
which seems to tend to put not a few fools at a still
greater distance from heaven.  Don Quixote has not
arrived at the age of the tedium of life, a condition that
not infrequently takes the form of that topophobia so
characteristic of many modern spirits, who pass their
lives running at top speed from one place to another,
not from any love of the place to which they are going,
but from hatred of the place they are leaving behind, and
so flying from all places : which is one of the forms of
despair.

But Don Quixote hears his own laughter, he hears the
divine laughter, and since he is not a pessimist, since
he believes in life eternal, he has to fight, attacking the
modern, scientific, inquisitorial orthodoxy in order to
bring in a new and impossible Middle Age, dualistic,
contradictory, passionate.  Like a new Savonarola, an
Italian Quixote of the end of the fifteenth century, he
fights against this Modern Age that began with
Machiavelli and that will end comically.  He fights
against the rationalism inherited from the eighteenth

[1] The wooden horse upon which Don Quixote imagined that he and Sancho
had been carried in the air.  See *Don Quijote*, part II., chaps. 40 and 41.—
J. E. C. F.

century. Peace of mind, reconciliation between reason
and faith—this, thanks to the providence of God, is no
longer possible. The world must be as Don Quixote
wishes it to be, and inns must be castles, and he will
fight with it and will, to all appearances, be vanquished, but he will triumph by making himself ridiculous. And he will triumph by laughing at himself and
making himself the object of his own laughter.

" Reason speaks and feeling bites," said Petrarch; but
reason also bites and bites in the inmost heart. And
more light does not make more warmth. " Light, light,
more light!" they tell us that the dying Goethe cried.
No, warmth, warmth, more warmth! for we die of cold
and not of darkness. It is not the night kills, but the
frost. We must liberate the enchanted princess and
destroy the stage of Master Peter.[1]

But God! may there not be pedantry too in thinking
ourselves the objects of mockery and in making Don
Quixotes of ourselves? Kierkegaard said that the
regenerate (*Opvakte*) desire that the wicked world should
mock at them for the better assurance of their own
regeneracy, for the enjoyment of being able to bemoan
the wickedness of the world (*Afsluttende uvidenskabelig
Efterskrift*, ii., Afsnit ii., cap. 4, sect. 2, *b*).

The question is, how to avoid the one or the other
pedantry, or the one or the other affectation, if the
natural man is only a myth and we are all artificial.

Romanticism! Yes, perhaps that is partly the word.
And there is an advantage in its very lack of precision.
Against romanticism the forces of rationalist and
classicist pedantry, especially in France, have latterly
been unchained. Romanticism itself is merely another
form of pedantry, the pedantry of sentiment? Perhaps.
In this world a man of culture is either a dilettante or a
pedant : you have to take your choice. Yes, René and
Adolphe and Obermann and Lara, perhaps they were all

[1] *Don Quixote*, part ii., chap. 26.

pedants. . . . The question is to seek consolation in disconsolation.

The philosophy of Bergson, which is a spiritualist restoration, essentially mystical, medieval, Quixotesque, has been called a *demi-mondaine* philosophy. Leave out the *demi;* call it *mondaine,* mundane. Mundane— yes, a philosophy for the world and not for philosophers, just as chemistry ought to be not for chemists alone. The world desires illusion (*mundus vult decipi*)—either the illusion antecedent to reason, which is poetry, or the illusion subsequent to reason, which is religion. And Machiavelli has said that whosoever wishes to delude will always find someone willing to be deluded. Blessed are they who are easily befooled! A Frenchman, Jules de Gaultier, said that it was the privilege of his country-men *n'être pas dupe*—not to be taken in. A sorry privilege!

Science does not give Don Quixote what he demands of it. "Then let him not make the demand," it will be said, "let him resign himself, let him accept life and truth as they are." But he does not accept them as they are, and he asks for signs, urged thereto by Sancho, who stands by his side. And it is not that Don Quixote does not understand what those understand who talk thus to him, those who succeed in resigning themselves and accepting rational life and rational truth. No, it is that the needs of his heart are greater. Pedantry? Who knows! . . .

And in this critical century, Don Quixote, who has also contaminated himself with criticism, has to attack his own self, the victim of intellectualism and of senti-mentalism, and when he wishes to be most spontaneous he appears to be most affected. And he wishes, unhappy man, to rationalize the irrational and irrationalize the rational. And he sinks into the despair of the critical century whose two greatest victims were Nietzsche and Tolstoi. And through this despair he reaches the heroic fury of which Giordano Bruno spoke—that intellectual Don Quixote who escaped from the cloister—and becomes an awakener of sleeping souls (*dormitantium animorum excubitor*), as the ex-Dominican said of himself—he who wrote: " Heroic love is the property of those superior natures who are called insane (*insano*) not because they do not know (*no sanno*), but because they over-know (*soprasanno*)."

But Bruno believed in the triumph of his doctrines; at any rate the inscription at the foot of his statue in the Campo dei Fiori, opposite the Vatican, states that it has been dedicated to him by the age which he had foretold (*il secolo da lui divinato*). But our Don Quixote, the inward, the immortal Don Quixote, conscious of his own comicness, does not believe that his doctrines will triumph in this world, because they are not of it. And it is better that they should not triumph. And if the world wished to make Don Quixote king, he would retire alone to the mountain, fleeing from the king-making and king-killing crowds, as Christ retired alone to the mountain when, after the miracle of the loaves and fishes, they sought to proclaim him king. He left the title of king for the inscription written over the Cross.

What, then, is the new mission of Don Quixote, to-day, in this world? To cry aloud, to cry aloud in the wilderness. But though men hear not, the wilderness hears, and one day it will be transformed into a resounding forest, and this solitary voice that goes scattering over the wilderness like seed, will fructify into a gigantic cedar, which with its hundred thousand tongues will sing an eternal hosanna to the Lord of life and of death.

And now to you, the younger generation, bachelor Carrascos of a Europeanizing regenerationism, you who are working after the best European fashion, with scientific method and criticism, to you I say: Create wealth, create nationality, create art, create science, create ethics, above all create—or rather, translate—*Kultur,* and thus kill in yourselves both life and death. Little will it all last you ! . . .

And with this I conclude—high time that I did !—for the present at any rate, these essays on the tragic sense of life in men and in peoples, or at least in myself—who am a man—and in the soul of my people as it is reflected in mine.

I hope, reader, that some time while our tragedy is still playing, in some interval between the acts, we shall meet again. And we shall recognize one another. And forgive me if I have troubled you more than was needful and inevitable, more than I intended to do when I took up my pen proposing to distract you for a while from your distractions. And may God deny you peace, but give you glory !

SALAMANCA,
*In the year of grace* 1912.

# INDEX

331

Printed and Bound in Great Britain by
Billing & Sons, Ltd., and James Burn & Co., Ltd., Guildford, Esher, and London.